ENCOUNTERS WITH CIVILIZATIONS

ENCOUNTERS WITH CIVILIZATIONS

FROM ALEXANDER THE GREAT TO MOTHER TERESA

GËZIM ALPION

WITH A FOREWORD BY GASTON ROBERGE

TRANSACTION PUBLISHERS
NEW BRUNSWICK (U.S.A.) AND LONDON (U.K.)

Transaction printing 2011

This book is printed on acid-free paper that meets the American National Standard for Permanence of Paper for Printed Library Materials.

Library of Congress Catalog Number: 2010051602
ISBN: 978-1-4128-1831-5
Printed in the United States of America

Library of Congress Cataloging-in-Publication Data

Alpion, Gëzim I., 1962-
Encounters with civilizations : from Alexander the Great to Mother Teresa / Gezim Alpion.
p. cm.
Originally published: Chapel Hill, N.C. : Globic Press, c2009.
Includes bibliographical references and index.
ISBN 978-1-4128-1831-5 (alk. paper)
1. Egypt--History. 2. Albania--History. 3. Teresa, Mother, 1910-1997. I. Title.

D7.A45 2011
962--dc22

2010051602

For Professor Gaston Roberge,
a fellow encounterer of civilizations
who made this book happen

Author's Note

Amidst talks about clashes of civilizations this book brings a message of hope: civilizations can co-exist, but not if some are written off as footnotes while others impose themselves as the norm. The fifteen articles included in this book will serve as essential reading for scholars, students and general readers who are interested in encountering the 'other' without prejudice.

Contents

Acknowledgements

Gëzim Alpion and Gaston Roberge would like to thank the following people for making this book possible:

Professor Bonita Aleaz, Dr Panizza Allmark, Abdul Rahim M. Al Mahdi, Dashi Alpion, Geila Alpion, Klendi Alpion, Ahmed Badawi, Stephen Bates (*The Guardian*), Dr Adrian Blackledge, Professor J. T. Boulton (Fellow of the British Academy), Alban Bytyçi, Aparajito Chakraborty, Bhagbat Chakraborty (Meteor Books), Dr Aroup Chatterjee, Tony Collins, Subhandra De, Subhromoni De, Anna J. Dingley, Usama A. Ebaid, David Edgar, Marcus Fernando, Dr Sadri Fetiu, Avik Ganguly, Dr Father Lush Gjergji, The Right Honourable John Grogan (Member of the British Parliament for Selby), Paul Groves, Bodo Gudjons, Eve Hancock, Professor John Holmwood, Dr Altin Ilirjani, Sami Islami, Artan Kutra, James Lamont (*The Financial Times*), Roland Lelaj, Lesley Leyland, Dr José Lingna Nafafé, Anthea Lipsett (*The Guardian*), Father K. T. Mathew SJ, Professor Enver Mehmeti, Anna Mitchell, Jeton Neziraj, Primrose Peacock, Xhemail Peci, Nicolas Pelham (Former Editor of *The Middle East Times*), Bashkim Rama (Head of the Albanian Diplomatic Mission in Kosova), Dr Nuhi Rexhepi, Lesley Riddle (Routledge, Taylor & Francis Group Plc), Kastriot Robo (Albanian Ambassador to the Court of St James's), Stephen Schwartz, Dr Matthew Scott, Dr Brian Shoesmith, Jivraj Singh, Dr Adrian Stokes, Lavdrim Terziu, Dr Michael W. Thomas, Xhevat Ukshini, Professor Cyril Veliath, Muhamed Veliu, Professor Seadin Xhaferi, Ozlem Young, Ahmed Yussry.

Grateful acknowledgement is made to the following for permission to reprint previously published material:

The Middle East Times (Cairo, Egypt)

- 'An interview with Mohammed Ali's ghost' (4-14 June 1993, p. 12).
- 'Foreigner complex': 'When in Rome' (20-26 July 1993, p. 12); 'Back to the army' (27 July - 2 August 1993, p. 12); 'Enslaved by the slaves' (3-9 August 1993, p. 16); 'Complete apathy' (10-16 August 1993, p. 12); 'Cultural invasion' (17-23 August 1993, p. 13); 'Cracked but not broken' (24-30 August 1993, p. 12); 'Becoming foreign to become Egyptian' (31 August - 6 September 1993, p. 12); 'Power returns to the people: the making of Egypt's politicians' (7-13 September 1993, p. 19); and 'Egypt for the Egyptians' (14-20 September 1993, p. 12).
- 'The genesis of Egyptian coffee shops' (23-29 May 1994, p. 6).
- 'The Bride of *Hapi*' (31 August - 6 September 1993, pp. 1, 3).
- 'A parade of porters': 'The Nubian doorman' (15-21 June 1993, p. 12); 'The peasant *bowab*' (22-28 June 1993, p. 12); 'The *simsars* in their prime' (29 June - 5 July 1993, p. 13); and 'Today's *bowab*' (6-12 July 1993, p. 12).

On Magazine (Durham, UK)

- 'The Bride of *Hapi*': 'The genesis of Miss Universe' (8.1 May 1994, p. 8; reprinted as 'The Bride of *Hapi*', also in *On Magazine*, 8 Fresher's Issue, October 1994, p. 6); 'The Nilotic *arousa*' (8 Fresher's Issue, October 1994, p. 7); 'The drowning of the rite' (8.3 November 1994, p. 10); and 'The resurrection of the rite' (8.3 November 1994, p. 11).

Besa Journal (Truro, UK)

- 'Images of Albania and Albanians in English literature: from Edith Durham to J. K. Rowling' (Vol. 6, No. 2, Spring 2002, pp. 30-4).

The Birmingham Post (Birmingham, UK)

- 'A corner of Europe still waiting for peace' (8 December 2003, p. 10).
- 'A rich land where poverty is the norm' (8 December 2003, p. 10).

The Guardian (London and Manchester, UK)

- 'Oh! not Calcutta' (6 September 2003, p. 25).

Globic Press, Chapel Hill, NC, and *Albanian Journal of Politics* (USA)

- 'Western media and the European "other": images of Albania in the British press in the new millennium' (Vol. 1, 2005, pp. 7-27).
- 'Review of Hiromi J. Kudo's book *Mother Teresa: A Saint from Skopje*' (Vol. 2, 2006, pp. 120-2).
- 'Brain down the drain: an *exposé* of social closure in Western academia' (Vol. 4, Issue 1, June 2008, pp. 41-63).

The New Leader (Chennai, India)

- 'A new book that asks: Is she a saint or just a celebrity?' (Combined issue of December 1-15 and 16-31, 2006, p. 51).

Continuum: Journal of Media & Cultural Studies (Australia)

- 'Media and celebrity culture – subjectivist, structuralist and post-structuralist approaches to Mother Teresa's celebrity status' (Vol. 20, No. 4, December 2006, pp. 541-57).

Foreword

This book is a selection of thirteen texts written by Dr Gëzim Alpion between 1993 and 2007. The essays deal with history, culture, the media, social issues and politics. They have all been published in leading journals and newspapers in the UK, Australia, the Middle East and beyond, and have drawn the attention of scholars and general readers. Each text is prompted by Dr Alpion's ongoing reflection on the problems people experience in their encounters with civilizations different from theirs. Thus, these texts pertain to philosophy. For, the subject of 'civilization' involves a consideration of the ultimate issues of life. Such a reflection is welcome anytime anywhere, but it is particularly welcome now, here in India, where there is a vibrant tradition of such a concern. For instance, shortly before his death in 1941, Rabindranath Tagore, then 80 years old, wrote a substantial testament, 'Crisis in Civilization'.[1] Continuator of Tagore, Satyajit Ray, in his last film *Agantuk* (*The Stranger*, 1991), has the hero say that the dominant contemporary civilization is one in which a man can destroy a whole city just by pressing a button, and remain unmoved.

The sub-title of the book may surprise: Alexander the Great (356-323 BC), one of the greatest conquerors in the history of humankind, and Mother Teresa (1910-1997), the saintly humanitarian nun of Kolkata. Do they have anything in common? There are many similarities, with as many differences. First. Alexander the Great conquered lands and nations. Through her love, expressed in service, Mother Teresa conquered the hearts of people the world over, across continents, races, religions and cultures. Second. Both Alexander and Mother Teresa were from Macedonia. Ethnically both were Albanians, although neither actually lived in what is today Albania. Third. Both of them went to India – Alexander in 326 BC, Mother Teresa in 1929 – and both have left their mark there.

Alexander the Great contributed to India's name through the Greek language. For, the term 'India' comes from the Sanskrit *sindhu*, the river. The Persians changed *sindhu* into *hindu*, and the Greeks dropped the 'h'. Thus from *sindhu* eventually came the word 'India', which is now embedded in the Indian Constitution as one of the two names of India, the other name being *Bharat*.[2]

Yet, Alexander the Great left the country soon after his arrival. On the other hand, Mother Teresa made India her home and became an Indian citizen. She was awarded the Nobel Prize for Peace in 1979, and India's highest civilian award, the *Bharat Ratna* (the Gem of India) in 1980. She was made an Honorary Citizen of the United States in 1996 (one of only six).[3] Upon her death in 1997, India gave her a state funeral similar to that given to Mahatma Gandhi, the Father of the Indian Nation. In 2001, the Indian filmmaker Amar Kr. Bhattacharya entitled his documentary film on Mother Teresa as *Mother of the Century*.[4]

I said there are similarities and differences between Alexander and Mother Teresa. I have mentioned similarities. The main difference is obvious. Alexander's attitude towards conquest was not shared by the people of India. According to the Greek historian Flavius Arrianus (c. 95 - c. 175 AD), Alexander engaged in discussion with Indian sages. In his book *The Argumentative Indian* Amartya Sen has this passage:

> [W]hen Alexander asked a group of Jain philosophers why they were paying so little attention to the great conqueror, he got the following – broadly anti-imperial – reply (as reported by Arrian): 'King Alexander, every man can possess only so much of the earth's surface as this we are standing

> on. You are but human like the rest of us, save that you are always busy and up to no good, travelling so many miles from your home, a nuisance to yourself and to others!... You will soon be dead, and then you will own just as much of the earth as will suffice to bury you.'[5]

One wonders...these words come from the apparently distant civilization of India, but they resonate afresh today as if they were addressed to the agents of globalization. Could they not engage in discussion with sages of various civilizations? Further, the phenomenon of *The Da Vinci Code* (book 2003 and film 2006) is a pathetic indication of the spiritual poverty of the self-styled rich global world. That world turns away from truth and goes for fanciful myths.

One more aspect of the subtitle calls for explanation: the subtitle is not complete. It should read, 'From Alexander the Great to Mother Teresa...and to you, gentle reader'. The encounters with civilizations continue today. And Dr Alpion's writings, dealing with both past and present encounters with civilizations, cultures and human communities, constitute an excellent pedagogy for our time. They provide models to emulate; they analyze the difficulties one is likely to face; they are an irresistible call to commitment and action. One may not always agree with Dr Alpion's opinions, but one can never discard them. One is challenged, whatever the place one happens to live in.

Indian readers belong to ancient and extraordinarily rich civilizations. As they encounter the civilizations of Egypt, the Balkans and the United Kingdom they may ponder over the fate of what is best in the human heart, and how much one can do to either nurture or poison that goodness.

As clearly appears from this book's table of contents, Dr Alpion deals with a variety of subjects. Moreover, he is equally at ease and successful as a playwright, a storyteller, a journalist and a scholar. Dr Alpion is not just a media scholar; he is first a media person. The essays of this selection are vibrant with the life, diversity and appeal of present day media.

Gëzim Alpion was born in Albania in 1962. He lived in Albania (1962-1985), then in Egypt (1985-1993) and, since 1993, in the United Kingdom with his wife – also a scholar – and their two children. One may well wonder, 'Why now in the United Kingdom?' I could not help asking Dr Alpion. Here is his reply:

> I finished my studies at the University of Durham in 1997, the year when Albania was in turmoil following the collapse of the fraudulent pyramid schemes. From 1985, when I began my studies at Cairo, until 1997, the year I received the PhD at Durham, Dashi [Dr Alpion's wife] and I had invested in nothing else but my education. As we had no savings, no house in Tirana and a young family (Geila was five years old, Klendi was not yet born) we decided not to return to Albania in 1997. In October 1997 I started lecturing on American literature at the University of Huddersfield.
>
> Dashi and I often wonder if we should have returned to Albania after 1997. We don't have a conclusive answer. We miss our parents, siblings and friends. Being away from our loved ones is a burden we have to live with for the rest of our lives.
>
> As a writer, however, I don't regret that I 'left' Albania because, in a sense, I have never left my country. My distance from Albania has been essential for me to develop a sense of critical appreciation of my background.[6]

Only recently (26 June – 2 July 2005) has Dr Alpion, for the first time, visited India – in fact, Kolkata – in connection with his study *Mother Teresa: Saint or Celebrity?* As an Albanian he is naturally interested in Mother Teresa. But Mother Teresa is not Dr Alpion's sole interest in

India. He is an avid reader of Asia's first Nobel laureate, Rabindranath Tagore, and during his short stay in Kolkata, he found time to go to Santiniketan and visit Visva-Bharati, the University founded by Tagore.[7]

Hence, the four parts of this book: Albania, Egypt, The United Kingdom, and India. Some of the essays could belong to more than one part, but their being placed in a particular part indicates the point of view that presided over the selection.

Part One: Albania

'An interview with the ghost of Mohammed Ali, former ruler of Egypt' (1993) introduces a theme that runs through the entire collection of Dr Alpion's texts: the Albanians living outside the Balkans, and their relationship with the ethnic group they belong to as well as with the people they have come to live with. Here is the astounding relationship of the Albanian Mohammed Ali (1769-1848) with the Egyptians he ruled from 1805 to 1848. The second essay of this part, 'Kosova – a corner of Europe still waiting for peace' (2003), deals with the political situation in this Albanian region,[8] and how that situation affects the difficult relationships between the Albanians and the Serbs.

Part Two: Egypt

Dr Alpion's seven-year stay in Egypt helped him understand the social evolution of the Egyptians over the centuries, namely, the feeling of 'inferiority' that has been instilled by different conquerors of Egypt on its inhabitants. With at least one exception, Mohammed Ali. That feeling of 'inferiority' and its devastating consequences is what Dr Alpion discusses in 'Foreigner complex' (1993). The three other articles of this part – 'Egyptian coffee shops' (1994), 'The Bride of *Hapi* – female sacrifice and cosmic order' (1993) and 'A parade of porters' (1993) – deal with specific aspects of the Egyptian culture. Indian readers will easily note cultural similarities between Egypt and India.

Part Three: The United Kingdom

In this part is reproduced Scene 4 of Dr Alpion's play *If Only the Dead Could Listen*, which, sponsored by the Arts Council England, was first performed by the Dreamscape Theatre Company at the MAC Theater, Birmingham, UK, in February 2006. The premiere was such an astounding success that shortly afterwards Dr Alpion and Marcus Fernando, the Sri Lankan-British Director, received invitations from several national theatres in the Balkans to tour the region. Theater made it possible for Dr Alpion to express his thoughts more forcefully than in an academic essay. The drama depicts the 'foreigner complex' as experienced by Albanians – from Albania and Kosova – who seek refuge in the United Kingdom. The two complementary essays on the images of Albania and the Albanians a) in English literature from Edith Durham's *High Albania* to J. K. Rowling's *Harry Potte*r (2002), and b) in the British Press in the new millennium (2005) are two perfect examples of what in literary circles is called 'imagology'. These images have a deep effect on the identity of the people concerned, and at times result in a foreigner complex.

Part Four: India

Part four begins with a short piece, entitled 'Oh! not Calcutta!' (2003), about Mother Teresa's supposed negative impact on the image of Calcutta. Calcutta (now Kolkata) has long been famous, if at times out of unthinking playfulness. The city has been depicted by numerous image-makers, like writer Mircea Eliade (*Bengali Night*) and filmmaker Louis Malle (*Calcutta*). It has been called 'a city of palaces', 'a hell of a place' (Joseph Lelyveld), 'the black hole', a sample of the 'sad tropics' (Claude Lévi-Strauss, *Tristes Tropiques*, 1955), 'the unintended city', 'the city of the poor' (Joy Sen), and 'the city of joy' (Dominique Lapierre).[9] In addition, the phrase 'Oh! Calcutta!', used by a Broadway revue of that name (1969), was borrowed from the caption of a painting by French artist C. Trouille (1889-1975), who made a vulgar pun on the name of Calcutta.[10] Neither the play nor the painting had anything to do with Kolkata itself.

Calcutta was not the only place in South Asia to be the basis of vulgar puns in French. So were Pondicherry, Ceylon and Bombay. I personally came to know these puns when I was a child. To make fun of cities and places of other worlds is not the best thing a child can learn from his/her own milieu.

Dr Alpion's masterly essay 'Media and celebrity culture – subjectivist, structuralist and post-structuralist approaches to Mother Teresa's celebrity status' will greatly contribute to develop an academic approach of the media phenomenon called Mother Teresa. Some of the themes of the essay are developed further in Dr Alpion's book *Mother Teresa: Saint or Celebrity?*,[11] recently published by Routledge in the UK, the USA and Canada. In this book, which attracted the attention of the world media almost three years before its publication, Dr Alpion shows, among other things, the influence of Mother Teresa's Albanian roots on her ministry among the poor. Then, as a secular thinker and media expert, Dr Alpion discusses how Mother Teresa became a media icon in the context of the contemporary lust for fame and cult of celebrities. Dr Alpion addressed these two issues also in the three talks he gave in Kolkata in 2005.

Dr Alpion's essays on Mother Teresa and his review of a book on her by Hiromi J. Kudo, a Japanese scholar, are of particular interest to both Indian and other readers. These works help readers know Mother Teresa better and appreciate her even more.

Dr Alpion has no axe to grind: he is committed to unraveling the facts. Whether one deals with Albania, Egypt, the UK or India, unraveling the facts is worth the effort, rewarding and even at times amusing.

In addition to Dr Alpion's three articles on Mother Teresa, I have written two essays especially for this book. One essay is a note on Dr

Alpion's above-mentioned book on Mother Teresa. The other essay deals with a controversial issue: Mother Teresa's thoughts about abortion, her statements about it, and the reaction of the press to these statements.

Envoi

The last part of this anthology, captioned 'Envoi', comprises a single essay by Dr Alpion, and earnestly entreats the reader to say 'No' to social closure. In this last essay, Dr Alpion offers an *exposé* of social closure in Western academia. Scholars are at the forefront of any successful encounter with civilizations, that is, if they are not socially excluded. But the fact is, as Dr Alpion clearly shows, many foreign scholars in the West are subjected to what Max Weber called 'social closure'. Here Dr Alpion, twice a foreigner – in Egypt and in the UK[12] – no doubt draws from his own experience, as well as from the experience of a large number of scholars who have been subjected to social exclusion. Although the collective testimony of these scholars might create dismay, Dr Alpion does not 'commit the grievous sin of losing faith in man'.[13] He trustfully affirms that to build a caring society no one should be treated as a disposable object.

Gaston Roberge
Professor of Film and Communication Studies
St Xavier's College
Kolkata, India
25th January 2007

Part One: Albania

– 1 –

An interview with the ghost of Mohammed Ali, former ruler of Egypt

In an exclusive interview with fellow Albanian comrade and one-time leader of Egypt, Mohammed Ali, Gëzim Alpion provides the answers to questions which have troubled historians for over a century.

The Middle East Times

The interview takes place alongside MOHAMMED ALI'*s white marble tomb at the Citadel in Cairo in June 1993. The* INTERVIEWER *is standing in an attitude of respect before the tomb.*

INTERVIEWER I am grateful to Your Majesty for granting me this rare opportunity to meet you. I do apologise for disturbing your eternal slumber.

MOHAMMED ALI (*smiles.*) Don't you worry about that! I don't like sleeping. As a matter of fact, I have never closed my eyes since I left your world. I am always on the watch, you know.

INTERVIEWER I am sorry, Your Majesty, but I don't follow.

MOHAMMED ALI It's all right. I don't expect you to. So, you are Albanian!

INTERVIEWER I am, Your Majesty.

MOHAMMED ALI What are you doing in Egypt? Don't you know that our days in this country came to an end in 1952?

INTERVIEWER I am a student at the University of Cairo.

MOHAMMED ALI (*eyes* INTERVIEWER *with interest.*) A student? What are you studying? Let me guess. You are doing an MA on (*Chuckles and points to self.*) MA. You are a historian, right?

INTERVIEWER No, I'm afraid not. I must admit your achievements as the architect of modern Egypt have yet to be acclaimed by Albanologists, but I am confident that much will be written in the near future about you and your progeny.

MOHAMMED ALI (*grinning.*) You think so!

INTERVIEWER Absolutely!

MOHAMMED ALI Hm! I have seen you coming to my… (*He hesitates.*) resting-place rather frequently for some years now, but you have never before asked me for an interview. Why now? Are you leaving Egypt for good?

INTERVIEWER (*smiling.*) No one who comes to Egypt leaves this country for good. You of all people should know this, Your Majesty.

MOHAMMED ALI (*thoughtfully.*) True! True!

INTERVIEWER Yes, I am leaving Egypt. But I am not here to bid you farewell.

Mohammed Ali I am listening.

Interviewer I have been studying your life thoroughly for quite some time now, but I still have some questions whose answers I have not been able to find in any book.

Mohammed Ali (*smiles.*) So you want to hear them straight from the horse's mouth!

Interviewer Well, I believe no one else but Your Majesty knows the answers to-

Mohammed Ali (*interrupts* Interviewer, *suspiciously.*) Have you made this pilgrimage to blame me for benefiting Egypt and not Albania?

Interviewer (*surprised.*) No! Not at all.

Mohammed Ali (*suspiciously.*) No? Why not? It's the truth, isn't it?

Interviewer Because... (*He hesitates.*) because I believe that you *did* benefit Albania.

Mohammed Ali (*grinning.*) Really! How's that?

Interviewer Although you rose and set in Egypt, you remain an ever-glittering star for Albania. Being born in Albania, the country of eagles, you were destined to fly. Your nest blessed your flight to enlighten Egypt at a time when it was suffering under the Turkish eclipse.

Mohammed Ali (*impatiently.*) Do you always beat about the bush like this?

Interviewer (*clearing his throat.*) Um...what I am driving at is this: although you never returned to Albania after leaving it as a child, you always took pride in being Albanian. You insisted on having only Albanians in your regiment when the Porte dispatched you to Egypt in 1802. That fact alone proves that you could never forget your roots.

MOHAMMED ALI Well, I am not the first Albanian military strategist to appreciate the valour of my fellow countrymen. Two centuries and a half before me our national hero Gjergj Kastrioti Skanderbeg did the same when he broke away from the Turkish Sultan to start his resistance. Twenty-five years long. Quite glorious, eh? Skanderbeg returned to Albania choosing three hundred tried and tested soldiers from his native Dibra as his loyal followers. I decided in Turkey to enlist in my regiment only Albanians because they were the most efficient officers.

INTERVIEWER Was there any time when you regretted your decision to select only Albanians?

MOHAMMED ALI (*smiles.*) Never!

INTERVIEWER (*baffled.*) Several historians claim that your chosen Albanian officers proved problematic for your safety.

MOHAMMED ALI (*smiles.*) They certainly did. So?

INTERVIEWER But if that's the case, how come you persisted in keeping them around you all the time?

MOHAMMED ALI (*smiles.*) It is as they say: 'Better the devil you know'. My hand-picked Albanian friends made an attempt on my life more than once. Each and every one of them was my potential assassin. But I already knew that since I was in Turkey. Some of them couldn't wait to see Cairo simply to get rid of me.

Interviewer So far I have found no records on how you punished these, shall we say, hand-picked traitors.

Mohammed Ali (*smiles.*) You haven't because such records do not exist. You see, I never punished any of them.

Interviewer But...

Mohammed Ali (*smiles.*) It's strange, I know. But I am not called Mohammed Ali the Great for nothing. The more my Albanian officers tried to eliminate me, the more precious they became. I never liked blind loyalty. Their disloyalty did not bother me. You know why? Because, being of the same blood, I always knew what they were up to. I could read the burning ambition in their eyes. I could hear their unspoken thoughts. They were my kindred spirits. That's why I could always curb them when they got out of hand. I considered myself blessed to be surrounded by such brave officers who, to the very last man, considered themselves abler and greater than me.

Interviewer (*surprised.*) Abler and greater than you!

Mohammed Ali (*smiles.*) But of course! And I admired them for that. Sometimes I even envied them. But I never dismissed, imprisoned or executed any of them. How could I, when no amount of gold could buy them? They were ever ready to die only to protect me, the one they wanted to be rid of. They were my inspiration.

Interviewer The Porte considered you a traitor. Do you accept the accusation?

Mohammed Ali (*thoughtfully.*) Treason and loyalty are relative. With my so-called treachery I served the Ottoman Sultan more venerably than I might have done with dogged devotion. If I was a traitor, at least I was an honest one.

INTERVIEWER Did you betray the Porte because you were too ambitious?

MOHAMMED ALI (*clears his throat.*) Well, I admit I was ambitious. I was convinced that my vocation was to be more than just an officer – never mind how high I might rise in the Turkish Army. I was hungry for conquest and only the vastness of deserts and seas could satiate my appetite.

INTERVIEWER (*smiles ironically.*) Wasn't the Ottoman Empire big enough for you?

MOHAMMED ALI (*dreamily.*) It certainly was, but I am not talking only about space. I wanted a kingdom of my *own* where I could implement my *own* ideas. I had a vision that I could never realise in any territory under the Turkish rule.

INTERVIEWER How did you know that?

MOHAMMED ALI (*thoughtfully.*) I could feel the deepening impotence of the Ottoman Empire long before it was finally paralysed. Even as a student I knew that it lacked the will to introduce any of the changes I had in mind. The Porte was intellectually dead, and the Sultan and his courtiers had long run short of new ideas when I volunteered to come to Egypt. I needed an escape and was delirious with joy when I found one.

INTERVIEWER So, were you after… (*Hesitation.*) instant fame?

MOHAMMED ALI (*smiles ironically.*) You should know! Do you not live in an age when everyone is obsessed with the idea of celebrity? You would do anything for your miserly fifteen minutes of fame.

INTERVIEWER (*smiles.*) Be that as it may, you were hardly less addicted to fame yourself. Living in Istanbul must have been quite an ordeal for any Albanian in your time.

MOHAMMED ALI (*frowns.*) We were competitive, yes.

INTERVIEWER I have the impression that you were afraid that it would take you a lifetime to be accepted at the Turkish court.

MOHAMMED ALI (*grinning.*) Hm!

INTERVIEWER Not being…(*Pause.*) that well-connected, it's understandable you lacked the patience of those more fortunate Albanians who made it to the top of the Ottoman Empire.

MOHAMMED ALI (*nervously.*) Nonsense!

INTERVIEWER And, when you established your *own* empire, you could not stand the Turkish Sultan because he reminded you of your humble origins and your treachery to your benefactor.

MOHAMMED ALI (*irritated.*) Preposterous!

INTERVIEWER For you to revel in your success, the Porte had to become history. Is that why you never stopped attacking Turkish territories?

MOHAMMED ALI (*smiles dejectedly.*) You don't understand. The Ottoman Empire had to die because it was setting a bad example. In 1833, I was only 150 miles away from that terminally ill patient. Had I practised euthanasia at that time, I assure you that the Porte would not have suffered its later degrading death.

INTERVIEWER Did the Egyptians dislike you for not being of their blood?

MOHAMMED ALI (*smiles.*) No, not really. The Egyptians are an open-minded people. Besides, by the time I arrived here, they had long forgotten how to govern themselves. Why, they couldn't even remember the name of a single Egyptian leader! These people never had the chance to rule themselves after their humiliation by the Romans at Actium in 31 BC. What is more interesting, very few Pharaohs could claim to have pure Egyptian blood. *De facto*, my descendant Farouk is the last link in the millennia-long chain of Egypt's foreign rulers.

INTERVIEWER In 1811 you invited some 470 guests at a banquet at this very Citadel only to massacre them in cold blood! That was pure madness, wasn't it? That gory feast must still haunt your dreams!

MOHAMMED ALI Not at all! To create a great country sometimes you have to make painful but necessary decisions.

INTERVIEWER Was the butchery a warning to the populace of Egypt that you wouldn't tolerate any trouble or dissent?

MOHAMMED ALI No, absolutely not. The banquet was a fitting send-off for Egypt's retarded Mamluk leaders. They had their chance to do something for this glorious ancient country. What did they do? Nothing. I did not get rid of all of them at once because I was afraid of them, but because it was not worth my time to deal with each of them individually. They were as blinkered as the courtiers I had left behind in Istanbul. That's why they had to go. As for the people of Egypt, you don't need to threaten them to rule them. Once they are convinced that you love Egypt and are true to them, they welcome you and obey.

INTERVIEWER You loved Egypt, but you weren't always true to the Egyptians, were you?

MOHAMMED ALI I was true to them as much as I could possibly be. A ruler can't afford to be true all the time to his loyal subjects. You see what I mean?

INTERVIEWER No, not exactly.

MOHAMMED ALI (*grinning.*) Hm! I knew since I was in Istanbul that it wouldn't be wise to take too many risks with the Egyptians.

INTERVIEWER So you didn't find ruling Egypt very easy, after all?

MOHAMMED ALI (*smiling.*) I quite understand King Farouk's last words to the Free Officers before finally leaving Alexandria in 1952: 'You will see that it is not very easy to rule Egypt'.

INTERVIEWER Is it true that Your Majesty never learned your subjects' language, even though you ruled them for more than four decades?

MOHAMMED ALI I'm not the only Albanian ruler of Egypt to disregard his people's native tongue.

INTERVIEWER You mean, some of your descendants also never learned Arabic?

MOHAMMED ALI (*rather irritated.*) But, of course they did. I am not simply talking about *my* descendants, but about *my*, *your*,

our predecessor.

INTERVIEWER (*completely at a loss.*) *Our* predecessor?

MOHAMMED ALI (*frustrated.*) Yes, the one who happened to be a Pharaoh.

INTERVIEWER (*amazed.*) A Pharaoh!

MOHAMMED ALI (*impatiently.*) Didn't you know that Alexander the Great was my hero since I was a child? Obviously not! But then you are no historian – you said so yourself.

INTERVIEWER If Alexander did not speak Egyptian he had a reason. After all, unlike Your Majesty, he did not come here to stay.

MOHAMMED ALI (*with narrowed eyes.*) Are you sure you are not a historian? I honestly don't understand why you are making so much fuss about this trifle. Do you know how many Ptolemaic rulers bothered to speak Egyptian? *None*, except for Cleopatra. And what did she achieve by being such a *gifted* linguist? The destruction of the Pharaonic civilisation.

INTERVIEWER (*hesitantly.*) Well, I wouldn't put it quite that way. It seems to me that Pharaonic Egypt came to an end when it did, not just because Cleopatra-

MOHAMMED ALI (*interrupts* INTERVIEWER, *irritated.*) Let me tell you something, my good scholar! A great ruler has no time to indulge in linguistic hobbies, and should *never* – you understand? – *never* mix business with pleasure, as (*Ironically.*) *your preferred queen* and some of my foolish descendants did. I was born to make history. All my life I was a man of action. I had no time for learning. I was here to teach. The

Egyptians had the will for change. I showed them the way. Could they have obeyed me, as they did, if they had failed to comprehend my language, or I theirs?

INTERVIEWER What would Your Majesty say to those historians who claim that you were, er…(*Hesitating.*) not in your right mind during the last years of your life?

MOHAMMED ALI (*smirks.*) Do they *really* say that? Perhaps I do them a disservice. (*Thoughtfully.*) Well, I was never more sane than when I was insane.

INTERVIEWER I understand that, before Your Majesty passed away, you issued strict orders against any attempt to mummify your body. [*Folklore says that if Albanians die abroad, their corpses do not decompose.*] Nevertheless, still…

MOHAMMED ALI (*sighs heavily.*) Still, I am an alien here, my son.

– 2 –

Kosova – a corner of Europe still waiting for peace

The eyes of the world remain focused on Iraq and the rest of the Middle East. But Dr Gëzim Alpion argues there is still much unfinished business to complete on our own doorstep in Europe.

The Birmingham Post

A word of advice if you fly to Kosova this winter. Make sure you are properly insured because you have no guarantee your plane will land at Prishtina airport.

It is not as sinister as it sounds. You will certainly land there – eventually. But not before your plane has taken you first on an unscheduled tour to another landing strip somewhere in Greece or Bulgaria or even further afield to Italy or Switzerland.

In my case, the Austrian Airlines plane took me first to Thessalonica in Greece, and from there back to Vienna International where my odyssey to Kosova had started some seven hours earlier.

The reason for the *ad hock* change of plans had nothing to do with any terrorist threat. The culprit in this case was the weather.

'Ending up somewhere in Europe is normal for us who fly regularly to Prishtina,' a United Nations official told me at Thessalonica where we were stranded for quite a while. 'Landing at Prishtina is still done visually. The pilots, of course, can't take chances.'

I asked whether it cost too much for the UN to modernise the airport. 'Well, no,' he replied hastily. 'The main problem with the airport is its location. It's been built in a most unsuitable valley. Anyway, as you'll see, the airport now is in a much better shape than when we first took control of it.'

The following day the weather in Kosova was much more welcoming and I was in for quite a pleasant surprise when the plane touched the tarmac. A brand new airport. Everything inside was clean and shiny.

For a moment, though, I had the feeling that I had landed in the wrong place. I certainly expected the UN military presence at the airport and everywhere in Kosova – a large number of passengers on my plane were in military uniform. What took me by surprise was the fact that all the signs at the airport were in English; not a single word in Albanian or Serbo-Croat. For a moment I thought I was in an English-speaking country and not in the heart of the Balkans.

'Do you understand what the signs read?' I asked a Kosovar immigrant returning home from the Czech Republic. He shrugged his shoulders, smiling helplessly.

Those who built the airport obviously had in mind first and foremost the comfort of thousands of Westerners and non-Westerners employed by the UN and other international organisations and charities throughout Kosova. And they were right. Who would like to get lost at Prishtina airport! Time is precious; never more so for those who have gone to Kosova purely to help out its people.

Albanian and Serbo-Croat are not used in the airport signs because the UN obviously wants a speedy integration of Kosova into the European Union. This, I thought, also explains why the Euro is Kosova's official currency.

The Kosovars are expected to tolerate an insignificant Orwellian linguistic transformation (some would call it humiliation) if they seriously want to join the European family. You do not join the most exclusive club in the world without making some small sacrifices.

If Kosovars expect foreigners working there to learn Albanian or Serbo-Croat, they must be joking. If they had linguistic hobbies, the numerous foreign do-gooders of Kosova would have very well chosen to pursue comfortable academic careers in their own countries. They are in Kosova mainly for the noble purpose of making this traditionally troubled patch of land a better place to live in.

I was picked up at the airport by Sami Islami, a Kosovar journalist now living in London. On our way to Prishtina, Sami gave me a very grim picture of the daily life in Kosova. 'There is real poverty here,' he told me. 'Which is a shame. Kosova is such a rich place.'

I only had to look out the window of the car to see that he was right. I have visited several countries in the Balkans, but never seen such a vast field as the Plane of Kosova.

Seeing the endless Plane of Kosova, I was not surprised the Serbs have been so reluctant to let Kosova slip from their tight grip.

Nowhere else in the Balkans is the land as fertile as in Kosova. But Kosova is not only a plentiful granary. This province is also rich in mineral resources such as gold, coal, lead, nickel, zinc and silver.

But the people of Kosova are still poor. Life is especially difficult for the elderly and those who have no family members in the West to help them out. They are expected to get by with only €60 (£40) a month they receive in the form of state benefits. Of course there are families who are entitled to less.

Salaries in Kosova are very low, which makes the introduction of the Euro a cruel joke. The Euro makes Kosova the poorest appendix of the European Union. The average salary in Kosova is €70 (£50), but there are people who earn only €30 (£18) per month.

The situation is a bit different for the white-collar workers. At the University of Prishtina, a deputy-dean told me that a lecturer earns normally €170 (£135) per month.

I asked a representative of the United Nations Interim Administration Mission in Kosova (UNMIK) why the economy was in such a poor state.

'Mainly because the Kosovans abroad are not investing in Kosova', was the reply.

Perhaps there is some truth in the claim. But I could hardly see how the 'rich' Kosovars in the West were the main culprits for the poverty of the people in Kosova.

It is eight years since the NATO-led alliance succeeded in evicting the ethnic cleansing Serbian army from Kosova. In all this time, however, the European Union and the UN have been unable to come up with a clear plan for the future of the province.

Who would like to invest in a place whose international status is nowhere in sight? Would any Western businessman be foolish enough to throw away his money in a place like Kosova whose future is shrouded in mystery and uncertainty?

Kosova is often described as one of the few UN success stories. Undoubtedly, the UN has done a good job in Kosova. Thanks to its military presence, the Albanians in Kosova no longer live in fear of being massacred by Serbian military thugs just because they are Albanians.

But the Albanians and the ethnic minorities in Kosova do not just want to remain alive. They have every right to govern their common country.

So far, however, the people of Kosova are virtually powerless. As in the past, their future is decided outside Kosova.

The UNMIK officials are quick to blame the Kosova leaders for their pathological *naiveté* – they are seen as a bunch of old-fashioned people who have failed to show real leadership. I could see for myself that the present leaders of Kosova have still a lot to learn when it comes to mastering democratic skills. As for the Kosovar media, it is hardly the independent vibrant force Kosova needs at this unique historic moment.

But then one could argue that the amateurish behaviour of the Kosova politicians is also a result of the limits imposed on them by the UN, which rules Kosova more like a colony than a democracy. The local politicians are not seen as partners by the unelected modern viceroys of the UN, who often are some over empowered shady bureaucrats thrown into the limelight of international politics hardly for any successful political careers in their own countries.

The people of Kosova are tired of promises and frustration. They are Europeans, who, as a result of their own faults as well as of the West's sins, have been artificially estranged from the rest of Europe for over six centuries.

It is about time they rejoin the family of European nations. Offering them a chance to decide their future through democratic means is not a favour we are doing them.

In giving them a chance to speak and in listening to them, the UNMIK and the EU are in fact meeting a sacred obligation towards them and other nations across the world that aspire to democracy.

There will be no peaceful co-existence between the Kosovar Albanians and the Serbs in this province as long as the voice of the people is ignored.

Europe needs to sort out the issue of Kosova, and sort it out for good, if it does not want a repeat of history. Full independence for Kosova is the road to lasting peace in the Balkans.

Part Two: Egypt

– 3 –

Foreigner complex

i. When in Rome

The Egyptians' *okda al khawaga*, or 'foreigner complex', has been built up over many centuries through the cunning policies of various alien rulers. It was the Romans, however, who first sowed the seeds of this deeply rooted complex.

Pharaoh Cleopatra was clever enough to choose Rome as a strategic ally, but she was tragically mistaken in picking Antony for her partner. Her political miscalculations culminated in her premature death in 30 BC and the demise of an extraordinary civilisation of unique temporal, spatial, spiritual and cultural dimensions. A very heavy toll was also paid by Egypt's powerful army, especially its much-feared fleet, which was the main target of Octavius's revenge.

And so in 32 BC, Octavius, who became the Emperor Augustus in 27 BC, crowned himself King of Egypt just over a century after 146 BC, when the fall of Carthage marked the rise of Rome to superpower status.

From the time of the first Pharaoh, King Mina, also known as Narmer, to the last, Cleopatra VII, many rulers of *Misr* (Egypt) were not of 'pure' Egyptian blood. But Octavius was different from them all. This new 'Pharaoh' ruled Egypt from Rome.

It did not take long for the Egyptians to realise that, unlike their Greek Ptolemaic predecessors, of whom Cleopatra was one, these newcomers did not love their country. The burial of the Pharaonic civilisation was of utmost priority for the new European conquerors.

With a mere 110 years of Empire, the Romans envied Egypt's success during almost 3,500 years of Pharaonic rule. The invaders felt deeply inferior, and sought to humble the Egyptians' pride.

To achieve this goal, they were brutally iconoclastic. The looting and plundering of temples and tombs became the norm. The Romans were the first to begin the shameful shipment of Pharaonic masterpieces to Europe.

But the Romans did not deal exclusively with the dead. The offspring of Pharaohs suffered from the invaders' cruelty just as well. On the pretext of heresy, Rome exterminated many Egyptians, including those who had converted to Christianity.

The Roman Empire itself converted and became 'holy' under Constantine in the fourth century. Naturally, the Christian Egyptians rejoiced. But not for long. The establishment of the Catholic Church meant that the common religion the Egyptians had hoped would finally bring them and their European invaders together simply set both parties further apart. Rome's conversion of convenience to Christianity strengthened further the Christian Egyptians' belief that only their Coptic Church preached the purest testament of Christ.

From the start the Romans knew that one of the main reasons the Pharaohs had defeated numerous enemies for over three millennia was military. With their well-equipped and highly trained army, the Egyptians had proved themselves to be staunch fighters. They had excelled as brave warriors especially under the command of legendary strategists such as Mina, Ahmus, Tohetemes III, Ramses II and Ramses III.

In order to prevent rebellion, the Romans, from the first, prohibited the Egyptians from entering the Roman forces, and also from establishing their own *corps*. The glorious military past of the Pharaohs made it vital for the Romans to suppress the bellicose arts of their contemporary Egyptians.

Egypt was declared Emperor Augustus's garden from the outset of the Roman yoke. Gradually, the Romans succeeded in forcing the Egyptians into peasant farming as their sole occupation. The foreigner complex stemmed from the enforced military supremacy of Rome, *à la* the Khmer Rouge.

But, to the disappointment of the Romans, the complex never bore the expected fruits. The Egyptian farmers in many cases would rise up to prove that they had not completely forgotten their martial arts. The revolution of Alexandria in the fourth century, otherwise known as the Age of Martyrs, marked a culmination of the Egyptians' pent-up hatred for the merciless invaders. After its bloody repression, the Romans were forced to slacken their harsh attitude towards the Egyptians by granting them more religious freedom and reducing taxes. But allowing the Egyptians to join the army would remain unthinkable for another three centuries.

If the Romans failed to turn the Egyptians into simple, obedient farmers, they at least succeeded in the indoctrination of a cultural revolution. It was during their rule that the Egyptians started to look at Pharaonic monuments as heaps of stone. This was to make the deepening of the foreigner complex a much easier task to achieve for future conquerors.

Throughout their long history the Egyptians had excelled not only as shipbuilders, fishermen and manufacturers of glass, leather and perfume but also as farmers of their fertile land. Under Roman rule, however, farming had become their obligatory labour. For almost six centuries Egypt was one of the foremost granaries of the Roman Empire.

ii. Back to the army

The introduction of Islam marked the beginning of Egypt's first renaissance after many centuries of ruthless Roman suppression. But the Romans had effectively cut off Egypt from its roots, and the Egyptian Muslims were unable to revive their glorious Pharaonic culture. Amr Ibn Al Azz, Medina's first 'viceroy' in Egypt, was the first ruler in seven centuries to allow the Egyptians to enrol in the army. But Egypt, as a Muslim nation, prevented Jews and Christians from serving in its army. This law came to an end for the Egyptian Christians only after the 1952 revolution.

The main reason why the Egyptians regained access to the army was that Egypt was destined to play a unique role in the whole region from the seventh century AD onwards. It is believed that the Prophet Mohammed more than once had praised the military skills of the Ancient Egyptians.

Egyptians joined the Arab armies that invaded Spain to overrun Andalusia. They also proved themselves brave fighters during the rule of the Omayyids, the Abbassids and the Fatimids. Up until the twelfth century, the Egyptians had their own army. The Fatimids established *Al Qahira* (Cairo) as the capital of their vast empire, which ruled over all North Africa.

Towards the end of their rule, the Fatimids were too weak to face the waves of the crusaders alone, and as such were desperate to find some allies. They sought support from Aleppo in Syria and Mosul in Iraq, from where came the military Kurdish genius, Salah Al Din Yusuf Ibn Ayyub, known in the West as Saladin.

For many years while under the command of Salah Al Din, the Muslims taught the crusaders a harsh lesson, above all by regaining Jerusalem in the Battle of Hattin in 1187. Salah Al Din died five years later, but from Hattin the foothold of the foreign crusaders was steadily undermined.

The Egyptian contribution in battling this first wave of Europeans was essential. During the reign of the Ayyubids, and particularly under Queen Shagarat Al Dor, the Egyptians earned a reputation as avowed defenders of their own country, Islam and the Arab world.

iii. Enslaved by the slaves

In the 1250s Queen Shagarat Al Dor transferred power to the Mamluk class. The Mamluks (meaning 'the owned', or 'slaves' in Arabic) were military men of various nationalities. Originally bought in the slave markets across Asia Minor, most of them were trafficked to Egypt as children, orphaned by the Tartars as they blitzkrieged their way through the Islamic world. In Egypt, the Fatimid and later the Ayyubid kings established special military schools for these traded orphans, nursing within them an intense desire for revenge against the Tartars.

The Mamluks were gallant warriors. Because of their conspicuous valour many of them captured the highest positions in the Egyptian army. Gradually some of those brave soldiers set their hearts on the throne of Egypt. Their chance to take the reins came when Queen Shagarat Al Dor, obliged to find a husband after her first one died, married General Azz Al Din Aybak.

The Mamluks retained the Egyptians as fighters, which was rather fortunate for the Mamluks, because right at the outset of their rule a serious threat had emerged, this time not from 'crusading' Europe, but from East Asia. After capturing Palestine, hordes of Tartars vigorously brandished their weapons at Egypt. With the support of the Egyptians, the Mamluks defeated the Tartars in Ain Galut in 1260, thus consolidating their power in Egypt.

But the Mamluks did not grow complacent. Long years of fighting shoulder to shoulder with the Egyptians had convinced them of their subjects' exceptional military skills. Unlike the Romans, the Mamluks did not need to consult history to see what Egyptians could do in war. The Mamluks had witnessed for themselves the fury and bravery of the Egyptian army.

To remove the domestic threat to their power, the Mamluks imposed military apartheid on Egypt. Many Egyptian fighters were demoted and gradually forced to retire from the army. Unless they were enlisted, the Egyptians had no right to keep arms. Those who could still join the army were not promoted even to the lowest ranks. This discrimination, which had started during the reign of the last Ayyubid king, Negm Al Din, reached its climax following the reign of the first Mamluk kings.

Once again in their long history Egyptians were told that they were born to be no more than farmers. The Mamluks started a campaign of Roman proportions to convince the Egyptian peasant that it had been an accident if at times he had carried a sword instead of a hoe. Very frequently, the Mamluks' frenetic brainwashing propaganda war was accompanied with capital punishment, and soon there was no place at all for Egyptians in the Mamluk-led army. The foreigner complex, first inflicted by the Romans, began for a second time to bite the Egyptian soul.

Only the early Mamluk rulers attempted to benefit Egypt. Among them, the third one, King Barbars was exceptional. Barbars (or Al Zaher, 'The Conspicuous', as he became known posthumously for his ideas and achievements) wanted to introduce a new civilisation, art and education into Egypt. The ignorance and cruelty of the Mamluk kings who succeeded Barbars eclipsed the rays of any potential enlightenment. The intellectual life came to a standstill when Barbars's reign was over.

To Egypt's ill-fortune, the narrow-minded military rulers,

whose sole interest was tax-collection, reigned for almost three centuries. The Mamluks, who had been slaves themselves, succeeded in making 'slaves' out of Egyptians.

iv. Complete apathy

The Mamluks were cruel not only to Egyptians but also to one another. By the beginning of the sixteenth century they were too busy plotting against their own military rulers to assess the potential threat from Constantinople. And when this threat became dangerously imminent, the divided Mamluks were left alone to face the huge Ottoman army.

The Mamluks' strenuous efforts to organise in haste an army of Egyptians came to nothing. The Egyptians had no desire to save their tormentors' skin, and so chose to ignore the call to conscription. The poor Egyptians thought that no other foreign rulers could be worse than the Mamluks. They couldn't have been more wrong.

Without the Egyptians' support, the Mamluks stood no chance against the Turkish hordes. The Turks took control of Egypt shortly after the Battle of Al Raidanoia in 1517.

The Ottomans imposed a new administrative system in Egypt and throughout the Arab world. The Arab lands were split up into emirates, or principalities, thereby seeking to weaken Arab countries so that they would be unable to start any large-scale rebellion against the Porte.

To the Egyptians' misfortune, the Turks did not dismiss the Mamluks, but turned them into blind tools. The Mamluks became the whip with which the Ottomans flagellated the Egyptians up until the end of the eighteenth century. The Turks burdened the Egyptians with heavy taxes, appointing the heartless Mamluks as their tax-collectors. The Mamluks, who had never forgiven the Egyptians for their initial blatant indifference to the Turkish invasion, overcharged the Egyptian farmers to compensate.

Under the Turks, the Mamluks lost their absolute power, but stayed on as knights and landowners. Perhaps their case is akin to that of the Abbassids, the eighth century absolute monarchs of the Islamic world, who were reduced to puppet vassals by their Tartar conquerors.

The Mamluks' main duty was to keep the people of Egypt busy tilling their fields. The Turks knew that the only way to avoid having trouble with the Egyptians was to keep them away from the army. The Romans' and the Mamluks' experience in dealing with this ancient nation proved especially useful to the Porte. The Egyptians' dream to fight and have an army of their own would remain taboo throughout the three centuries of Ottoman rule.

During those hard times of twofold exploitation, Egypt crawled back into the Dark Ages, as did the entire Arab world. The Turks opened no schools in Egypt and limited the number of Egyptians who attended the University of Al Azhar.

It is hardly surprising, therefore, that the foreigner complex reached its peak among Egyptians under the Turks. Many years of deprivation were bound to increase their feeling of inferiority towards the aliens. The Mamluks and the Turks were viewed as superior particularly because of their military status. Egyptians felt humble in front of the military men.

The Arabic word for 'foreigner' is *agnaby*, but gradually the Egyptians came to refer to the Mamluks and mainly to the Turks as *khawaga*, a word which was probably introduced into Arabic with the coming of the Ottomans. Perhaps, its etymology is to be found in the Turkish word *hoca* which is pronounced as *hoja* or *hoga*. *Hoca* means 'university lecturer' or 'religious instructor'. Spelt as *hoxha*, the word can be traced across the breadth of Ottoman rule to Albania, where the Ottomans stayed for almost five centuries. But for the Albanians, *hoxha* never meant more than 'teacher of Islam' and *imam*.

Throughout the long and painful Ottoman rule, Egyptians used the word *hoca/khawaga* to refer to the Turks and their cruel yet obedient servants, the Mamluks. Apparently, for Egyptians the word *khawaga* gradually came to mean not just a 'stranger', or someone belonging to the aristocracy, but also, or rather mainly, a foreigner who was primarily a master in the art of fighting. The poisonous tree whose seeds were carefully sowed by the Romans continued to bear fruit under the Mamluks and especially under the Turks.

v. Cultural invasion

The fate of the Mamluks and the Turks in Egypt changed dramatically with the arrival in 1798 of the French expedition, headed by Napoleon Bonaparte. The Mamluks, who some three centuries earlier had tried unsuccessfully to drum up Egyptian support against the Turkish invasion, did not want to risk losing face once again. This time, however, the Mamluks left the Egyptian farmers to their fields not only because they feared their indifference, but also because they did not take the French threat seriously. At first the Mamluk officers ridiculed the European soldiers for their 'femininity'.

After their crushing defeat at the Battle of the Pyramids in Imbaba on 21 July 1798, the Mamluks were in no doubt that they had foolishly underestimated the uninvited European guests. Their sabres and swords were no match for the Frenchmen's weapons.

Unwilling to accept defeat and knowing that Egyptians were religious by nature, the Mamluks sought to represent Napoleon as the leader of an infidel European army out to besmirch Islam. After all, the French came from the same continent as the crusaders.

Following the Imbaba battle, Napoleon made it clear in his speech relayed in Arabic that the French were not invaders but transmitters of light and culture who venerated Islam. If Napoleon expected the Egyptians to welcome him with open arms as soon as his speech was over, he could not have been more mistaken. The Egyptians remained suspicious, and they were right. History had often taught them that foreigners came to their country to exploit them. It is true that prior to 1798 Egypt had never been invaded by an army that also had a 'battalion' of scientists. The Egyptians were wise to suspect, however, that some of France's brightest minds at that time had not sailed all the way from Toulon simply to benefit them.

In retaliation to the Egyptians' defiant indifference and mistrust, Napoleon rode his horse through Al Azhar Mosque, one of many since Caligula to prove that a genius and a madman have much in common. The Egyptians were outraged and rebelled, forcing Napoleon into negotiations with the Azhari leaders, Sheikhs Omar Makram and Sadat.

Napoleon left Egypt almost a year after his arrival, but many of his scholarly entourage preferred to stay on. For the Egyptians, the French represented a new type of foreigners. These *khawagas*' primary motive in conquest was not military but economic and cultural – if raping antiquities can be termed 'cultural'.

When Napoleon left for France to have himself crowned Emperor, the conditions were uniquely favourable for the Egyptians to declare their independence from the Porte and rule themselves. But the Egyptians had been brought up as slaves for quite a long time, and so lacked the inclination and confidence for self-rule. They were psychologically and politically unprepared to gather together and govern their own country. The foreigner complex had seriously paralysed the Egyptians' will.

vi. Cracked but not broken

Availing himself of Egypt's political apathy, the Turkish Sultan dispatched a large and highly efficient Albanian regiment to fill the vacuum left behind by Napoleon. Commanded by their fellow countryman, the thirty-three-year-old Mohammed Ali, the Albanian soldiers and officers were ordered to restore the authority of the Porte to a chaotic Egypt.

But unbeknown to his superiors and subordinates alike, Mohammed Ali entered the Egyptian labyrinth as his own master. Wearing two masks, he acted both as a loyal military envoy to the Ottomans and as a reliable ally of the ambitious Mamluks.

Ali won the hearts of the Egyptians mainly through his skills as an exceptional fighter. They saw in him a saviour to rid them of the cruel, turbulent Mamluks and of the backward Turks. Ali was the Egyptians' first genuine hope in so many centuries, and they were determined to make the most of this opportunity. Sheikh Omar Makram and Sheikh Sadat beseeched the Turkish Sultan to recognise Ali as the governor of Cairo.

But being the governor of Cairo was not all this *khawaga* from Albania wanted. Ali's burning ambition was to become the absolute monarch of Egypt. And the Egyptians did not have to wait very long to see for themselves what Ali was prepared to do to reach his regal goal. Lacking the time to eliminate each Mamluk opponent one by one, Ali plotted their common death. In March 1811 he held a banquet at the Citadel in Cairo and, after passing the Porte, exterminated some 470 Mamluks.

Following the massacre, Egyptians breathed freely for the first time in six centuries. This does not mean, however, that their foreigner complex came to an end. The Egyptians could not get rid of their crippling inferiority by themselves. They needed help to do so.

Mohammed Ali sensed from the first that the Egyptians' ingrained foreigner complex could seriously hamper his plans to retain power and later on to expand his own empire. That was why he considered it very important that he should do something to liberate the Egyptians from this crippling spell. His success depended on the restoration of this ancient nation's self-confidence and prestige.

At first the Egyptians marvelled at their treatment by Mohammed Ali. Unlike their previous *khawaga* rulers, Ali befriended prominent religious and lay Egyptians, and in his early years at least, never made any step without first consulting the Azhari sheikhs; establishing a *Shura* council (something of a people's parliament) for them to discuss matters of state. Their support justified his purge of the Mamluks and very soon Ali became a popular, though uncrowned, 'king'.

It was only after the Mamluks were dead and buried that the Egyptians discovered that they had been duped. Ali had eliminated the Mamluks not to share power with his subjects but to be the unrivalled leader of the country. With the Mamluks gone, he set about firing key members of his Egyptian team. Unexpectedly, Sheikh Sadat found himself exiled to Assiut and Sheikh Omar Makram to Damieta. Unhappy with its performance, Ali dissolved the *Shura* soon after.

Obviously, Ali had no intention of erasing the foreigner complex from the psyche of Egypt. On the contrary, like his foreign predecessors since the Romans, he sought to instil in the Egyptians once and for all the belief that if they were ever to excel in anything, it would be farming.

It is not by chance then that, perhaps, Mohammed Ali's greatest achievements were in the field of agriculture. He wanted the Egyptians to be not merely peasants but modern farmers. Irrigation projects were implemented without regard to either time or money.

Two new crops, cotton and tobacco, were introduced into Egypt during his reign. Above all, this new ruler knew that a highly developed agriculture was a must in order to maintain the huge army which he was planning; with this he would establish absolute control over Egypt and conquer neighbouring countries and beyond.

Initially, Ali upheld the characteristic trait of the foreign ruler – keeping his subjects out of uniform. He waged successful campaigns in Nubia and several African countries, capturing thousands of Africans and conscripting them into his army. Suleiman Pasha, a French military expert who had converted to Islam, was appointed to oversee the creation of a standing army. His bid to establish military schools in Aswan and Cairo with African recruits was not a success. Despairing, Suleiman tried to persuade Ali to abandon his colonial bent, thus allowing the Egyptians to join the army. The stubborn Albanian monarch finally agreed, and so for the first time in six successive centuries, and for only the second time in two millennia, the Egyptians were given the chance to prove that they could fight as well as farm.

Under the command of Mohammed Ali and his Albanian officers, one of whom was his son Ibrahim, the Egyptian soldiers sought out and found the fountainheads of the River Nile in the heart of Africa, the first time foreigners had done so in history. Allowing Egyptians to join the ranks of his army paid dividends for Ali in no time. It was thanks to their military skills that the ambitious Albanian conqueror could establish an empire which quickly reached into Africa, including Sudan and Ethiopia, and most of the Arab world, stretching from Yemen in the south through Palestine to Syria in the north.

Ali also restored Egypt's status, lost since Pharaonic times, as a naval power. His fleet ruled the Nile and much of the Mediterranean waters, bringing Europeans as slaves to Egypt following his swift successful campaigns in Crete (1822) and Morea (1824). And were it not for European military intervention to stop Ali's army in Lebanon, by the early 1840s the Ottoman Empire would have become the Egyptian Empire.

Under the leadership of a military strategist of Mohammed Ali's calibre, the Egyptians re-emerged as victorious conquerors much in the same way as they had been when they were led to battle by epic Pharaonic warriors like Mina and Ramses II. Several successful military campaigns boosted the Egyptians' self-confidence to an unprecedented level. Ali's loyal subjects were becoming ever more confident that he was a new age ruler determined to erase their enslaving foreigner complex once and for all.

vii. Becoming foreign to become Egyptian

Benefiting from the French instructors who remained in Egypt after Napoleon's departure in 1799, Ali worked hard to make the Egyptians explore their latent potential beyond the limits of farming and soldiering. Only during his reign could farmers dream of becoming not only army officers but also historians, architects and scientists. Ali initiated the military, economic and cultural rebirth of Egypt, something which the French would have been unwilling to do had they retained their military presence there after 1801.

The French expedition proved to be a momentous event in the history of modern Egypt. The year 1798 marked the end of the backward Ottoman rule and of the notorious cruelty of the Mamluks in Egypt as well as the country's first contact with the modern world.

If the Egyptians were lucky when Napoleon came to them, however, they were even luckier when he and his army left Egypt. The French were the first modern Europeans to 'rediscover' the long-lost world of the Pharaohs. This, of course, does not mean that they came to Egypt with the purpose of opening the eyes of the Egyptians to the grandeur of their past. The main purpose of the French was to turn this ancient and resourceful country into one of their colonies. Their expedition was an ambitious political, military and economic undertaking both by Napoleon and the French Directory. Egypt was deemed by the French as an ideal spot where they could undermine Britain's colonial interests, especially by blocking off the Suez trade route. Egypt was also a good consolation prize for the French at a time when they had already lost several sugar-producing colonies in the West Indies. Despite the cultural legacy of their conquest, had the French ruled Egypt for longer, they could have hardly brought about the rebirth of the Egyptian nation in the way that Mohammed Ali did.

For the Egyptians, Ali remains a unique European, for, unlike the French before his arrival and the British after his death, he did not come to Egypt to exploit it for the good of his native Albania, or of his former master, the Turkish Sultan. He wanted Egypt to belong to the Egyptians. Had Napoleon ruled Egypt for much longer, it is most likely that the foreigner complex would have deepened. No colonial power has ever been interested in making subjugated peoples aware of their glorious heritage.

Ali made excellent use of the French experts to rediscover Egypt's Pharaonic past, but he did not rest all hope in them. Egypt's new foreign ruler was keen that Egyptians should also be closely involved in the long and challenging process of unearthing and recording their long-forgotten and ignored Pharaonic civilisation. Coming from one of the most ancient peoples of Europe, the Albanian ruler knew the value of antiquity. He was convinced that Ancient Egypt did not have to be uprooted to France and other European countries to be appreciated. Pharaonic treasures, Ali believed, could be best enjoyed, studied and valued in their native country.

Ali sent many promising Egyptian students to France, hoping they would acquire there the education and culture of the European superpowers, as well as retrace their Pharaonic roots which, with the plundering of Egypt's antiquities, were being replanted in the museums and plazas of Paris.

It was during Ali's reign that the Egyptians first realised the scale of the desecration of what for so long they had considered to be 'piles of stones'. For centuries, the Egyptians had 'sinned', albeit unwittingly, against Pharaonic monuments by erecting religious buildings and other structures with their blocks of stone. Even since the pyramids were built, the Egyptians had been robbing tombs for the wealth they contained.

viii. The making of Egypt's politicians

With Mohammed Ali's death in 1848, Egyptians, armed with their increasing exposure to the new ideas sweeping Europe in the wake of the 1848-1852 revolutions, began to challenge the other long-established taboo that the farmer could not be a politician. This hardly meant that the Egyptians were challenging or posing any threat to Ali's progeny. It would take more than a century before the modern descendants of Pharaohs could convince themselves and the world that they were capable of ruling their ancient motherland on their own again.

Upon the death of Mohammed Ali, the Porte in Istanbul struggled to regain Egypt for its empire. In spite of some success, the Turkish sultans never again achieved the influence they had enjoyed in the Mamluk days. This time, however, British imperial interests, rather than defiance of Mohammed Ali's successors, stood in their way.

But a new force of resistance to the foreign overlords was about to emerge. In 1882, Colonel Ahmed Orabi, who came from fairly humble rural origins and was recruited into the army during the reign of King Said (1854-1863) as part of his programme to Egyptianise the armed forces, led a siege on Abdeen Palace in central Cairo. Orabi insisted on a meeting with Tewfik, who was ruling Egypt as a *Khedive* (a viceroy of the Turkish Sultan). One of Orabi's demands was that the ruler should stop appointing Turkish officers to the Egyptian military.

At first Tewfik refused Orabi an audience. Threatening to storm the palace in Egypt's version of the Bastille, Orabi rallied his fellow countrymen: 'We were born free and we will never be slaves.' Only an urgent plea to the British to intervene could save Khedive Tewfik and his family's fortunes. The British duly obliged and put Egypt under direct military control.

But not all the Alis obeyed the British instructions. One such stubborn ruler was the ambitious Abbas Helmi. Helmi was an outspoken opponent of Turkish and British influence in Egypt. Unhappy with a ruler like Helmi at the helm, no wonder the British banned him from entering Egypt on his way back from Turkey.

Helmi loved Egypt and was loved by his subjects. The Egyptians' foreigner complex was further eroded when his reign brought about the country's cultural revival. King Helmi opened many colleges, including the Schools of Medicine, Architecture and Law. These schools later evolved into the faculties of Cairo University, the first state university in Egypt.

From the outset of the School of Law, several graduates proved that they would be the dominant players in the modern history of their country. Prior to the establishment of the School, all Egyptian lawyers were *sheikhs* – Al Azhar graduates who judged cases according to Islamic jurisdiction. Now it was the time for 'lay' lawyers to become Egypt's *vox populi.*

The most charismatic of the turn-of-the-century lawyers was Mustafa Kamel, founder of the National Democratic Party. In the 1890s, Kamel toured France and England proclaiming his country's violated rights. With his powerful speeches, Kamel restored pride and optimism among his countrymen. 'Were I not an Egyptian,' he once said, 'I would have wished to be an Egyptian'.

The most prominent Egyptian lawyer at that time was Saad Zaghloul. In a spontaneous referendum in 1919 – the first unofficial opinion poll in Egypt – the Egyptians recognised Zaghloul as their legitimate representative to the Versailles Peace Conference. The Egyptians sent an uncompromising message to the recalcitrant British: were it necessary to sign the canvassing letters with their blood, they would be happy to do so. In signing the letters, the Egyptians penned the 1919 revolution and the beginning of the end of the British military presence in Egypt.

The 1919 revolution was not the sole prerogative of lawyers. Egyptian poets, musicians and singers also devoted their talent, energies and art to the national cause. Media Khairi's verses such as 'Wake up, Egyptians, because Egypt is calling you', 'Egypt is saying serving me is a debt you have to pay', and 'I am of the noblest birth' served as clarion calls. Ahmed Showky's 'My country, you are my blood and my heart' became the text of the national anthem. With his voice and music, Said Darwish became the forerunner of the legendary singer Om Kelthoum (1904-1975). Nicknamed 'star of the East', 'empress of Arab tunes' and 'ambassadress of Arabic arts', Kelthoum's songs remain living hymns of patriotism to this day in Egypt.

The year 1919 was a turning-point in the history of modern Egypt. The Egyptians were united in their first popular revolution in centuries.

Egypt's new political leaders emerged triumphant from the revolution. Zaghloul became Egypt's first Prime Minister as head of the *Wafd* (delegation) Party. In 1920 he established constitutional rule in Egypt.

ix. Egypt for the Egyptians

The 1919 revolution proved ominous for the Alis. From then on the question for them was no longer *if* they would ever be deposed but rather *when*. The Egyptians needed only a pretext to get rid of their Albanian rulers, and the moment came in 1948. King Farouk's handling of the Palestinian War in the same year was the last straw.

Egypt's army together with independent Egyptian military units, one of which was formed by the Muslim Brotherhood, were obliged to withdraw after suffering heavy casualties. Egypt boiled with anger and turned against the king. A group of men from the army, in the main graduates from the Military Academy in 1938, who called themselves 'Free Officers', launched the 23 July 1952 *coup d'état*.

The *coup* was bloodless. The Free Officers asked veteran politician Ali Maher to form a government and persuade Farouk, who at that time happened to be in his Muntaza palace in Alexandria, to leave Egypt with his family and most of his wealth. At the insistence of Mohammed Naguib, who headed the Free Officers' Revolutionary Council, ceremonial gunshots were fired as the royal *Al Mahrusa* set sail for Italy with the dethroned Farouk on board. Two years later in January 1954, the 150-year-old Ali monarchy was formally abolished, and Naguib, who was half-Sudanese, became President of Egypt.

But this was not the time for an Egyptian with 'foreign blood' in his veins to rule Egypt. After many frantic efforts, open and secret, the Free Officers of 'pure' Egyptian blood finally sidelined Naguib. In May 1954 he was replaced by Gamal Abdel Nasser.

The spring of 1954 remains special for Egyptians. For the first time in many millennia an Egyptian – an Assiut-born peasant and soldier – was sworn in as President of Egypt. Nasser was not unaware of the significance of this. After narrowly escaping assassination in Al Manshia Square in Alexandria at the end of that year, he angrily addressed the crowd: 'How could you do this to me? I gave you back your self-esteem.'

Nasser's contribution to his country's overcoming its inferiority complex towards foreigners is inestimable. In 1955, this ambitious leader expelled foreigners, especially Albanians and Jews, from Egypt. In 1956, he put an end to the British military presence along the Canal Zone, and nationalised the Suez Canal. In 1957, when the White House failed to keep its promises to help Egypt build the High Dam, Nasser turned to the Kremlin and flooded Egypt with thousands of Soviet experts, particularly after the 1967 war with Israel, when defeat compelled him to import Soviet socialism.

With his moral and military support for the Algerians in their war of a million martyrs in 1956-1957, Nasser proved himself to be the most important leader in the Arab world; two years later he was President of the United Arab Republic, a short-lived union of Egypt and Syria, a union that was attempted even though the two countries share no borders; by the 1960s he was the idol of the Arab world.

In the international arena Nasser sent Egyptian troops to fight alongside freedom fighters in Algeria (against the French), in Congo (against the Belgians) and in Yemen (against the Imams). He also sent assistance to anti-imperialist movements in Ghana, Kenya and Central Africa. In 1955, the young president – he was only thirty-seven – found himself the equal of Tito and Nehru when together the three led the call in Bandung, Indonesia, for a movement of the non-aligned.

After Nasser's sudden and rather mysterious death in 1970, Anwar Sadat, another Egyptian peasant, this time from Monoufiya, became Egypt's head of state. The new leader promised to pursue Nasser's policy and, as the Egyptians put it, Sadat kept his word, but with an eraser in his hand.

In 1971, Sadat declared that he no longer required the Soviets' help, and in October 1973 restored the Egyptians' pride with a war, which was to regain for Egypt all the territories captured by Israel in 1967. Three years later he pre-empted Gorbachev by a decade exchanging war for the taboo of peace with an implacable enemy. He declared he was looking for peace anywhere and everywhere. In order to secure peace he was ready to go even to Tel Aviv. Sadat was the first world leader to search for a peaceful solution to the Arab-Israeli conflict, not through endless rounds of talks, but through concrete actions.

In 1981, this ingenious statesman paid the ultimate price for his efforts to establish peace in the Middle East. His assassination remains a painful reminder of the dark forces still strongly opposed to peace in this volatile region.

Under the presidencies of Nasser and Sadat, the Egyptians led their country in war and peace. In just over a quarter of a century, Egypt became a regional power that was taken seriously by foes and allies alike. Never before in thousands of years had the Egyptians felt so confident about themselves as a nation as during the 1952-1981 period. They could not remember the time when their country had been such an important regional and international player.

In spite of their marked economic and political achievements, ghostly remains of the foreigner complex continue to haunt the Egyptians. Nowadays, the developed countries of the West and the Far East have swapped their armies for sophisticated technology to 'conquer' Egypt, and thus revive the Egyptians' inferiority towards the *khawagas*.

During the long reign of President Hosni Mubarak, who came to power in 1981, Egypt is trying hard to serve as a mediator and a peace broker in a region where conflicts never seem to end. In this mediating role, however, Egypt is hardly an independent player. The current Egyptian president is more of a 'spokesperson' for *khawaga* leaders, mainly the US presidents, than an initiator of the Nasser or Sadat type.

Egyptians, who are far from happy with the influence of the West on their government, can do nothing but grumble. And they will continue to do so until Egypt implements true democracy, and thus gets rid of the infamous *okda al khawaga* once and for all.

– 4 –

Egyptian coffee shops

i. The ancient drinking-places

From time immemorial the swapping of goods in marketplaces in Egypt as well as around the world has been a vital part of daily life. In Ancient Egypt the main market was always located close to the Pharaoh's palace.

The disparate nature of the Pharaonic families meant each fiefdom had its own capital, which would contain a thriving market in its own right. To reach them both Egyptian and foreign merchants had to travel long distances on foot, or drive their loaded camels and horses for miles through the interminable desert and the scorching sun. As one can expect, on arrival at the market the first thing they would ask for was a drink.

Drinks were always there and always profitable. The first vendors would stroll around carrying animal hides filled with water and other refreshments.

With time, the mobile drink peddlers settled in a special area on the fringes of the market, where dealers went to refresh themselves. While drinking, they talked to each other, made new friends and initiated fresh deals. Traders would relax in the shade of leafy trees and pieces of cloth turned into makeshift tents. These places were the antecedents of what some 4,000 years later came to be called *qahwas*, or coffee shops – Egypt's rub-a-dub-dub.

At first, drinks were served in stone or earthenware goblets, later to be replaced by copper cups. Favourite beverages were those now known as *helba*, *karkade* and *ork esus*, all still popular in Egypt.

The Ancient Egyptians' national drinks, however, were wine and beer. It is believed that during Pharaonic times the Egyptians made no less than twenty-four varieties of wine and seventeen of beer. That alcohol was very important to the Egyptians can also be seen from the high esteem in which they held Sesmu, the god of wine. Unlike other deities, this god was worshiped throughout Ancient Egypt.

The Egyptian beer was made from wheat or barley and dates. The Egyptians produced it at home for their own consumption, or bought it from their preferred brewery. One brand of heady and rather toxic beer, known as *buza*, is still made in Egypt.

Beer was the main beverage served in taverns and brothels in Ancient Egypt. So much so that they were known as 'beer houses'.

As markets expanded into cities, the drinking-places spread further afield. The separation of the drinking-place from the market became inevitable with the introduction of money. Until then, customers used to offer some of their own goods in return for refreshments.

These drinking-places were open all day, every day, though they were most busy in the afternoon before sunset. People went there not only to drink but also to unwind, dispute and play games. Throughout Egypt's Pharaonic history these establishments drew people together for daily 'conferences'. It was in such places that ordinary Egyptians learned and talked about royal scandals, new products imported from the magical Land of Punt, festivals, military successes and defeats, and the heretical ideas of Pharaoh Amenhotep IV – who changed his name to Akhenaten – (c. 1352 - 1336 BC), one of the earliest known founders of monotheism. And later, throughout the centuries they were suffering under the Romans, Egyptians used these places to vent their spleen against the tyrannical European invaders.

The drinking-places acquired a special importance particularly by the time the Arabs introduced Islam to Egypt. After listening to an *imam*'s preaching, ordinary Egyptians would discuss among themselves the recently introduced holy message of *Allah*.

From the seventh century, Islamic architecture became an integral part of these refreshment spots. Islamic decorations, designs and styles were found almost on every piece of furniture. Wood, shells and straw were widely used in the design of *mashrabaya* (arabesque).

ii. The advent of coffee

These watering holes, which started during the Pharaohs and outlived them and numerous later rulers of various races, underwent a deep transformation in 1802 with the accession to power of Albanian-born Mohammed Ali. Ali was the first to bring to Egypt tobacco and cotton for cultivation. But if he succeeded with these crops, Ali failed to make the Egyptian farmers cultivate coffee beans – Egypt's soil, climate and humidity, unlike those of Yemen, India and Brazil, are unfavourable for coffee cultivation. All the same, coffee was hardly scarce in Egypt because Ali never ceased importing it from India (*tigara al Hind*).

At first, coffee was never on the menu of the public drinking-places. Being an imported commodity, for many years this exotic drink remained a luxury, which only the Albanian rulers and other people of the élite could afford. Instead, ordinary Egyptians, either at home or in the drinking-places, drank tea, not just because it was cheap, but also because it was hot – hot drinks serving to lower body temperature in warm climates.

Coffee started to be served in the public drinking-spots only when it entered Egypt in large quantities. This was quite an event, and as a result, the drinking establishment began to be named after its newest beverage. This is how *qahwa* (coffee shop) came into being in Egypt.

For many years afterwards, coffee was considered as the drink of older and sophisticated people. Youths frequented cafés, but they neither ordered nor were served coffee.

During the second half of the nineteenth century, many new coffee shops were opened in Cairo, mainly in the Hussein and Al Azhar areas. Al Fishawi Café near the Hussein Mosque continues to welcome customers after almost one hundred and fifty years.

The people who made coffee in the cafés, usually the owners or their sons, were professionals. They knew each *zubun* (customer) personally, as well as his preference for *qahwa zieda* (coffee with extra sugar) or *qahwa sade* (coffee with no sugar).

By the beginning of the twentieth century, because of many internal and external factors, the Egyptian cafés became important institutions of public thought, debate and social life. They began to monitor the pulse of the Egyptian nation.

By the 1920s, there were many coffee shops throughout Egypt. They could be classified into three major kinds: the Alexandrian *bursa*, the Cairo club, and the rural *gharza* (inn). While all three types evolved independently, they played more or less the same role in Egyptian life. They gradually became significant centres where Egyptians sipped the spirit of integration and unity.

iii. The Alexandrian bursa

These drinking-places had a huge impact on the Egyptians. They were also equally important for many Europeans, mainly the Italians and the French, who came to Egypt during the 1914-18 period to escape the horrors of World War I. Their immigration to Egypt continued after the bloodshed was over, and soon they were joined by many poor Greeks, who were looking forward to a better economic future.

One reason why so many Europeans chose to come to Egypt during and after the First World War was because from 1802 onwards Mohammed Ali and his reigning progeny constantly steered Egypt towards Europe. This explains why throughout the one-hundred-and-fifty-year-long reign of the Ali dynasty, the Albanians were not the only Europeans to feel at home in Egypt.

The Italian and French immigrants settled mainly in Alexandria. During the 1920s, they became partners with some Egyptian coffee shop owners before they could open their own cafés. The Greek immigrants were initially employed as waiters in the Alexandrian coffee shops. Unlike their fellow Europeans in Egypt, it took the Greeks quite a long time before they could own their own cafés.

The presence of so many foreigners in Alexandria was bound to have an impact on the city's coffee shops. The cafés employing or owned by European immigrants made this traditionally cosmopolitan city even more so.

In spite of the foreigners' influence, on the whole, most of Alexandria's coffee shops remained traditionally Egyptian. Imitating the idea of big, traditional Egyptian houses, where blood relatives lived together or very near their next of kin, the Alexandrian cafés were big in size as they were meant to 'accommodate' clients belonging to the same 'tribe'. The old, the middle-aged and the young had their own designated corners in those coffee shops.

To attract as many clients as possible, the Alexandrian coffee shops were located close to ministries, courts and other public institutions and places. The walls of these cafés were always decorated with originals and replicas of still-lifes and portraits. Alexandria boasted many such small 'art galleries' in the early decades of the twentieth century.

As time went by, the Alexandrian cafés came to be known as *bursas* mainly because they became popular places for people to meet, discuss business, and make deals.

The *bursa* was different from the Cairo club and the rural *gharza* because of its attitude towards women. The Alexandrian cafés were the only coffee shops in Egypt to welcome female customers. The *bursas* were frequented by women either on their own or in the company of their husbands, sons and male relatives.

Gradually, some Alexandrian *bursas* started serving alcoholic drinks. The move was hardly welcomed by many Egyptians, who immediately boycotted them. But those early semi-bars were not short of customers. They were regularly visited by thousands of soldiers and officers of the British Army from the UK, India and Australia. Those Egyptians who dared to go to such 'infamous' drinking-places had to make sure they were not seen by their fellow teetotal friends.

The majority of the *bursas*, however, did not serve alcohol. This was the main reason why they were always full of loyal Egyptian customers, most of whom were poor and middle-class. As for the rich, they entertained themselves in their imposing villas.

In the 1920s, Alexandria was more sophisticated and cosmopolitan than Cairo. This explains why the first *salons* in Egypt emerged initially in this Mediterranean city. Members of the aristocracy made a habit of welcoming writers, painters and musicians to their mansions to discuss art and literature. Likewise, fellow artists began to invite each other and members of the Alexandrian social élite to their own houses.

Those *salons* would later spread to Cairo. The *literary salons* of Alexandria and Cairo were one of the main reasons why Egyptian literature flourished in the first half of the twentieth century.

Both the *literary salon* and the *bursa* played a significant patriotic role throughout the 1930s and 1940s. The difference between them was that while the former brought together and catered for the privileged few, the latter accommodated people from all walks of life.

The Alexandrian *bursa* became the preferred venue for singers and poets to meet ordinary Egyptians and make them conscious of their responsibility to their country. Among those artists frequenting the *bursas* were singer-composer Said Darwish and poet Beram Al Tonsi. Darwish was a builder. After work he would often go to a *bursa* to play the lute and sing. As a composer he is considered to be the founder of a new music school in the Middle East. He composed and sang many songs about love, life and nature. On the whole, however, his repertoire consisted mainly of patriotic songs.

Al Tonsi was born in Egypt to Tunisian parents. Yet he never considered himself a *khawaga* (foreigner). The founder of modern Egyptian poetry, he was one of the country's leading poets throughout the 1920-1960 period. Al Tonsi made a habit of reciting his verse in several *bursas*. He wrote his poetry mainly in *amaya* (colloquial Arabic) so that he could appeal directly to ordinary Egyptians.

Al Tonsi's patriotic poetry gave great cause for concern to the British and the monarch of Egypt who sent him into exile to France and Tunisia several times between the 1920s and 1940s. Each time he was sent away, however, Al Tonsi managed to return to Egypt.

Musicians and poets like Darwish and Al Tonsi turned the Alexandrian *bursa* into a living theatre where, almost on a daily basis for many years, they not only entertained their fellow countrymen, but also filled them with patriotic pride and hope for a better future. It is possible to trace the roots of the 1919 revolution largely to the powerful poetry and music of these Alexandrian *bursas.*

Unfortunately, Darwish died on the day when thousands of enthusiastic Alexandrians were welcoming home Saad Zaghloul as he returned from exile. Darwish had been poisoned in mysterious circumstances. No poison, however, could kill the patriotism his music and Al Tonsi's poetry had inspired.

The Alexandrian *bursas* remained centres of ardent patriotism up until the 1950s. It was there that students organised and began their massive strikes and demonstrations against the British rule. These coffee shops played a vital role in making the Egyptians understand and support the 1952 revolution.

Paradoxically enough, the successful outcome of the revolution marked the end of the Alexandrian *bursas*. The new rulers of Egypt, who were delighted by the popular support they enjoyed when they came to power, had no time for the *vox populi* once the revolution was over. The Alexandrian *bursa* was not the only unfortunate casualty of the Free Officers' revolution. The Cairo clubs also suffered when the reins of power changed hands.

iv. The Cairo club

In the first two decades of the twentieth century some coffee shops came to be known as 'clubs' because their customers gathered together to thrash out political and religious issues. Art and philosophy in the capital were initially discussed in the *literary salons* of famous artists and thinkers like Abbas Al Akad. The *salons* in Cairo were particularly fashionable in the 1940s.

The infiltration of the ideas of the 1917 Russian revolution into Egypt in the 1920s made politics a much-favoured topic in many Cairo coffee shops. Debates on social in/justice and Communism attracted many ordinary Egyptians to some cafés, which came to be known as the coffee shops of the Communists. Those who loathed or mistrusted Marx and Soviet propaganda held their lively discussions in the coffee shops of the capitalists. While most customers were loyal to their 'political clubs', it was not unusual for political opponents to exchange visits to each other's cafés for fiery debates.

Communist propaganda was forbidden in Egypt during the 1930s. This explains why many coffee shops frequented by the Communists were often closed down during this period.

Throughout the 1930s and 1940s, Cairo witnessed an increase in the number of cafés where the main topic of discussion was religion. The Muslims, the Christians and even the Jews – 'Metetia' in downtown Cairo was the most well-known Jewish café in Egypt – had their own religious coffee shops in the capital during this time. Most of the religious coffee shops were situated in the Hussein area and near Al Azhar Mosque. Angry and disappointed with their moderate colleagues, many hard-line sheikhs and other spiritual leaders used the religious cafés to preach in favour of implementing 'pure' religion in every aspect of life.

Many were the Egyptian patriots who opened their own cafés in Cairo in the 1930s and 1940s. These coffee shop owners offered shelter to young Egyptian scholars who opposed the British rule. The British failed to catch the troublemakers because every time they followed them to the patriots' cafés, they left the premises through secret doors.

If many café owners in Alexandria and Cairo were successful in their attempts to shelter patriots and often saved them from the British, they found themselves helpless in the wake of the 1952 revolution when the Egyptian regime itself started chasing 'mischief-makers'. Egypt's new masters were military men who craved absolute power. Afraid of any opposition to their totalitarian rule, they stifled the free debates their fellow countrymen had been enjoying for almost half a century in cafés across the country.

The Egyptian coffee shops, which had been the cradle of democracy, suffered a serious blow immediately after the revolution. Many *bursas* in Alexandria and clubs in Cairo were shut down and some of their owners and customers arrested and thrown in jail. No wonder the number of coffee shops and their activity declined considerably throughout the 1950s and 1960s. Egyptian democracy began and unfortunately ended with the Alexandrian *bursas* and the Cairo clubs. The only indirect criticism of the Nasser regime thereafter would come from the theatre.

Customers visiting the coffee shops that had escaped the wrath of the military rulers continued to debate literary and social issues. They would no longer, however, discuss politics or prices of food. One such café where politics became taboo was that owned by Hag Ibrahim Nefa. This coffee shop, which was opened in the 1940s and outlived both the 1952 revolution and Nasser, is still found in Dokki.

'Apolitical' as the cafés of Cairo became in the wake of the 1952 revolution, they continued to play a major role in promoting cultural debate in Egypt. With their frequent visits to several Cairo clubs throughout the 1960s, Beram Al Tonsi and other artists ensured that the capital's coffee shops remained important centres of culture and art. The discussions held there inspired many promising young artists, writers, scholars and thinkers such as Joussef Idris, Noaman Ashur, Saad Al Din Wahba, Alfred Farag and the 1988 Nobel Prize Laureate in Literature, Naguib Mahfouz (1911-2006). The coffee shops of Cairo were the original birthplace of some of the best literary works in Arabic written in the second half of the twentieth century.

v. The rural gharza

The only kind of coffee shop in Egypt that did not suffer as a result of the 1952 revolution was the rural *gharza*. Up until the revolution, the Egyptian farmers, whether they lived in the Delta or in Upper Egypt, were largely unaffected by urban life. As they were able to sustain themselves on their own, they imported almost nothing from the city, and if occasionally they went there it was mainly to trade their agricultural and animal products.

Historically, Egyptian peasants had been conservative to the core. They always shunned the city primarily because of their ingrained 'citizen complex'. To the *fellahin* (peasants), city folk were 'tricky' people, whose aim was to cheat, abuse, rob them of their *filus* (money) and, of course, make fun of their simple-mindedness. Whenever farmers visited the city for health reasons or to offer their condolences, they wasted no time in hastening back to their undisturbed, rural life.

In the early 1920s, some business-minded citizens and daring farmers bought coffee beans in the city and carried them to several rural areas where they built *gharzas* (small country inns made of wood) and started serving coffee to peasant customers. This marked the beginning of the end of the frosty relationship between country people and city dwellers.

For many years, those farmers who wanted to open coffee shops in the countryside would not dare do so in their own villages. It took their fellow *fellahin* a long time to stop viewing the new profession of the coffee shop owner with suspicion. Many were the peasants who saw the coffee beans as the seeds of corruption, as a sophisticated tool in the hands of the shrewd city people to spoil their quiet, rustic life.

Most Egyptian farmers shied away from opening coffee shops

themselves, but they did not hesitate to frequent these new attractions from the start. The arrival of the 'drink of the élite' was quite an occasion in the life of the Egyptian peasantry. Its unheard-of name and strange flavour were too tempting for them to ignore the exotic beverage. Little did they know that by entering the *gharza* they were in fact making an irreversible step towards the city.

From the beginning, the rural *gharza* was something of a supermarket in miniature. The *gharza* owner imported from the city not only coffee but also other goods, which were displayed in a special corner. Thanks to the *gharza*, for the first time ever Egyptian farmers no longer needed to go to the city to buy lipsticks and skin creams for their wives. The *gharza* gradually brought the city to them. Cosmetic products, new shapes of *takaya* (caps), *galabyias*, watches, slippers and veils of lovely colours appeared in the stalls of the *gharza* as if by magic.

The rural *gharza* also introduced something new to the farmers' rustic daily routine. If for centuries life for them had meant nothing more than working in the fields and praying in churches and mosques, during the 1920s and 1930s the *gharza* offered them a chance for recreation as well. From its early days, usually at sunset, the *gharza* would draw the farmers away from their wives, children and family problems. Naturally, women and young girls were not allowed in.

In the *gharza* the peasants could order not only coffee but also tea, *naana* and other traditional Egyptian drinks. Of course, no one expected alcohol to be served there.

The rural coffee shop also became an ideal place for the village elders who would spend much of their time there smoking and drinking coffee. These regulars had permanent seats that younger farmers would never dare to occupy.

Like the Alexandrian *bursa*, the rural *gharza* was not short of entertainers. In common with their fellow countrymen, the Egyptian farmers were addicted to music. The *gharza* offered the peasant musicians a unique opportunity to display their talent in front of enthusiastic admirers. Music was an essential part of the village coffee shop from the first.

But the rural *gharza* was more than just a place where farmers of all ages could while away their time, drink, do their shopping or entertain themselves. From the onset, it also became the village news centre. The *gharza* was the most reliable source of information on village births, deaths, engagements, marriages and divorces. There quarrels, disputes and feuds were thrashed out and, in most cases, settled amicably. Those who were not on speaking terms would often become friends again in the *gharza*, celebrating the event with a coffee of reconciliation.

The rural *gharzas*, especially those located alongside national roads, were soon destined to play another reconciliatory function. They became in no time what are now known as 'rest houses', where citizens travelling across the country would stop for food and drink. The hospitable *gharza* served as a unique place for the suspicious farmers and stuck-up city dwellers to get to know each other better. It was in these modest coffee shops by the side of the road that country and city people began to look at each other with less distrust and to consider one another not as aliens but as partners. The frequent contacts encouraged many farmers to visit the city more often. The rural *gharza* was instrumental in tempting thousands upon thousands of farmers to migrate to the city in the wake of the 1952 revolution.

On the whole, the number of coffee shop clients declined during the Nasser regime, partly because many Egyptians – city people and farmers – found employment up and down the country in ambitious projects such as the Aswan High Dam and Lake Nasser. With his totalitarian tactics Nasser may have undermined the spirit of free debate that used to thrive in coffee shops prior to his 'accession', but he also offered his people a common purpose. He made them feel proud of their identity as an ancient nation, convincing them that they had the potential to build a better future for themselves.

Between 1967-1975, most cafés in Egypt were often closed or empty because of the war with Israel. After 1975, many coffee shops sprang up in Cairo. President Sadat's open-door policy meant that for the first time in the history of the Egyptian coffee shops, the new owners would no longer hope simply to survive but also to make profits.

Nowadays the Egyptian coffee shops are not short of customers. However, they are no longer important centres in the country's political, cultural, artistic or religious life. The majority of Egyptians are too busy making a living in a materialistic world that demands all their time and energies. The only time cafés bring this nation together today is when crowds of ecstatic fans are glued to television screens to support their national football team. The referee's final whistle is a painful reminder of the rat race they, like most of us, have to face day in day out.

– 5 –

The Bride of *Hapi* – female sacrifice and cosmic order

i. The genesis of the rite

Nearly five thousands years ago the people of Egypt had their own version of what is now known as the Miss World contest. When exactly this annual event came into being in Ancient Egypt is difficult to say. The general belief is that it was initially held as a state-run activity from the first stage of the Pharaonic civilisation, known as the Early Dynastic Period (c. 3000-2700 BC).

Although a yearly event, the contest was almost as important as the *Sed* Festival (jubilee celebrations) held after the first thirty years of the Pharaoh's rule or whenever he felt the need to replenish his strength. The erratic behaviour of the River Nile was a disturbing reminder to the Pharaoh that, 'divine' as he was, he could do with some special rituals to keep the much-needed, flowing monster under control. This, perhaps, explains why the Ancient Egyptians' version of today's beauty contest was religiously motivated, and as such conducted by the Pharaoh's high-ranking priests.

In Ancient Egypt the beauty contest was open to every young

woman; the only requirement was that she had to be a virgin. Having succeeded in the preliminaries organised along the banks of the river from Nubia to the Nile Delta, Egypt's most beautiful girls, dressed as brides, headed for the Royal Palace to take part in the finals. This important national event was hosted by the Pharaoh himself, and took place towards the end of summer.

The finalists were mainly upper-class young ladies, including daughters, sisters, nieces and other female relations of the Pharaoh. Often it was one from the royal household, or someone closely connected with the court, who ended up winning the much-coveted, if fateful, title. This distinction brought honour not only to the winner, but also to her royal or aristocratic parents, and the entire household. In the rare cases when the chosen one was an 'outsider', honour was shared with the people of her tribe, village, town or city.

No matter who the winner was, the whole country rejoiced every year for the Bride of *Hapi*, who was destined to make happy a god venerated for his generosity, and dreaded for his tantrums.

Ancient murals depict the voracious bridegroom as a bloated hermaphrodite with a pregnant belly. The bisexual image symbolised the River Nile which the Ancient *Misrain* (Egyptians) had baptised *Hapi*. In Pharaonic mythology *Hapi* was both a god and a goddess.

The Nile has always been Egypt's fountain of life, and Egyptians, ancient and modern, have remained grateful to their benefactor although he was not always bounteous, and droughts were not rare.

The caprices of the river, however, did nothing to undermine the Egyptians' veneration for it. Together with their 'divine' rulers, they strongly believed that their life-provider was sacred. This is the reason why in the colourful Pharaonic pantheon of gods and goddesses *Hapi* always had a place of special distinction.

As opposed to other ancient deities, *Hapi* was not worshipped at a permanently designated, monumental temple. His shrine was a makeshift diving-board erected annually at different places by the river side. From there, the high priest offered the winning bride as a sacrifice to the Nile, thus cruelly terminating the bloom of her youth on her nuptial day.

The deep conviction of the Pharaoh (the living god), the clergy (considered as the only mortals having the power to communicate with the gods), the fated bride, and the exalted crowd attending the 'blessed' execution, was that in 'marrying' the female beauty, *Hapi* would not violate his lasting covenant with Egypt. They believed that, having acquired the prize, in return, the deity would ensure that the waters of the Nile would ceaselessly flood their parched land, and so their granaries would always be full.

The Ancient Egyptians had for centuries observed that their valley was often heavily flooded in autumn. It is difficult to say if, or when exactly, they realised that the floods followed the spring rainfall and summer snow-melt in the Ethiopian mountains and Ugandan highlands that fed the Nile. What is known is that they never failed in their attempts to pacify this capricious ally. The Egyptians continued for centuries to drown their most beautiful 'bride' at the beginning of autumn, adamant that the sacrificial ceremony was their only hope for survival. This explains why it outlived the very civilisation whose longevity remains mysterious and unique in the history of mankind.

Antony and Cleopatra's defeat at the naval Battle of Actium in the year 31 BC sealed the end of the three-century long Greek presence in Egypt, a period which formed the last chapter in the long Pharaonic history. Soon after this momentous event, the Roman lover and his Egyptian enchantress took their own lives. Legend has it that Cleopatra died from snake poison. The serpent that bit the last wearer of the Pharaonic crown put an instant end to her life, but not to the ancient civilisation she had tried so hard, though without success, to serve. Many Pharaonic rites and traditions, including the annual sacrifice of a beautiful bride, outlived Cleopatra.

Octavius, the new ruler of Egypt, had no intention of stopping the recurrent tragedy. He did not have the spiritual motivation to care. The cruel rite continued to take its toll on Egyptian beauties not only when Octavius was in Egypt but also throughout his long reign as the first Emperor of Rome.

For centuries the Romans plundered the Egyptian temples and tombs, thus seriously eroding the Pharaonic heritage. As a direct result of the Romans' iconoclastic attitude towards the Pharaonic civilisation, the number of Egyptians who believed in the once popular gods and goddesses diminished considerably. As for the few staunch believers who were eager to perform the ancient rites, they gradually stopped seeing the Pharaonic creed as an organised religious system. It was during the early part of Rome's domination of Egypt that, in the words of the French writer Chateaubriand, the hieroglyphs became 'like a seal placed on the lips of the desert'. No wonder the names of the Ancient Egyptians' deities sank into oblivion, and together with them, that of *Hapi*.

But if time whitewashed the name of *Hapi*, the Nile retained its annual appetite for a bride. With the sunset of the Pharaonic era, however, the winning contestant could no longer claim to be Miss *Misr* (Egypt), as her selection was not the result of a nationwide event.

The main reason why under the Romans not all Egyptians participated in the long selection process of the annual *arusa* (bride) was that by then they had gradually ceased sharing a unifying creed. Tolerant Egypt had already begun to shelter Jews, and to welcome Christianity. The Egyptian Jews and Christians were unable, or perhaps unwilling, to completely stop the sacrificial ceremony. On the whole, they did not commit themselves to altering the long-established popular conventions and traditions of Egypt.

While Christians were in very large numbers in Egypt from the first century AD, Christianity became the state religion in the land of Pharaohs only in the fourth century. This was the time when the Egyptians made their first organised effort to stop some of the persistent pagan rites and practices. And they largely succeeded because by that time the Romans too had already converted to Christianity. The cruel invaders, who had remained pagan despite many temptations, had finally adopted Christianity during the reign of Constantine in the hope that the conversion might save their gigantic, ailing empire.

The dramatic changes in Egypt's religious landscape in the fourth century AD, however, did not necessarily mean that the annual ceremony of offering a 'bride' to the Nile came to an end. Egyptian farmers proved far too stubborn to stop this ancient and cruel rite. They were confident that their bond with the river was unique and, as such, no religion, not even Christianity, had any power or right to intervene. The Nile was their everlasting source of life and hope. If they had to sacrifice a beautiful girl every year to keep the flowing giant happy, then so be it. Apparently, the farmers did not consider this as one of their many heavy taxes. And so beauty remained a cursed blessing for many more Egyptian *belles* until the middle of the seventh century AD.

ii. The drowning

The decade during which Omar Ibn Al Khatab officiated as the second *Caliph* marked a steady increase in the number of Muslim believers in what is now known as the Arab world. Al Khatab, who was committed to spreading Islam worldwide, was particularly keen to introduce the new religion into Egypt. His appointment of Amr Ibn Al Azz (an expert in Egyptian mentality and mores) as the first Muslim envoy in Egypt was a well-calculated choice.

Al Azz loved Egypt and was determined to persuade as many Egyptians as possible to convert to Islam. As he had already visited Egypt prior to his religious mission, he knew a great number of Egyptians, and was welcomed by the country's most renowned families. It was perhaps during one of these early visits to Egypt that he had first learnt of the sorry fate of the annual bride of the River Nile. His coming to Egypt as the official envoy of Islam in the 640s coincided with a severe drought. The River Nile had dried up to such an extent that it is believed that in some places it could be crossed on foot. Water was badly needed for drinking, sanitation and irrigation throughout Egypt. Desperate for a miracle, the Egyptians were making the final preparations to offer the Nile the yearly bribe of a bride.

Al Azz was keen to bring this cruel ritual to an end, but he did not intervene at once. He first sought urgent advice from Medina. Caliph Omar wasted no time in replying, and his message was unequivocal. The Caliph ordered his dutiful representative in Egypt to stop the pagan sacrifice once and for all.

By that time, however, the calamitous drought had already claimed its first victims. Egypt was in a state of panic and despair. Monitoring the mood of the country carefully, Al Azz decided to reason with the thirsty Egyptians before showing them Omar's message. The patient negotiator met with a deputation of frustrated Egyptians, and tried hard to dissuade them from going ahead with that year's drowning of a beautiful girl. His efforts, however, came to nothing. Much to his disappointment, the Egyptians turned a deaf ear to his reasoning and pleading.

Feelings were running high, but even at that critical moment Al

Azz did not hasten to ban the sacrificial act outright. His intervention had already inflamed the populace's resentment toward him and Islam across the country. He knew that one hasty move on his part, and the situation could get worse. Having convinced some moderate Egyptians (who themselves had serious misgivings about the rite) to delay that year's planned execution for a little while, and foreseeing further unhappy developments, Al Azz decided to contact Omar again. The *Caliph* responded without delay. He instructed Al Azz to read out his message to the enraged Egyptian *fellahin* (farmers).

Numerous dejected Egyptians reportedly gathered on both banks of the stream-like Nile. They were told that *Caliph* Omar had sent them a message, but they could hardly guess what it was about, or why that particular site had been chosen for them to receive it. They were all ears when Al Azz produced the scroll, which is believed to have read as follows:

> *Hey, Nile! If you claim to be a god and to flow of your own free will, we do not need your water because we believe only in Allah. But if you flow of Allah's will, then we pray to the Almighty, and to Him only, to have mercy on us and bless us with your water.*

To the Egyptians' great surprise, after Al Azz finished reading the message, he threw the scroll into the river. That was the Nile's 'bride' for that year. As Caliph Omar's message sailed away, it took with it one of the most enduring Pharaonic traditions. A cruel practice that had been going on for almost three millennia finally came to an end.

But not forever. It would resurface unexpectedly after twelve long centuries when Pharaonic Egypt was rediscovered.

iii. The revival

The Middle Ages sank in Europe to re-emerge in Egypt. The Napoleon-led French expedition to Egypt in 1798 was the country's first glimmer of hope in three centuries of Ottoman darkness. But if the French initiated the Egyptian revival, it was the Albanian-born genius Mohammed Ali who masterminded it. Ali was the driving-force behind the Egyptian renaissance. To a large extent, his success resulted from his ability to make the best use of the work done by the French prior to his arrival in Egypt. Ali was also ever willing to support and encourage the members of the French expedition who chose to stay in Egypt after Napoleon's departure, as well as several other inspired European scholars interested in his newly adopted country.

Jean-François Champollion's decoding of the *cartouche* bearing the name of Ramses II, and later of the Rosetta Stone, finally put an end to the long silence of the Pharaonic civilisation. Thanks to Champollion and a host of devoted Egyptologists from France and several other European countries, Ancient Egypt was brought back to life after almost eighteen long centuries of hibernation.

While Ali benefited from the inestimable contribution of many European Egyptologists in resurrecting the Pharaonic civilisation, he also made sure that the Egyptians themselves did not remain idle spectators in the process. Ali believed that without the Egyptians' direct involvement, any effort to study and bring Ancient Egypt back to life would be incomplete.

By the time Ali started his rule, there were no Egyptians who could match the expertise of the European Egyptologists. But Ali had a solution to this problem. He provided every opportunity for many bright Egyptian youths to study in France so that they would be able to decipher for themselves the texts of their ancient scribes.

When the long-frozen hieroglyphs finally began to melt in front of their eyes, Ali's Egyptians realised for the first time that, unlike the Europeans during the fourteenth, fifteenth, and sixteenth centuries, they did not need to draw inspiration from the ancient Greek and Roman civilisations to bring about the Egyptian revival of the nineteenth century. Much to their amazement and delight, they now discovered that they were the descendants of a much older and even more refined culture. Their long-forgotten civilisation had been the cradle of ancient and modern Europe, the very seedbed of what we now know as Western civilisation.

The Paris-educated Egyptian intellectuals had two main aims when they returned home: first, to open their countrymen's eyes to the European civilisation and, second, to make them feel proud of their own glorious ancient heritage. Brilliant scholars like Rifat Al Tahtaui, who wrote widely and memorably about Paris, and Ali Mubarak, one of the founders of the Egyptian Museum in Cairo, were instrumental in building the much-needed cultural bridges between their ancient country and Europe.

It was mainly because of Mubarak's zeal for studying ancient myths, legends and creeds that many long-forgotten gods and goddesses were reawakened. Of all the Pharaonic deities, however, *Hapi* had the most dramatic resurrection.

In the 1820s, Mohammed Ali made several successful attempts to discipline the River Nile. Because of the *hawis* (iron gates) at Kamatr Al Khairia, water no longer flowed wastefully into the Mediterranean. Thousands of hectares of desert were reclaimed as a result of the Monoufiya and Baheiri Canals.

The Egyptians rejoiced because for the first time in several millennia they felt strong enough to take on the Nile. The achievement was impressive and as such deserved to be celebrated in style. It was during this surge of national euphoria that *Hapi* was suddenly brought back to life. Mubarak was probably the first to think of inviting the infamous 'bridegroom' to the celebrations.

And so in the 1830s *Hapi*'s annual 'marriage' routine started all over again. Since then, every year towards the end of summer, many Cairenes carouse alongside the river to celebrate the Bride of *Hapi*, just as their ancient counterparts did every autumn from the Old Kingdom to the Islamic conquest.

But today's Nile is no longer in luck. Instead of 'wedding' a beautiful virgin, the modern bridegroom marries a stone doll, usually dressed up as a bride. In 1993, a mortal *arusa* was chosen not for her 'blue' blood, beauty and chastity but for her swimming skills. A champion diver hurled herself from the Abbas Bridge on 27 August for a brief fling with *Hapi* rather than a lifetime commitment.

Nowadays, the five-day *Hapi* festival is organised by the Governorate of Cairo, and the Ministries of Youth and Sport, Culture and Tourism. On the final day of the hoopla, several people in Pharaonic costume sing and dance along the riverbanks, as the ship with the doll-bride on board approaches the centre of the 'lake' near the University Bridge, which is the widest point of the Nile in Cairo. A fleet of smaller, decorated boats packed with ecstatic sailors surrounds the bride-ship. When the moment comes to give the 'bride' away, the sailors blow their horns in unison, imitating the exaltation of the ancient 'wedding guests'. The spectacular event always attracts huge crowds, with many more watching the colourful ceremony on television.

Today, thanks to the Aswan Dam, *Hapi* has been brought to heel. Bride or no bride, the Nile remains high throughout the year, every year. *Hapi*'s periodic fits of pique that caused droughts are a thing of the past. But as a symbol of what unifies all Egyptians, the Nile remains worth celebrating.

It is anybody's guess if *Hapi* is content with his doll-brides now.

But then few care about this notorious serial bridegroom, least of all the beautiful girls of Egypt. A lot of water has flown since they last had nightmares about muddy marriage-death-beds.

– 6 –

A parade of porters

Not all Gëzim's articles, it must be confessed, were well received. As MET [*Middle East Times*] editor, I was used to complaints, most of them from the censor's office and touchy western diplomats. But I was struck when one arrived from the doormen's association, objecting to the publication of Gëzim's essay celebrating the Sudanese import of the *bowab*, or porter. At first I feared this was another ploy by Egypt's Information Ministry to attack the MET and defend a key institution in its intelligence arm: tucked into their cubby-holes under the stairwell of every apartment block in Cairo, the *bowabs* were widely regarded as official informers on the tiniest of domestic ripples. But after Gëzim and I traipsed the five flights of chipped stairs to the grubby home of the Nubian Association in Cairo, it became apparent that the *bowabs* were defending their honour. They objected to Gëzim's slur that they had been dragooned *en masse* from Sudan by that ubiquitous Albanian, Mohammed Ali. Worse, they accused Gëzim of propagating the smear that *bowabs* would punish ungenerous residents by trapping them in lifts between floors, or withholding their mail. Gëzim, it seemed, was as guilty of damaging Nubia's cultural pride as Nasser was in drowning Nubian civilisation with his construction of the Aswan dam. *Bowabing* is an Egyptian taboo not to be mocked.[1]

Nicolas Pelham, Former Editor of the *Middle East Times*

i. The Nubian doorman

Not long ago, a dark-complexioned doorkeeper in red livery was a fixture at the front entrance of Cairo's best hotels. His only duty seemed to be putting on a smile whenever opening the doors in welcome and farewell.

Nowadays, hotel doors open and close by themselves, and this dandy *bowab* has had to leave his post. Porters still scamper about, carrying luggage or hailing taxis, but something is missing without the courteous and friendly black doorman at the entrance to usher guests in and out.

The origin of this profession is as old as the polarisation of society into haves and have-nots. More recently, the great-grandfathers of the black porters emerged in Egypt during the era of the Albanian ruler, Mohammed Ali. After his successful campaigns in Nubia, the region that bridges Egypt and Sudan, Ali brought back to Cairo man-slaves to serve in the palaces and villas of the members of the military hierarchy.

At first the new slaves spoke only their native Nubian language which, to this day, remains unwritten. When the sons of the Nubian slaves grew up, rich and middle-class Egyptians employed them as doorkeepers. The Citadel, Abdeen, Garden City and Zamalek were areas populated by the well-to-do. Not far from there lived the families of the Nubian porters. Up to the present day, the progeny of those doormen have dwelt around the palace of Abdeen, near the Citadel, in Boulk Aboulaila, and in Mounira.

The Nubian porters were highly trustworthy people. That is why up until the end of the Ali monarchy, the overwhelming majority of civil sentries were chosen from among them. They were considered by their masters as 'members' of their families, and the faithful employees were eager to do all they could to please their employers. They were satisfied with what they earned and had their hearts in whatever they did. Their main duty was to stand beside the front door, but they were ever willing to perform other chores such as cooking, shopping, gardening or sending messages.

Amity between the porters and their masters continued until the revolution of 1952. Shortly after this turning point in the history of modern Egypt the situation started to change. President Nasser's socialism undermined the long-established Egyptian social pyramid. His policies were also to affect the doormen who by then had a century-old tradition behind them. He offered the Nubian porters Egyptian nationality, which they accepted readily.

After July 1960, with the beginning of a nationwide policy of nationalisation, the Nubian doorkeepers and especially their sons, not wanting to see themselves as 'inferiors' amongst 'equal' citizens, were unwilling to serve in their traditional jobs. Instead, they chose to work in state-run factories and shops, or opened their own cafés. Many returned to their tribes in Nubia.

Others started smuggling goods across the southern borders of Egypt. Their familiarity with the nooks and crannies of their ancient native land helped them avoid detection as they sent goods like cheese, sugar, tea and coffee, which were inexpensive in Egypt, to parts of Africa, mainly Sudan, Ethiopia and Chad, in exchange for leather, feathers, cacao, monkeys, wood products, to mention a few. This is how the Pharaonic-old tradition of doing business with the Land of Punt was revived in Egypt in the twentieth century.

The Nubian porter, always dressed in his long and loose *galabiya* with a red *tabush* on the head and a *nabut* on the hand, had become history in the 1960s and 1970s. But very soon the Egyptians came to understand that they could not do without the doorman. That was why the much-loved and trustworthy figure of the *bowab* appeared again. This time, though, he did not come mainly from

Nubia. The modern doorkeeper emerged from areas not far from Greater Cairo.

ii. The peasant bowab

By the end of the 1970s, masses of dejected *fellahin* (peasant-farmers) had temporarily deserted the Egyptian countryside for various reasons. Some could not afford to buy a piece of land of their own. Others were unable to support themselves with what land they had. And there were those who could not cultivate their fields throughout the year.

Many of these fortune-seekers came from Fayoum, a region which, since its climate began to dry up some six millennia ago, has always been one of the poorest in Egypt. Fayoum, as a populated area, dates back to the beginning of the Middle Kingdom (c. 2055-1650 BC) of the Pharaonic civilisation, or to be more precise, to the XII Dynasty.

The XII Dynasty Pharaoh Sesostris II ordered the building of what was perhaps the first high water dam in the world, the Lahun Dam. The completion of the Lahun Dam was one of the Ancient Egyptians' successful attempts to discipline the unruly Nile. Since then, the sunken Fayoum land has never been flooded again. Through another canal, Sesostris II also made it possible for peasants to get water from the river. Hundreds and thousands of *feddans* were put into cultivation as a result of these remarkable feats of engineering.

In spite of such long-term benefits from Sesostris II's agricultural developments, the Fayoum farmers have never had enough arable land. To this day their governorate remains something of an oasis. This explains why many people from the region have always eyed nearby Cairo with hope.

By 1970, Cairo had ceased being the villa capital of Egypt as many of the old single-family residences were pulled down to make way for modern housing. New multi-storey buildings mushroomed, biting into considerable areas of cultivated land. While the Egyptian capital was being transformed into a gigantic building site, it attracted many farmers not only from Fayoum, but also from Sharkia, Tanta, Said and beyond.

The farmers were employed in demolishing numerous villas. Many of them were too unskilled to be trusted with the mortarboard of the bricklayer, but they could prepare mortar, put up scaffolds and carry building materials.

As the rate of construction of new blocks of flats began to decline, the one-time farmers gradually started to lose their jobs. Some of them returned to their villages. Many, however, especially those from Fayoum, chose to stay in the bustling metropolis. A new occupation, one that no Fayoum farmer could have at first thought of, was opened to them. They became the doorkeepers of the newly built buildings and of the few villas which were lucky to avoid demolition.

This marked the revival of doorkeeping in Egypt. The new *fellah* doorman filled in the gap left by the disappearance of his black Nubian predecessor.

Unlike the Nubian porter, the new doorkeeper is a farmer to the core. Physically he is in Cairo, but his mind is in the countryside with which he retains a very close relationship. This explains why in many cases he refuses to take his family to live with him in Cairo. Being a traditional man, he is unwilling to let his children, and especially his wife, see those aspects of city life of which he does not approve.

The main reason however why the Fayoum farmer has doggedly pursued the life of a hermit in his underground 'cell' is that he has never abandoned his dream of returning home to buy a few *feddans* of land. In spite of his many years of devoted service in the capital, the *fellah bowab* considers himself an outsider to city life. He is obliged to work in Cairo for a spell until he is ready to return again to the bosom of his simple life in the fields.

To realise this dream, however, the farmer-turned-porter of the Sadat years had to be an agile participant in an increasingly competitive society. Being a *bowab* in the 1970s was not the same as in the pre-1952 revolutionary period. The new farmer doorkeeper had to be not just a fixture at the entrance of new buildings and villas but also a businessman with a creative mind. He had to grab every business opportunity available as well as create new ones, something which was not difficult to do when Sadat embraced capitalism. It was mainly because of the enterprise spirit initiated by this Egyptian leader that the doorman signed on again in Cairo.

iii. The simsars in their prime

Like their Nubian predecessors, the new *bowabs* did very good business with their fellow countrymen. But not only with them. More often than not the porters also dealt with non-Egyptian clients. With Sadat's 1974 open-door policy, foreigners, especially from the Gulf, soon came in their droves to pay short-term visits to Egypt. Many preferred to hitch up in private apartments rather than hotel suites, and with such a demand, the Egyptian *nouveaux riches* invested much of their money in building and furnishing new flats. It was a worthwhile investment because the short-term *khawaga* (foreigner) tenants were generous in paying.

The new lease business also attracted less wealthy Egyptians. Unable to afford the construction of new buildings, they hired out the furnished flats they lived in, and moved into smaller apartments.

The new landlord needed a liaison officer to attract clients.

And who could do the job better than the new doorman, ever alert to a profitable co-operation? This is how a new type of porter, the *simsar*, came into being.

Many doorkeepers in the 1970s at first had thought they could work both as doormen and as *simsars*. But they soon realised that performing at the same time the duties of a porter and those of an estate agent was virtually impossible. A building needs its porter every minute like a new born baby its mother. This explains why so many *bowabs* had no other option but to become full-time *simsars*.

Every well-to-do area soon had its own *simsar*, who had full information about the network of furnished flats on offer for the alien tenants. The landlords and landladies notified their respective *simsars* of the exact addresses of the apartments, the layout of the flats, the furniture available and, of course, the fees.

To some extent the *simsar* was a shareholder of the flats because he was given his own percentage of the profit in addition to a rather insignificant fixed salary. But like the doorkeeper, the *simsar* didn't depend only on this meagre income. To boost his earnings he also performed services for the apartment dwellers. This was how many *simsars* were able to hoard up considerable sums of money. Some even graduated to the middle class and bought their own flats.

The *simsars*' heyday came to an end when President Sadat made peace with Israel in 1978. After the Camp David Accords, Arab countries unilaterally severed diplomatic ties with Egypt. Egypt, which has historically served as a devoted doorkeeper and *simsar* of peace and understanding in the region and was the only reliable mediator between the West and the Middle East, was unjustly punished for taking a step that none of its neighbours had the will, the courage, or the credibility to take.

As the number of visitors from the Middle East and the Arab world reduced drastically, many *simsars* were made redundant. Most of them resumed their jobs as porters.

The profession of the *simsar*, however, did not die out. Many of those who were successful *simsars* in the seventies passed the secrets of the trade on to their sons who are not doing badly either. No one knows better than the present day *simsars* how many thousands of vacant furnished flats are ready to accommodate the army of foreign tenants, mainly Arabs, who flood Egypt either for relaxation or, as the Gulf War in the early 1990s showed, because they are afraid that the situation in their own countries has become too dangerous for themselves and their money.

iv. Today's bowab

Either because Egypt has never stopped welcoming foreigners, especially Arabs, or because the Egyptians have established a lasting bond with their doorkeepers, porter-mania shows no sign of flagging in this country. In the big cities, but especially in Cairo, it's still a pre-condition of construction that a prospective *bowab* as well as a *simsar* be found. A wooden stool remains an essential piece of furniture at the entrance of every apartment building. A wrong turn at the elevator still means falling over the *bowab*'s bed.

But the bench covered with a faded blanket – perhaps a mattress, perhaps not – is more than just a resting-place for the doorman. It also serves as a reminder that there is someone close at hand responsible for the safety of the tenants and for attending to day-to-day building matters.

The *bowab* porter still predominates in the well-to-do areas of Cairo. Some think that not all *bowabs* are born with the same silver spoon in their glasses of tea. But this is hardly true. Porters in a rich residential and commercial district like Zamalek, for instance, are not necessarily luckier than those in Heliopolis, Al Haram, or elsewhere. A Zamalek *bowab*'s monthly salary these days rarely exceeds eighty Egyptian pounds (E£), which is the equivalent of about £15.[2]

It is true that those who *bowab* about in Zamalek, Garden City and other affluent parts of Cairo take tips from their tenants and visitors. But such tips are hardly 'substantial'. One would have considered E£200-300 per month a lot in the 1960s, but not in the early 1990s.

The rat race has changed the porter into an obedient servant of many masters. He carries the satchels of the children of his building to the school bus in the morning, and escorts the children home in the afternoon. He is the mobile post office box of the building. He meticulously collects all the tenants' bills for electricity, gas and telephone. He does not volunteer to do so many chores because he is greedy. It's just that for people like him the cost of living nowadays is not very cheap.

Many are the watchmen who have succeeded in buying their own houses somewhere in Cairo. However, as they have to be on the look-out round the clock, they cannot afford being away from their post. This makes it indispensable for them to live in a tiny room on the ground floor or under the stairs, where in many cases some of them accommodate their large families.

Not all doorkeepers, however, are lucky enough to have such an 'apartment'. The less fortunate ones, and they are many, have no choice but to settle in their 'own' building's underground garage, curtaining off a nook with old sheets or scraps of cardboard.

Many porters continue to live in Cairo alone, leaving their families in the countryside. When these solitary *bowabs* pay a visit to their families in places such as Nubia, Said, Fayoum, Tanta and Sharkia on the occasion of a religious feast, a wedding or a funeral, they often return with quantities of home-cooked foods. A *bowab*'s underground 'mess' usually contains earthen jars, *balas*, and *qulas* for storing the food parcels.

Porters, like everybody else, can't help turning 'materialistic' in a selfish social environment. They are grateful when tipped, but never fail to remind anybody who pretends to forget coughing up for services rendered. The *bowabs* who don't forgive will not hesitate to retaliate; it is not unusual that the elevator will get stuck between two floors with a miser inside, or that a tight-fisted tenant will receive his mail several days late.

But the porters do not mean any harm. They just tip careless people off. The *bowabs* are professionals well aware of their own worth. No matter how little they earn these days, the Cairenese porters are always thankful servants and very reliable sentries. It is because of their vigilance that most buildings in this gigantic city are burglar-proof. After almost two centuries of co-existence, they and their landlords share the strong belief that they cannot do without one another.

In the wake of the terrorist attacks in Egypt in the early 1990s, a new type of porter in police uniform has emerged in Cairo. But the civil doorman is not envious or jealous of this armed doorkeeper. He is convinced that he is irreplaceable in the capital of porters.

Part Three: The United Kingdom

– 7 –

If Only the Dead Could Listen

(Scene Four)

If Only the Dead Could Listen is a controversial play on the treatment of refugees and asylum seekers in Britain. The play is based on Gëzim Alpion's six-scene tragedy *Vouchers* (2001). Directed by Serbian-born dramaturg Dr Duška Radosavljević, *Vouchers* was first performed at the Festival of Contemporary European Plays in Huddersfield, UK, in March 2002, with English academic Dr Steve Nicholson cast as the character of Dr AGIM Kodra, and Jordanian actor Mohammed Aljarrah playing the role of LEKA Trimi.

Sponsored by Arts Council England and the Birmingham and Midland Institute, and staged by Dreamscape Theatre Company, *If Only the Dead Could Listen* had its world première in February 2006 at the MAC Theatre, Birmingham, UK. The March 2008 performances at the MAC Theatre and the Arena Theatre in Wolverhampton were sponsored by *r:evolve*, a Consortium of the Arena Theatre, the Midlands Arts Centre (MAC), and Black Country Touring.

Following the success of the British première, Alpion and Dreamscape received invitations from the National Theatres of

Albania, Kosova and Macedonia, all offering their resources for the show to be staged in their countries. Serbia and Croatia also expressed a keen interest. Information on the 2006 and 2008 performances is available at: *http://www.ifonlythedeadcouldlisten.co.uk*

If Only the Dead Could Listen was first published by Globic Press, Chapel Hill, NC, USA, in 2008.

Cast and Crew

BILL Wright, police sergeant	Andrew Cullum (2006) Laurence Saunders (2008)
JOHN Moseley, police officer	Peter Collis
ALMA Stone, Albanian researcher from Tirana	Tina Hofman
LEKA Trimi, Albanian asylum seeker from Kosova	Richard Attlee (2006) Andrew Cullum (2008)
WOMAN	Tina Hofman
BARTENDER	Peter Collis
MAN	Andrew Cullum (2006) Laurence Saunders (2008)
PARAMEDIC	David Wake

Director & Designer – Marcus Fernando
Production Advisor – Duška Radosavljević (2006)
Stage Manager & Website Designer – David Wake
Movement – Tina Hofman
Music – Mark Taylor

The events in the play take place at a police station in a small town near London, UK, in December 2001.

Synopsis

Scene One – Office in a Police Station

Bill Wright, a police sergeant in his late forties, is anxiously awaiting the arrival of Dr Alma Stone, an Albanian researcher in London. She has volunteered to act as an interpreter at the interview of Leka Trimi, an Albanian asylum seeker from Kosova, who has been arrested on suspicion of theft. The conversation between Bill and Alma reveals that she suffers from an inferiority complex because of the bad press her country and expatriates receive in the British media. Bill is taken by surprise by her low opinion of her fellow Albanians.

Scene Two – Interview Room in a Police Station

John, a custody officer, orders Leka repeatedly to sit down when Bill and Alma enter the interview room. Leka is profusely apologetic to Bill for having hit him unintentionally the day before during a fight that had broken out between Leka and a fellow Albanian interpreter. Leka speaks broken English throughout the scene. He is very courteous towards Alma. When John leaves the interview room Bill and Alma fail to convince Leka that Alma is Albanian. Leka's self-esteem and his opinion of his fellow Albanians are apparently so low that he cannot comprehend that some of his compatriots in the UK are not refugees. At some point Leka compares Alma to another woman with a Serbian name, something which makes Alma very curious. She tries without success to learn from Leka about the Serbian woman. Alma could sense that Leka has perhaps a Serbian wife/girlfriend, which, in her view, is very strange considering the hostility between the Albanians and the Serbs in Kosova. John interrupts the interview to inform Bill that the Chief of Police needs to see him immediately.

Scene Three – Same Interview Room

With Bill gone, Leka remains in the interview room, while John and Alma have a chat in the corridor. John is not aware that Alma is Albanian. Alma is eager to enter the interview room and ask Leka about the Serbian woman. She manages to get rid of John temporarily by flirting with him. When she is alone in the interview room with Leka, Alma asks him about the Serbian woman, but he avoids answering her questions. Always believing that she is British, Leka praises her and the British for their generosity towards asylum seekers and refugees. His speech, however, is often peppered with ironic remarks, which indicates that he is saying to her what he believes she wants to hear. Alma tells Leka she is Albanian but he does not believe her because, in his view, this is not the time for Albanians to pursue academic careers in the West. Alma grows increasingly fond of him. Their conversation is interrupted by Bill who is shocked to find her alone with Leka. John is rude to Alma when he learns that she is Albanian. Leka is traumatised when he realises for the first time that he has behaved with such humility in the presence of a fellow Albanian. Bill, Alma and John withdraw from the interview room, leaving Leka behind. John keeps guard in front of the door of the interview room while Bill takes Alma to his office telling her he will collect her personally once he has dealt with the emergency which caused him to interrupt the interview in Scene Two.

Interval

Scene Four – Same Interview Room

Leka is seated at the opposite side of the table. He is in the same position as at the end of Scene Three: his elbows on the desk, his forearms raised, and his hands over his face. He seems as if he has frozen.

John is in the corridor, sitting on a chair close to the door of the interview room. He is reading through Alma's newspaper, enjoying his tea. After a while, Alma appears at the far end of the corridor, watching John furtively. John looks at the door of the interview room, and scratches his head. Alma hides away. John puts the newspaper on one of the chairs and stands up. He is obviously in some discomfort.

John (*to himself*) Bloody tea!

John opens the door of the interview room and looks at Leka angrily. Leka looks at John in fear then lowers his head. John closes the door and walks away on tiptoe. Shortly afterwards Alma appears in the corridor, also on tiptoe, approaching the door of the interview room. She enters the interview room grinning. Leka looks at Alma angrily then lowers his head. Alma closes the door very gently and takes her former seat close to the door. She rubs her hands all the time.

ALMA Back to our little chat. Had to slip past the guards. So? Where were we? Oh, yes, your family back in Kosova. I am not sure I understand why you cannot send them money. Besides, they say refugees in this country receive generous benefits.

Leka shakes his head.

LEKA Fuck you!

Alma is taken aback – not sure she has heard him correctly.

ALMA Sorry? What did you say?

LEKA Are you deaf or what? I said, fuck you!

ALMA I'm sorry, but I don't understand.

LEKA *I'm sorry, but I don't understand.* Fuck you and your understanding. So, you tricked me, eh? You fooled me, you bitch!

ALMA I really don't know what you are talking about. (*Forces herself to smile.*) Is this a joke?

LEKA No, this is not a joke. Do you think this is funny? Do I look funny to you?

ALMA *Le të flasim shqip. Të lutem, më shpjego-*

LEKA Oh, you want to talk in Albanian now! Why? My English is not good enough for you?

ALMA Your English is excellent, but I think-

LEKA Shut up! You hear me! Shut the fuck up! I don't give a damn what you think.

ALMA Mr Trimi, listen to me, please!

LEKA Oh, I'm *Mr Trimi* now! You bitch!

ALMA How dare you use such abusive language!

LEKA Abusive language! You have the nerve! You've made such a fool of me, and now I am the abuser? You scumbag! What do you expect me to do, thank you?

ALMA I didn't make a fool of you! How did I make a fool of you?

LEKA Oh, you didn't! So, I'm making it up now, yes? I'm a liar, eh?

ALMA No, of course, not! I'm only explaining that-

LEKA What's to explain, mother fucker? You led me on purpose to believe that you were bloody British.

ALMA No! That's not true! I told you from the first that I am Albanian. It's another matter that you didn't believe me.

LEKA Believe you! I'll see you hanged first. Then I'll believe a shifty bitch like you.

ALMA If you continue with that tone, I can't see any point in having this discussion.

LEKA Who's discussing with you, shithead?

ALMA That does it!

Alma stands up. Leka abandons his seat at once, rushes towards Alma, and pushes her back into her seat.

LEKA Sit down! You had your fun. Now it's my turn to enjoy myself.

ALMA What are you doing? You're mad!

Leka grabs Alma's chin.

LEKA You call me mad again, and you'll be sorry you were born.

ALMA Sorry! I didn't mean it. Just go back to your seat, and we can sort out any misunderstanding. OK? Can't you see that I'm here to help you?

Leka releases Alma's chin but still towers over her threateningly.

LEKA Stupid me! Of course, you're here to help me! You're the 'civilised' Albanian who has come to the rescue of a 'beastly countryman'. I'm a brute to you, eh?

ALMA No, I think you're unlucky.

LEKA Go fuck yourself! Who needs your opinion!

ALMA Another insult, and I'm out of here. You understand?

LEKA (*pretends he is scared.*) Ooh, I'm scared! I'm terrified! Please, don't leave me! Please, don't abandon me now! (*Kneels.*) Please! Please! Please! Forgive me.

ALMA You were a much better actor before. And what happened to your English? Or did it improve (*snaps her fingers imitating Leka.*) just like that?

LEKA Fuck you!

ALMA I've had enough of this.

Alma stands.

LEKA You don't get it, do you? You're going nowhere. No one can come to your rescue now. No one! Not even your spymaster!

ALMA My spymaster? What are you talking about?

LEKA Bill, of course. You are his spy. Like many fucking interpreters, you are a fucking British spy.

ALMA Oh, come on.

LEKA You are, you are. Oh, I know your type very well! You sell every thing for money. You sell your arse, even your mother for a bit of cash. How much do the British pay you?

ALMA I am not a spy. I'm a researcher, a scientist.

LEKA Yeah! Yeah! Who's sponsoring you – Billy boy or one of his weirdo friends? You fucking arse-licker!

ALMA Do you have to use such words? Why don't you calm down so that we can have a civilised conversation.

LEKA You see! I told you that you think I'm uncivilised. I'm an ape-man to you, a beast from the jungle. This is how you see me (*Points at the door.*), just like them?

ALMA No!

LEKA No? How do you see me then? Tell me!

ALMA I will, but not before you take your seat. Please!

Leka turns his head to the empty chair, then looks at Alma.

LEKA Aren't you a smart-ass! You think you can fool me again? You want me to go to my seat so that you can run away screaming for help?

ALMA The way I see it, we're both in the same boat.

LEKA Shut up. I don't need your lectures. I am smarter than you without your fucking degrees. (*Points to the chair at the other end of the desk.*) Go and sit there. Move your arse! March!

Alma gets up, shaking her head. She starts walking towards the chair at the other end of the table under Leka's watchful eyes. As she sits on the chair, she folds her arms and looks Leka straight in the eyes. Leka is still on his feet.

ALMA Why don't you sit down? Let's talk. We need to talk. I can help you. We can help each other.

LEKA *We*? Who's *we*?

ALMA Well, you, me, us, all Albanians.

Leka Thank you very much, but I refuse to be part of a community that includes a chameleon like you.

Alma Chameleon!?

Leka And a cheat. Like every Albanian, you have come to Britain with false papers.

Alma I don't know about every Albanian, but I guarantee you that I did not come here with false papers.

Leka Yes, you did! Yes, you did! God knows how much you've paid for a Yugoslav passport. Shame on you! Scumbags like you in Albania are taking advantage of our misfortune in Kosova.

Alma OK, let's suppose that what you say about some refugees from Albania is true. How does this-

Leka Some refugees! You call thousands of cheats some refugees!

Alma OK, thousands, if you like. But you're still missing the point.

Leka Which is?

Alma Which is that all Albanians have come to Britain hoping to secure better standards of living.

Leka Oh, no! No! No! No! Don't you dare mix us with you. You from Albania are simply economic refugees. We Kosovars are different. We've come here to escape Serbian state terrorism.

Alma Some of you, yes.

Leka No, arsehole! Not some of us. All of us.

Alma Nonsense! Like most other immigrants in Britain, we Albanians – whether we are from Albania or Kosova – have chosen to come here mainly for economic reasons.

LEKA Really!

ALMA Of course! A few years ago it was only natural that some of you would apply for political asylum in Britain. Now the situation has changed. Kosova is a free country. And still you don't return home? Why? Because, like all Albanians, you are essentially economic immigrants.

LEKA You think so?

ALMA Oh, yes. The decent thing would be to tell the truth and stop making up excuses to stay here.

LEKA You don't say!

ALMA Absolutely! Some refugees seem to have no self-respect. Who do you think you are fooling, anyway! The British know who you are and why you are here.

LEKA Is that so?

ALMA No doubt. The only reason why so many immigrants are allowed to stay in this country is not because British authorities are fools but because people like you are needed here. You are the cheap labour Britain cannot do without at the moment.

LEKA Bravo! Encore! Where have you been before? That's exactly what I've been dying to hear all these years in England! Oh, how eagerly I've been waiting for this revelation!

You stupid cow! You think I don't know this? I realised all this from the first day I set foot in this country.

ALMA I was only-

LEKA Shut your face!

Leka grabs the tape recorder and holds it above his head in an attempt to hurl it at Alma. Alma is scared but does not move. Leka puts the recorder back on the desk.

Don't you dare lecture me like that stinking piece of shit yesterday.

Pause.

ALMA Why did you fight with the interpreter yesterday?

Leka hesitates to speak.

LEKA I asked him if he could first listen to my story. I wanted no favours from him. I just wanted to unburden myself to an Albanian. Is that too much to ask?

ALMA What did he say?

LEKA He said: 'I'm not paid to listen to your confession. This job puts food on my table, and I'm not stupid to risk it for no thief.'

ALMA I'm sure he did not mean that!

LEKA Are you saying that I'm making this up? But, of course, he meant it. Someone from my own country, someone who speaks my own language, has no time to listen to a brother because all he is worried about is his lousy food.

That lowlife wasn't happy the war in Kosova was over because it had reduced his only source of income. Do you have any idea what this means? He wanted people to keep on dying there so that he could earn his dirty living here.

ALMA Even if he said that-

LEKA Even if he said that!

ALMA Life's a struggle for everyone.

LEKA Will you stop lecturing me!

ALMA We have to keep our dignity.

LEKA What do we Albanians know about dignity! We've always been each other's worst enemy.

ALMA No, that's not true!

LEKA Really! Remember 1997? With whom were you fighting in Albania when the pyramid schemes collapsed – Martians?

ALMA What happened in 1997 is a complicated story. The important thing is that we have moved on. Albania is looking up. Things are changing for us.

LEKA Nothing is changing for us. We Albanians can't work together. It's not our style.

ALMA Are you always so pessimistic?

LEKA I'm not pessimistic. I'm a realist, not a hypocritical dreamer like you.

ALMA Why am I a hypocritical dreamer – because I believe in our potential as a nation? Because I'm confident that we Albanians can and will work together? And not only us. Everyone in the Balkans – Albanians, Greeks, Slavs – we must learn to live together. We have to, and we can.

LEKA Yeah! Yeah! Is that why you left Albania – to preach in England that we in the Balkans can love each other to death. Oh, you are all the same! Scholars, scientists, artists – you are all rats. You've abandoned Albania.

ALMA People are entitled to make their choices. You made your choice when you came here.

LEKA Yes, but my choice was that of a hero, yours of a deserter.

Alma You really are an expert in Albanian mentality, aren't you?

Leka Oh, shut up! Stop behaving like royalty. You may think that the English treat you with respect but in their eyes you are just another bloody refugee.

Alma I am not a refugee, and I simply don't care what the English think of me.

Leka Hold your horses, Lady Stone! You must know by now that people in this country are very touchy, and you don't want to upset them, do you? Not until you secure a British passport.

Alma I already have one.

Leka What? You're a British citizen? Typical! Just fucking typical!

Alma What?

Leka You and your lies! How come someone like you qualifies for British citizenship! What lies did you tell? Let me guess-

Alma I told you I am a scientist, not a refugee. I didn't have to tell any lies to anyone.

Leka Yes, you did! Lying is the only way for an Albanian to be accepted in this country. And the funny thing is that people like you lie so much that you have come to believe your own lies.

Alma Is there anything you don't know about me? Anything at all?

Leka Absolutely nothing! I know all about you University types. Who gives a fuck about an Albanian scholar outside Albania! And, oh God, in England of all places! What did you say you do at this Institute of Genetics? Research? What kind of research – cleaning the floor or giving blow jobs to brainy perverts?

Alma Fuck you! You sick, bastard! I don't give a damn whether you believe me or not. I have earned my position and am very proud of my achievements. Academics in this country can be as narrow-minded as anywhere else. For ten years now it's been an uphill struggle and I will not allow a little shit like you to besmear what I have achieved.

Leka Ooh! Gutsy woman! Passing judgements on British academics! Are you so stupid to think that you've come here to civilise them? Whether we are refugees or world-class scientists, to the British we are some low-life scum.

Alma I had the impression earlier that you thought very highly of the British.

Leka Of course, you did because you bitch fooled me. But how was I supposed to know that a clown like you is not British? You dress like the British and you talk like the British. (*Imitates her.*) *Thanks, Bill! My feet are killing me. I haven't finished my cuppa yet, Bill.*

Alma You are pathetic, you know that.

Leka And you're as fucking calm as the fucking British. I call you 'bitch' several times, have been calling you every name I can possibly think of for so long, and you have answered me back once! Only once! Oh, you've really become British. You cock sucker! You mother fucker! You see? Not a single word. British to the core!

Alma You've obviously watched quite a lot of American movies. Do you feel any better now?

Leka Shut up! Shut the fuck up! You really think you're British? Don't you know that to qualify as British you must be a master of hypocrisy? You are a hypocrite, alright, but, take it from me, no matter how hard you try, you'll always be a fake copy of a British hypocrite.

Alma Have you told the British what you really think of them?

Leka Have you? Of course, not! You wouldn't risk your career. But don't you worry about me! I'll soon tell these fucking hypocrites what I really think of them.

Alma You are impossible!

Leka I bet you have an English lover.

Alma That's none of your business!

Leka I knew it! I bloody knew it!

You're used as a prostitute.

Alma How dare you! I'm engaged to-

Leka Oh, please! I know all about your filthy engagements and rotten marriages. To secure your citizenship you'd shag any shit here.

Alma You need help!

Leka When are you marrying this shit?

Alma Not yet. Not until my divorce comes through.

Leka Whoa! Whoa! Whoa! Until your divorce comes through? You were married? In Albania?

Alma Yes, but it didn't work. My ex didn't want me to come to England. He thought I had studied enough!

Leka So, you left him!

Alma What else could I do?

LEKA No! Of course! To have a career one must make some small sacrifices such as destroying the marriage. Oh, you have become more British than I thought. What does this lucky shithead do for a living?

ALMA Michael is Head of Department at the Institute.

LEKA I'm sure he is. And what Department is that – Studies in East European Cheeky Girls? I bet he is old enough to be your father.

ALMA That's none of your business, either!

LEKA And I bet he was married before. (*Pause.*) His wife must hate you, Queen of Sheba. Or are you one big happy family?

ALMA I have never met her.

LEKA And you, of course, make a devoted stepmother to his children. His kids must adore you. I bet some of them are old enough to love you more than just as a stepmother.

ALMA I told you, you're a sick man. I don't need to play mother to Michael's children. I have my own son from my first marriage.

LEKA You do? Where is this poor child now?

ALMA I don't want to talk about it.

LEKA You don't want to talk about *it*! Your son is just an *it* to you, eh? What have you done with him?

ALMA Stop it!

LEKA Dumped him in a public toilet as soon as you arrived here?

ALMA Stop it! My son is in Albania!

LEKA You have a son in Albania and you stay in England!

Alma lowers her head visibly shaken.

How often do you see this son of yours?

Alma does not reply.

When did you last see your son!?

Alma sobs.

When!?

ALMA (*struggling to control herself, sobbing.*) I haven't seen him for ten years now. My husband would not allow me.

LEKA Serve you right! What kind of a fucking mother are you! Not only you wreck your marriage for your bloody career, but you also abandon your own flesh and blood. Don't you see what you've done? You had everything one could possibly want and you just threw it away!

Leka stands up, starts walking away from Alma.

You threw it all away!

Leka sobs uncontrollably. Alma watches him with curiosity, stands up, starts walking towards the door, but then changes her mind. Finally, she returns to her seat.

Leka appears to have frozen.

ALMA If only you knew how much I've suffered when I left my son. I still have nightmares, every night. You know it yourself what it's like to be separated from the loved ones. But we gain nothing by allowing grief and bitterness to overpower us.

LEKA What do you know about grief and bitterness!

ALMA A lot! And I can imagine how you feel. I know you must miss your family terribly.

Leka You leave my family alone.

Alma You've been through so much, but-

Leka Stop it!

Alma Your ordeal will soon be over, believe me. You know the situation is getting better in Kosova. You'll return there any day now.

Leka I said stop it!

Alma All you have to do until then is to keep yourself busy. Try to find some work, a job, any job. Have faith!

Leka Shut up! Who are you, Mother Teresa? I used to believe in God once. But not now, not anymore, not ever. And if I can do without God, I can manage without your pity. I don't need anyone's pity.

Alma stands up, walks slowly towards Leka, and stops close to him.

Alma You're a strong man. You've coped remarkably well, and I admire you for that. I really do! You can't give up – not now!

Leka Shut up! Shut up! Shut up!

Alma If you can't be strong for yourself, then think about your family.

Leka moans painfully.

You must be strong for the sake of your wife-

Leka moans again, this time uttering something inarticulate.

and your son. They all are waiting for you.

Alma pats Leka on the shoulder. Leka's moaning intensifies.

And they've been waiting for far too long. They're longing to see you.

Leka turns towards Alma.

LEKA They are dead! They are all dead.

Shocked, Alma makes a few steps back.

ALMA Oh! No! No! No!

Leka moves slowly towards Alma, his stretched arms shaking. Alma is apprehensive of Leka's threatening look, but she finally makes a couple of steps towards him. They embrace.

Synopsis

Scene Five – Same Interview Room

Alma, slumped over the desk, appears to be resting on the chair near the door, her arms on the desk, supporting her head. In a long monologue Leka opens his heart to Alma about his own family tragedy, i.e. the gang-raping and killing of his pregnant Serbian girlfriend by Serbian policemen in Kosova; witnessing the killing of his parents by Serbian soldiers; and his painful experiences as an asylum seeker in the UK. Leka also tells Alma why he shoplifted in London: *A few weeks before the arrest he had gone to a pub for a drink. As he did not have enough money, he offered to pay for drinks with a voucher. A racist bartender does not accept the voucher humiliating Leka in front of some drunken louts.* As Leka's confession to Alma is over, Bill and John enter the interview room. Leka attacks them thinking that they are the Serbian policemen, who had raped his girlfriend. Leka is finally overpowered and taken away while a doctor examines Alma. The scene ends with Bill looking at the tape and the audience.

– 8 –

Images of Albania and Albanians in English literature – from Edith Durham's *High Albania* to J.K. Rowling's *Harry Potter*

The Albanian State was born at the turn of the twentieth century, but the history of Albania predates that of Greece. History has been cruel to the Albanians since the Roman conquest. Except for the 1443-1468 period, when the Albanian national hero Gjergj Kastrioti Skanderbeg (1403-1468) was successful in his mammoth task to defeat the Ottomans (thus defending both the Albanian nation and Catholic Europe), the fifteen years (1925-1939) when Ahmed Zogu (1895-1961) ruled Albania first as a president and then as a monarch, and the post-World War II period, for the last two millennia the Albanians have been constantly living under occupation.

In this respect, Albania is the closest European equivalent to Egypt. Like the Egyptians, who had to wait for almost three millennia until they finally could govern themselves again in 1952, the Albanians never abandoned the dream of self-rule. Unlike the Egyptians, when the Albanians finally succeeded in proclaiming their country's independence in 1912, they were not left with much of a country to govern.

The Albania that resulted from several dreadful historical miscalculations and injustices culminating in the London Conference of the Ambassadors of the Six European Great Powers in 1913, was a dismembered nation, something of a still-birth whose long-term survival was never taken seriously.

But survive the fledgling Albanian State did, and so did the Albanians living in Albanian territories unjustly left outside Albania. Survival has been a basic instinct of the Albanians since 169 BC when Gent, the last Illyrian king, was captured by the Romans at Shkodra. This has always baffled foreign Albanologists.

This specific Albanian characteristic also surprised Edith Durham (1863-1944), one of the most well-known, some would say controversial, Western Albanologists of the first half of the twentieth century.

Durham was not a scholar when she first visited the Balkans and the Albanian territories in 1900. It would probably be unwise to consider everything she wrote on the region as being indisputably correct.

Durham did not go to the Balkans to do fieldwork; she went there on medical advice when she was ill and depressed. She left England for a cure and found a vocation. She was one of the first Western travel-writers to discover that the Balkans could be a career.

Many British and European hopefuls are trying to emulate Durham's example, especially recently when so much has happened in the Balkans: the collapse of Communism, the disintegration of the former Yugoslavia, the wars in Bosnia, Croatia and Kosova, and the fighting in Macedonia.

As opposed to some recently self-proclaimed Western experts in Balkan and Albanian affairs, Durham appears to have gone to the region rather free of preconceptions and prejudices. While it is true that more often than not she wrote favourably about the Albanians, her 'preference' for one of the most ancient European nations was not inspired or motivated by the interests of her own country in Albania or the Balkans.

Durham was her own spokesperson when she defended the Albanians. With her determination to speak her own mind, she set an example seldom followed by her contemporary British and Western Balkanists and Albanologists.

Durham was a scholar by instinct rather than by trade. She based her judgements on her own observations. She wrote about what she saw. In this respect she is different from some Westerners, like the nineteenth-century German writer Karl May, who offered their readers an almost entirely fictitious picture of the Albanians.

Durham upset many one-sided and often blinkered Balkans experts because she championed the cause of a long-neglected people. But this was not done for reasons of self-interest. Despite her initial motive for visiting the Balkans, Durham benefited the region more than it benefited her. The Albanians were so impressed with her relentless efforts on their behalf that they referred to her as their *Kratlitse* (Queen).[1]

Durham, however, did not see herself as the Queen of the Albanians. She took an interest in the Albanians without a desire to lead them. Unlike her contemporary Hungarian aristocrat Baron Franz Nopcsa (1877-1933),[2] Durham had no ambition to claim the throne of Albania; she approached and vigorously defended the Albanian question mainly on humanitarian grounds.

By the time Durham 'discovered' Albania, especially Northern Albania, the country was in a state of hibernation as a result of successive invasions by the Celts, the Romans, the Slavs and the Turks. The Albanians appeared ossified. Although geographically near, they were politically and economically far from the European Powers that had perpetually chosen to ignore, and often abandoned them in favour of their own imperial interests.

When Durham visited Albania, Europe had little time for this long neglected country. She found the Albanians isolated, but not of their own volition. They had been forced into isolation. Cut off from Europe, the Albanians had no alternative but to ensure their survival by relying on their ancient mythology, laws and traditions. These were bound to change and in some cases become distorted in order to suit the often extraordinary circumstances the Albanian nation had experienced since the beginning of the Roman occupation. *The Canon of Lekë Dukagjini* (also known in English as *The Code of Lekë Dukagjini*), for instance, is probably the best example of the need the Albanians felt to revive, preserve and update their ancient traditions of self-governance in order to meet the challenges of surviving under the Turkish rule and the constant threat of assimilation by their neighbours.[3]

Much as she regretted the Albanians' imposed isolation from Western Europe, Durham often made no secret of her exultation at discovering the exotic Albania and Albanians. She differs from many past and present-day European 'experts' on Albania because of her unfashionable sympathy for the Albanians. Yet, the exotic occupies as central a place in her writings, as it does in the work of many other Western travel writers.

Durham travelled widely throughout the Albanian territories but her most inspired work *High Albania* (1909) concentrates on one of the most isolated and as such, one of the most exotic parts of Albania and the Albanian nation. The northern part of Albania offered Durham a unique opportunity to see a 'backwater of life' at the heart of Europe, which has 'primitive virtues, without many of the meannesses of what is called civilisation. It is uncorrupted by luxury'.[4] It was in this particular region of Albania, well known for its breathtaking and epic landscape and its people's proverbial hospitality, that Durham felt transported into an alien yet majestic world of living myths and legends, about which her European education had taught her nothing. Charmed by a reality she had never thought existed, Durham remarks:

> I think no place where human beings live has given me such an impression of majestic isolation from all the world. It is a spot where the centuries shrivel; the river might be the world's well-spring, its banks the fit home of elemental instincts – passions that are red and rapid.[5]

Northern Albania was for Edith Durham the land before time, or as she puts it, 'the Land of the Living Past'.[6] In this newly discovered reality she had no wish to be reminded of the civilisation she had left behind. High Albania was a place of such an 'absorbing interest' for Durham that she often 'forgot all about the rest of the world'.[7] In this part of the country, Durham came into contact with an enchanting wilderness, which explains why when she was there she commented: 'I never want books. They are dull compared to the life stories that are daily enacted among the bare grey rocks.'[8]

This mountainous part of Albania was for Durham something of an exotic oasis at the heart of Europe, which she generally felt was better left unspoilt. In her book *High Albania*, Durham, the champion of the rights of small nations, is at times subdued by Durham, the selfish Western tourist, who seems to believe that the world and especially small nations exist primarily for her own recreation and entertainment. Thus Durham emerges as judge and jury; she alone knows best what is good or bad for the Albanians and what they should and should not do. This is clear from the comments she makes upon hearing that the farmers in one of the most fertile regions in Albania would welcome the building of a new railway:

> I looked at the room full of long, lean cat-o'-mountains, and wondered whether it would benefit anybody – let alone themselves – to turn them into fat corn and horse dealers
>
> 'Civilisation is vexation,
> And progress is as bad,
> The things that be, they puzzle me,
> And Cultchaw drives me mad.'[9]

Durham was not the only one who would have preferred the Albanians to remain 'uncivilised'. 'God cast you into Hell,' a priest once said to her, 'that you might tell of it in England – that you might cry to every Catholic in England: "Save these people!"'[10]

Durham understood the Albanians well enough to realise that they were not 'wild' and 'uncivilised'. She tried hard to comprehend and explain, sometimes successfully sometimes not, why they were lagging behind other European nations. Occasionally, however, Durham glorified the 'primitive' life which some Albanians apparently lived at the turn of the twentieth century. Dazzled by the exuberant atmosphere she witnessed throughout the feast of St John, she remarked:

> I thought how dull London dinner-parties are, and wondered why people ever think they would like to be civilised. This was as good as being Alice at the Mad Hatter's Tea-party.[11]

If not taken out of context, Durham's remarks on the Albanians' 'lack' of civilisation are on the whole light-hearted. I personally enjoy reading her work but not because, on the whole, she wrote favourably about Albania. She had the ability to rediscover and reinterpret the country, the people and their culture firstly for the European audience still largely ignorant of this '*terra incognita*', but also for the Albanians themselves. Her independent mind, her eye for details and her sincere and fresh narrative are bound to continue to attract the attention of open-minded readers who do not judge Albania and the Albanians simply on the basis of hearsay or hostile literature.

In *High Albania* Durham depicts only one Albanian region. She makes it clear from the beginning of the book that, in her opinion, the conditions there 'are very different from those in South Albania, and it is with the wildest part of High Albania alone that this book deals'.[12] Did Durham offer this explanation simply because she wanted to clarify to the readers the scope and focus of her book, or because she was afraid lest her work would be seen as the 'definitive' picture of *all* Albania? Whatever her reasons, it cannot be disputed that in *High Albania* and other works, Edith Durham introduced Albania and the Albanians to the British readers in a sympathetic light hardly seen before.

Edith Durham's work belongs to the best tradition of the British travel writing where foreigners are depicted not as the alien and hostile 'other' but as fellow human beings who try hard, at times against all odds, to retain and protect their individual and national identity and integrity. Writers like Durham, D. H. Lawrence, George Orwell and E. M. Forster presented a new picture and perception of overseas peoples and cultures to a largely ignorant and at times misinformed British readership.

Like most people in the West, on the whole, the British remained largely ignorant of and misinformed about East Europeans throughout the twentieth century, especially during the Cold War. The chasm between the two Blocks (what a telling word this is!) became so pathetically wide, creating the impression that the Berlin Wall was a great divide between two completely different species, which, by a weird coincidence, had the same physique. Rarely before had humanity dehumanised itself more than during the 1950-1990 period. We humans have hardly been completely at peace with each other, but the bitterness in the relationships between East and West in the second half of the twentieth century is almost exceptional. That human beings could display such an intense hatred for fellow human beings is very unsettling in itself. That this happened immediately after the horrors of World War II became common knowledge makes this hostility even more inexplicable and disturbing.

The Berlin Wall but not its legacy is now history. When the Berlin Wall was demolished in 1989 (and remember that its destruction commenced on the East side) it did not take us East Europeans long to notice other 'imaginary' walls in the West. We were the unfortunate creatures deserving the charity of the West. The possibility of being seen as equals was beyond Western imagination. We were perceived and unfortunately continue to be seen as 'different' and 'inferior'.

Brick walls are easily demolished, but not the walls in our minds. And the most resistant of all walls are those built by works of fiction. Since the collapse of Communism, Western literature has hardly presented Eastern Europe sympathetically. There is an ongoing tendency to patronise and pigeonhole East Europeans. The phantom of Bertha in *Jane Eyre* (1847), for instance, is still present in contemporary English fiction. British writers should learn from the courage and far-sightedness of George Eliot and Wilkie Collins who portrayed some of their 'alien' characters as hard-working and decent individuals quite able and willing to give to society perhaps more than they received from it. Whereas the Silas Marners of today are expected to be grateful to Britain for the humiliating charitable pittance that comes in the form of vouchers.[13]

The stale remarks made by some British politicians in recent years may create the impression that the United Kingdom is the most welcoming country in the world. Yet, we do not really welcome foreigners, if we demean their country of origin, which is what often happens in English literature and the British media today.

Eastern Europe, for instance, continues to be depicted by some British journalists as a distant and mysterious land, where almost everything is corrupt, and everybody extremely poor, and so at the mercy of Western charity. Contemporary English literature is hardly more amicable in its treatment of Eastern Europe.

This is not surprising. After all, there has always been an element of dogma and propaganda in English literature. Willy-nilly, even the best of English fiction writers have expressed directly or indirectly their allegiance to the British Empire, thus undermining their credibility and independence as artists. No national literature is completely impartial to outsiders, and English literature is certainly no exception to this rule.

It is no surprise that Charlotte Brontë presented Bertha, a foreigner, as mad and inarticulate. After all, Brontë did in *Jane Eyre* what the Bard had already done a couple of centuries earlier in *The Tempest*. Bertha is Caliban's daughter. Shakespeare and Brontë are some of the first-rate English writers whose works uncover eternal truths about human nature, yet are hardly entirely free from restricting nets of allegiances to nationalism, empire, colonialism, religion, and more disturbingly, 'race'.

Twenty-first century Britain is, of course, different from the Britain of Shakespeare and Brontë. So much has changed for the better in the way the British perceive and receive foreigners. All the same, some references to 'aliens', especially to East Europeans in contemporary English literature seem to have been taken *verbatim* from the early boys' magazines, many of which appeared after the First World War. Referring to the *Gem*'s tendency to stereotype different nationalities in 1939, George Orwell remarks in his essay 'Boys' Weeklies': 'The assumption all along is not only that foreigners are comics who are put there for us to laugh at, but that they can be classified in much the same way as insects.'[14]

Children's magazines should not be considered serious literature but, being read by many young people, they are bound to make these impressionable readers think that those who live overseas are strange, uncivilised, ridiculous and as such not worth taking seriously. Their misperceptions become even more of a serious issue considering that, as Orwell rightly notes, many of such young readers would never read anything else in life except newspapers.[15]

Considering that most of these boys' weeklies were the property of the Amalgamated Press and were closely linked up with the *Daily Mail* and the *Financial Times*, one is bound to think that, after all, the 'free' and 'fair' British press has never been and hardly is that 'free' and 'fair'. According to Orwell, the purpose of this literature is to convince the young readers that:

> the major problems of our time do not exist, that there is nothing wrong with laissez-faire capitalism, that foreigners are unimportant comics and that the British Empire is a sort of charity-concern which will last for ever.[16]

Orwell even goes so far as to suggest that in England, popular imaginative literature, indeed all fiction from the novels in the mushroom libraries downwards, is censored in the interests of the ruling class.[17]

The denigration of foreigners, East Europeans and especially the Albanians is an ongoing process in the British media and English literature. This denigration manifests itself in the works of authors like Robert Carver and Malcolm Bradbury and especially in J. K. Rowling's *Harry Potter* series.

Whether or not Rowling will still be a celebrity writer in the future is perhaps not very important. That her legacy is likely to endure, however, and not necessarily for the right reasons, is very important.

Harry Potter invites young and not so young readers into a world of fantasy, where things are often as complicated and ugly as in the real world, but where, with a bit of magic, good eventually wins over evil. As a piece of escapism, Harry Potter is among the best. This escapist work, however, takes the easily impressionable young readers on a journey to foreign lands similar to that described in some of the boys' weeklies in the first half of the twentieth century. Whereas the weeklies' scribes ridiculed and dehumanised the French, the Italians, the Chinese, the Indians, or the Arabs – some of the usual victims in the boys' magazines – Rowling demeans Albania and the Albanians in her 'imaginative masterpiece'. In *Harry Potter*, Albania is the country where the evil 'Dark Lord' and his dedicated followers find a perfect hideout. In *Harry Potter and the Chamber of Secrets* (1998), we learn that Lord Voldemort is 'currently hiding in the forests of Albania'.[18] In *Harry Potter and the Goblet of Fire* (2000), the witch Bertha Jorkins is said to have gone on holiday to Albania and 'never came back'.[19] She is believed to have disappeared in Albania where Voldemort was rumoured to be last.[20] That Bertha Jorkins definitely arrived in Albania is confirmed by the fact that 'she met her second cousin there. And then she left the cousin's house to go south and see an aunt...and she seems to have vanished without trace, en route'.[21] In the same book, Voldemort himself explains that his loyal servant Wormtail:

> 'sought me in the country where it had long been rumoured I was hiding...helped, of course, by the rats he met along the way. Wormtail has a curious affinity with rats, do you not, Wormtail? His filthy little friends told him there was a place deep in an Albanian forest, that they avoided, where small animals like themselves had met their deaths by a dark shadow that possessed them'.[22]

Later on in the book we learn from Crouch, another servant of Voldemort, that his master 'had captured Bertha Jorkins in Albania', tortured and finally killed her.[23]

I do not know why, of all countries, Rowling has chosen Albania as the place that harbours evil creatures. If she has done this for a laugh, then this is a cheap laugh at the expense of a European country that has become small, 'insignificant' and 'voiceless' largely as a result of political witchcraft and wizardry practiced beyond its artificially drawn and imposed borders. I am inclined to believe that Rowling's choice of Albania is an indication of the intellectual arrogance and ignorance often displayed by Western authors when writing about, to borrow Edward W. Said's phrase, 'lesser peoples'. By choosing Albania as the right habitat for evil to reside in, Rowling reveals how little she knows about the world beyond the British shores, and in particular about a tiny spot like Albania.

Harry Potter could be a well-researched book as far as witchcraft and wizardry go. Rowling is obviously out of her depth, however, when she tries to connect her world of magic with the real world. Her references to Albania reveal a disturbing tendency in contemporary Western literature which seems to go unnoticed in the West. Writers like Rowling, and more experienced scribes than her, seem to think that 'vivid fantasy' is an excuse and a cover for their limited knowledge of the real world. In the works of writers like Rowling, reality, especially overseas reality, is at times sketched through some incoherent and incorrect sweeping statements, which often undermine the value of the best works of fiction.

A little learning is always a dangerous thing, especially when this is manifested in books intended for children. The worst books, Orwell warns us, 'are often the most important, because they are usually the ones that are read earliest in life'.[24] This is not to say that *Harry Potter* belongs to this category of books. Rowling, however, does no favour to millions of young readers in the United Kingdom and overseas by introducing them in such an irresponsible way to a country about which she obviously does not know much. Albania and other East European countries deserve a more objective and sympathetic treatment in Western and English literature. It is not very rare that a heart of darkness starts on the pages of a book.

– 9 –

Western media and the European 'other' – images of Albania in the British press

i. Introduction

Edward W. Said's *Orientalism* invigorated as never before the debate on the biased representation of the Orient in the West. In the first part of the article, after highlighting the significance of Said's work, I identify some weaknesses and limitations of the Saidian approach arguing that, like the Near and the Middle East, other countries and regions around the world have an unsavoury image in the West as a result of an ongoing academic and media demonology. Concentrating on the coverage that the Balkans, especially Albania, have received in the West from the start of the nineteenth century onwards, in the second part of the essay, I argue that the West has traditionally denigrated the European 'other' no less than the non-Europeans thus resulting in a cultural, historical and political fragmentation of the European continent which continues to have negative implications for Albania and the neighbouring countries, and more generally for the European Union. In the third part of the paper, through content-analysis of several articles that have appeared in the British press during the 2001-2006 period, the focus is on the disturbing tendency to denigrate the Albanian nation, a tendency which reveals a Euro-centric, post-imperial approach apparent in the Western media towards 'estranged' Europeans like the Albanians.

ii. Expanding the Orient

In the introduction to his acclaimed 1978 book, *Orientalism*, Edward W. Said states that '[t]he life of an Arab Palestinian in the West, particularly in America, is disheartening'[1]. Said was a devout champion of the Palestinian cause but his above remark, like the book in question, was not inspired only by patriotism and nationalism. This is a point he was keen to reiterate throughout his life, and especially in the preface to the 2003 edition:

> I do want to affirm yet again that this book and, for that matter, my intellectual work generally have really been enabled by my life as a university academic.... [F]or all its urgent worldly references [*Orientalism*] is still a book about culture, ideas, history and power, rather than Middle Eastern politics *tout court*. That was my notion from the very beginning, and it is very evident and a good deal clearer to me today.[2]

The book certainly exonerates Said from any 'accusation' of patriotism but, on the whole, what he claims in this particular work is mainly about how the Orient and the Orientals, especially Muslim Arabs, have been and continue to be misperceived and misrepresented in the West since the 1798 Napoleon expedition to Egypt onwards. In his own words:

> The web of racism, cultural stereotypes, political imperialism, dehumanizing ideology holding in the Arab or the Muslim is very strong indeed, and it is this web which every Palestinian has come to feel as his uniquely punishing destiny. It has made matters worse for him to remark that no person academically involved with the Near East – no Orientalist, that is – has ever in the United States culturally and politically identified himself wholeheartedly with the Arabs; certainly there have been identifications on some level, but they have never taken an 'acceptable' form as has liberal American identification with Zionism, and all too frequently they have been radically flawed by their association either with discredited political and economic interests (oil company and State Department Arabists, for example) or with religion.[3]

The Saidian predicament is felt in the West not only by the Palestinians or the Arabs (be they Muslims or Christians). The web of 'racism', 'cultural stereotypes', 'political imperialism' and 'dehumanizing ideology' holds in not only the Arab or the Muslim but any 'foreigner' in the West originating from other 'lesser' peoples and 'subject races'.

The degradation of the 'other' in the West is not done only for religious purposes, as Said often seems to suggest in this particular work and throughout his *oeuvre*. The negative image of the Orient in the West may have something to do with Islam, but the faith of the Muslims is hardly the main reason why Oriental countries, especially the Middle East, are often misrepresented in the literature produced by and intended for Westerners.

Moreover, contrary to Said's belief, the West's denigration of the Orient started in earnest not at the start of the nineteenth century, but in 32 BC when Octavius crowned himself King of Egypt just over a century after 146 BC, when the fall of Carthage marked the rise of Rome to superpower status.[4] The Romans envied Egypt's success during almost 3,500 years of Pharaonic rule and to silence the Egyptians' pride they were brutally iconoclastic. This is the time when the West first started the looting and the plundering of 'inferior' cultures and civilisations. On the pretext of heresy, Rome exterminated many people in Egypt and across the Middle East, including those who had converted to Christianity.

With the advent of Islam in the seventh century AD, West European countries, now Christianised, would use religion as a pretext any time they tried to exert their power over the peoples in the Middle East and across the expanding Muslim world. The crusades indicate clearly the extent to which the 'pious' West was prepared to use religion for the sake of justifying its looting and pillaging of the 'infidel' Orient. Portugal and Spain also employed religion as an excuse for the colonisation of the 'heathens' in both hemispheres. Christianity offered a smokescreen also to European powers like Britain, France, Denmark, Holland, Belgium and Germany to give 'legitimacy' to their colonial policy and to convince public opinion at home about, to use Rudyard Kipling's infamous phrase, 'the white man's burden' to civilize the 'barbarians'.

If Islam is the only reason why the West apparently has something against the Orient, one would expect the European powers to maintain a friendly attitude towards any Christian country that is not geographically in the West. This, however, has never been the case. The Portuguese, the Spaniards, the Dutch and the Danes, for instance, behaved as cruelly towards the converts to Christianity in the Far East and South East Asia over the last five centuries as they behaved in the colonies where the people refused to accept the Europeans' religion.

The same can be said about the way colonisers from Western Europe treated the peoples of Latin America. In spite of the fact that all the countries in this region adopted the white conquerors' faith, they were hardly treated with any leniency. Nor did their standing enhance in the eyes of the European masters throughout the colonisation period. To this day, in the West, the image of countries like Peru, Brazil, Argentina and Columbia is similar to the image they had when they were colonies. These countries are not geographically speaking in the Orient. All the same, their image in the West is not very different from that of any Oriental country.

Nowadays, the stigmatization of non-Western countries is done mainly through the media. Referring to the negative impact of Western media representations of the Orient, especially the Near East, on the image of the peoples of these regions and their cultures, Said notes:

> Television, the films, and all the media's resources have forced information into more and more standardized molds. So far as the Orient is concerned, standardization and cultural stereotyping have intensified the hold of the nineteenth-century academic and imaginative demonology of 'the mysterious Orient'.[5]

Television, the films and all the media's resources, however, have had the same negative impact also on other non-Western countries. The Latin Americans, for instance, are stereotyped and pigeonholed in the West no less than the Orientals. Like the Near East, Latin America makes headlines in the West mainly for the wrong reasons. Referring to this constant negative media coverage of the region, Richard S. Hillman notes that:

> [a]ttitudes, values, beliefs regarding the conduct of politics, business and life in general remain vastly and profoundly misunderstood by many. The media has sensationalised issues such as political corruption and instability, narcotics trafficking and immigration problems, overshadowing attempts to promote democracy, trade and development, tourism and regional co-operation.[6]

In his 'quarrel' with the West, Edward Said also seems to ignore the important fact that European powers have a long tradition of denigrating countries and regions which geographically, historically, religiously and politically speaking are part of Europe. One such region is the Balkans, and one such country is Albania.

iii. Racial prejudice towards the Balkans

In the Western psyche the Balkans have been traditionally seen as Europe's 'bad appendix', a region where ethnic tensions and conflicts are endemic. In the last two hundred years several European leaders have often expressed their low opinions about this region. In the 1820s, for instance, the German-born Chancellor of the Austrian Empire, Prince Klemens von Metternich, who was known as 'the coachman of Europe', made it clear that as far as he was concerned, the Balkans are not part of Europe. In his words, 'Asia begins at the Landstrasse', the highway leading south and east of Vienna into Hungary. In the late nineteenth century, 'the Iron Chancellor', Otto von Bismarck, one of the founders of the German Empire, held that the Balkans were not worth the bones of a Pomeranian grenadier.

Likewise, several European leaders have often made disparaging remarks about individual Balkan and central European countries. Bismarck, for instance, had no qualms in declaring that 'Albania is merely a geographic expression; there is no Albanian nation,' and Archduke Franz Ferdinand considered it 'an act of bad taste for the Hungarians to have come to Europe'.

As a rule, West Europeans do not consider the people living in the Balkans Europeans. In spite of their contribution 'to the general progress of European civilization',[7] these 'outsider' Europeans continue to have a negative image in the West. There are several reasons for this: – geographical, ethnic, religious, economic and political.

Western Europe's dominance and its unsavoury opinion of the Balkans have their beginnings in the days of the Roman Empire. Rome's victory over Gent, the last Illyrian king, in 169 BC signalled the start of the colonisation of the Balkans. Since Rome's annexation of Illyria, apart from some spells of self-rule, the Albanians in particular have been constantly living under occupation.

The mass arrival of the Slavs in the Balkans from the fifth century AD onwards, meant that the region became a contested space where tribe-nations would constantly vie for and fight over territory. The conflicts in the Balkans since the dawn of the Slavic migration have often been and remain to this day essentially conflicts about expansion, colonisation, consolidation and protection of ethnic borders.

This ongoing ethnic strife has often given the Balkans an unsympathetic image in the West. Conflicts between different and similar ethnic groups in the Balkans have made the peoples of the region easy targets for strong colonial powers, whether they came from the West or the East. This was particularly the case in the fourteenth century when the Ottomans' progress into the peninsula was facilitated by the lack of unity among princes of different ethnic groups. In spite of some valiant attempts to unite against the common enemy, initially in 1389 and throughout the 1443-1468 period, the Balkan rulers were too divided to form a common front against the Turks. The old Roman motto *divide et impera* was used skilfully by the Turks throughout their long stay in the Balkans. The Hapsburg Empire was equally eager to exploit the bitter rivalries between the Balkan countries.

The Balkan peoples have also suffered as a result of the several schisms that have befallen Christianity since the fourth century, and the religious decisions they have made at particular moments in their history. In the case of the Albanians, the conversion of a considerable number of them to Islam in the wake of the death of their national hero Skanderbeg in 1468, a conversion which was made possible partly through coercion, partly through bribery and partly as a matter of convenience for the local rulers who wanted to retain their power, was to have a detrimental impact on the image of the Albanians in the West.

The European Powers considered Albania as a Turkish colony for almost five centuries mainly because they wrongly believed – some still do – that all Albanians are Muslims. The West's perception of Albania as an 'Islamic' country has also been reinforced since the end of the nineteenth century by a powerful Serbian propaganda to present the Albanians as 'fanatic adherents' to the Islamic faith, and as such 'non-Europeans'. Documents made public recently by the US government reveal that, during the Cold War, the West as well as the USSR often referred to Albania as a 'Muslim' country in spite of the official atheistic stance adopted by the Communist government in 1967.

Following the disintegration of the Turkish Empire in the early twentieth century, the European Powers were quick to intervene in the Balkans to serve their own interests. The decision to carve up the Balkans, especially Albania, in 1913, remains to this day a blatant act of international thuggary initiated by powerful European states at the expense of one of the oldest European nations. The dismembered Albanian nation is a constant reminder of a festering wound at the heart of Europe which will not simply disappear unless Western leaders today own up to the dreadful miscalculations of their colonial predecessors for whom the territorial integrity and sovereignty of some small nations were hardly an issue.

Western powers' influence over the Balkans waned considerably during the Second World War and especially throughout the Cold War. Except for Greece's lucky escape, thanks to the financial support coming from the United States in 1947, something which proved vital later for the integration of Greece into the European Community, all Balkan countries adopted Communism.

The Cold War was essentially an irreconcilable ideological conflict during which the differences between the East and the West were often seen as a manifestation of the battle between 'good' and 'evil'. In this bitter contest between two contradicting social systems – Capitalism and Communism – the image of the Communist Balkans suffered further.

The end of the Cold War in 1989 brought to the surface once again the ancient issue about the 'Europeanness' or 'non-Europeanness' of the Balkans. For their part, after several decades of Communist propaganda and isolation, only now the Balkan citizens could see for themselves the negative image they had in the West. The violent disintegration of Yugoslavia throughout the 1990s dented their image in the West even more.

As for Albania, its image was greatly tarnished by the exodus of numerous impoverished Albanians heading towards Italy and other Western countries in the early 1990s, and the civil unrest in the wake of the collapse of the fraudulent pyramid schemes in 1997.

iv. Identity crisis

After the collapse of Communism and the violent fragmentation of Yugoslavia, every Balkan country was keen to join the European Union. So far, however, only Slovenia in 2004 and Romania and Bulgaria in 2007 have been able to join this expanding club. Some of the Balkan countries that have yet to become EU members apparently believe that their accession has been delayed partly because of the negative image the region has in the West. This is the reason why such hopeful candidates are keen to distance themselves from the Balkans.

The tendency to present themselves as 'non-Balkans' is strong among the region's EU member states Greece and Slovenia, and among the frustrated hopefuls like Croatia. Many Croats are insulted if foreigners consider their country as part of the Balkans.[8] The Croats' aversion towards the Balkans seems to have intensified as a result of the advice given by their Western 'promoters'. One such 'promoter' of Croatia in the UK is Brian Gallagher, who has repeatedly advised the Croats to distance themselves from the Balkans. In his article 'Will Croatia join a Balkan NATO?', which appeared in *Hrvatski Vjesnik* on 26 July 2002, Gallagher praises the Slovenes for their farsightedness to wean themselves from 'the problem region'. In his words, '[b]y simply saying "no", Slovenia has avoided all regional nonsense and has escaped the Balkan image'.[9] Sensing a 'hidden' agenda on the part of NATO to create what he calls 'a West Balkan NATO', Gallagher concludes that 'NATO clearly considers Croatia to be fully part of this troubled region, which cannot be good news for Croatia's image'. Having argued that 'Croatia and Serbia are not "like-minded" countries', Gallagher 'reprimands' the Croatian government for its 'naivety':

> Why is Croatia anchoring itself to these problem countries? Is Zagreb unaware of the appalling image these countries have in the EU? The British media – often hysterically – is continually running stories about Albanian criminal gangs in the UK. General Sylvester, Head of NATO in Bosnia-Herzegovina, in relation to dealing with terrorism described the BiH border as 'porous' in *TIME* magazine. Such an image means that Croatia will never join NATO and the EU on an individual basis. But it will certainly end up in some 'West Balkan' structure. The EU makes things clear on their website. They wish to 'encourage the countries of the region to behave towards each other and work with each other in a manner comparable to the relationships that now exist between EU Member States'. A West Balkan EU in other words....Croatia will be economically impoverished by 'West Balkans' association. Many investors will take their money to 'safer' countries, not linked to basket case economies such as Serbia. And if there are any conflicts in Serbia or elsewhere, tourism may suffer. Croatia needs to get away from the West Balkan image, not plunge straight into it.[10]

Gallagher is right to warn the Croats about 'the appalling image' all Balkan countries have in the West, but he seems to have a rather narrow view about its origin. While the turbulent 1990s hardly endeared the peoples of the Balkans to Westerners, their image as 'uncivilised' had been sealed in the West at least two centuries earlier.

v. The exotic archive

From the early nineteenth century onwards, the West knew the Balkans mainly through the works of Western travel writers and accounts of diplomats and military experts posted across the region. There were even cases when Westerners wrote about the Balkans without ever setting foot in the region, thus constructing, what K. E. Fleming calls, 'fictional Balkan worlds'. In the twentieth century such 'fictional' Balkan worlds appeared in the works of Georges Remi (known mainly as Hergé), Agatha Christie and, towards the end of the twentieth century, in the novels of J. K. Rowling. If the first two writers used fictional names for their Balkan countries ('Syldavia' and 'Borduria' in Hergé's *Le Sceptre d'Ottokar/King Ottokar's Sceptre: Tintin Visits an Exotic Country* (1939), and 'Herzoslovakia' in Christie's *The Secret of Chimneys* (1925)), Rowling has no qualms in using the name of Albania in her *Harry Potter and the Chambers of Secrets* (1998) and *Harry Potter and the Goblet of Fire* (2000) as a country where the evil 'Dark Lord' and his dedicated followers find a perfect hideout.[11]

While the West has quite an extensive archive of literary works in which the Balkans and Albania are continuously presented mainly as 'uncivilised', with the exception of the last few decades, over the last three centuries Western scholars have hardly considered Albania, any other Balkan country or the Balkan Peninsula worthy of a lengthy academic study. As K. E. Fleming notes in her 2000 article '*Orientalism*, the Balkans, and the Balkan Historiography', there is no history of 'Balkanism' as an established academic field.[12]

In the same work, Fleming holds that, different from *Orientalism*, the Balkans scholarship has traditionally been produced by a 'free-lance', 'pseudo-academic', 'cottage industry of "specialists"' who, as in the case of the break-up of Yugoslavia, are interested in the subject matter because contemporary conflicts render it 'timely'. I myself have written elsewhere that in the case of Albania, some of its Western image-makers in the past ended up writing about it quite by chance, and not as part of a long thought-out plan to study its people, history and culture.[13] In most cases, such Western 'specialists' on Albania and the Balkans took to travelling abroad either to escape bad publicity at home, as was the case with Lord Byron, or on medical advice, as in Edith Durham's case. Albania offered to eighteenth, nineteenth, and twentieth century Western travellers like Byron, Durham, Roland Matthews, Karl May, Franz Nopcsa, British military personnel operating in Albania and elsewhere in the Balkans during World War II, and more recently to Paul Theroux, Robert Carver, Marianne Graf, A. A. Gill and Mike Carter a chance to encounter the 'exotic', the 'primitive' and the 'uncivilised' at the threshold of Western Europe.

It is no coincidence that for most of these Albanian 'experts', what is of particular interest is not the 'civilised' Albania, but its backwardness, not the thriving towns and cities like Tirana, Shkodra, Korça and Vlora with a rich and varied cultural, historical, civic and natural heritage but some distant villages, and especially the less developed Northern Albania. Following the example of Durham and Nopcsa at the start of the twentieth century, contemporary travel writers like Carver and Graf pay attention almost exclusively to this particular region of Albania to tell Western readers about their sensational discovery of a 'backwater of life' and its 'primitive virtues'.[14] Some of the preferred themes of these devoted chasers of the exotic are *besa* (Albanian for 'word of honour'), the Canon of Lekë Dukagjin, blood feuds and the sworn virgins. Such exotic themes are given priority in the biographies of Albanian personalities penned by Westerners like Gwen Robyns, the author of *Geraldine of the Albanians: The Authorised Biography* (1987), and in the writings of some Mother Teresa scholars such as Eileen Egan and Kathryn Spink.

The American novelist Paul Theroux once said that writing travel books is 'a pretty harmless activity'.[15] This is true as far as the authors of this kind of literature and their intended readers are concerned; after all, most published travel writers in the West are Westerners.

As far as the countries described in this made-in-and-for-the-West travel literature are concerned, however, travel-writing is anything but a harmless activity. As a result of works written by authors who have visited Albania or virtual travellers who used to and still describe this 'exotic' place without ever setting foot there, as was the case with the German writer Karl May and more recently with the Spanish novelist Susana Fortes, the author of *El Amante Albanés* (*The Albanian Lover*, 2003), the West now possesses quite an 'exotic archive' on Albania. This 'exotic archive' is largely responsible for the predominantly negative image Albania has in the West at the moment.

Albania's image as a 'primitive', 'uncivilised' and 'dangerous' but still fun-to-visit place, prevails nowadays in spite of the fact that this corner of the Balkans is no longer an isolated country. It is as a result of this long-established tendency to describe this place only in black and white that to this day the West remains largely ignorant of anything positive about Albania in the past, and especially since the fall of Communism in 1991. Anything reported in the West about Albania, even an international football match, has to be politicised for the sake of highlighting this country's 'backwardness'. In his messy article 'Good grass and gun law', that appeared in *The Observer* on 25 March 2001, for instance, Simon Kuper takes the reader on a journey that has more to do with the 'primitiveness' of the host country, corruption, the donkey carts its people allegedly use as a mode of transportation to travel to Tirana to see international matches, and contract killings than with Albania's World Cup fixture with England. Referring to a photograph an Albanian football historian had taken of the England team before the kickoff when they played Albania in 1989, Kuper cannot contain his surprise when he notices that in the picture 'Bryan Robson, Peter Shilton, John Barnes and Gary Lineker [were] looking as if they had no idea they were visiting Europe's strangest state'. The England team, it seems, had let Kuper and Britain down by looking normal in an 'abnormal' country, surrounded by 'abnormal' football fans.

This biased, sensationalist and exotic literature on and tabloid-like media coverage of Albania have long become 'the norm' in the West especially in the United Kingdom. The articles cited in this part of the essay have appeared in national British newspapers and magazines between 2001 and 2006. The reason for their selection has been determined purely by the fact that during these years Albania has experienced political stability, law and order have been maintained across the country, and many Albanians have seen an increase in their savings[16] and a significant improvement in their living standards. As a result of more opportunities to work and higher salaries, the Albanians who went on holiday abroad in 2004 spent $560 million.[17]

All indications are that the Albanian government is working hard to follow the advice of the European Union on several issues regarding its monetary policy and the management of the economy. Albania is also playing a positive role in the Balkans to further regional cooperation. More recently, the Balkan Council for the Ministers of Culture, which was founded in Copenhagen on 31 March 2005, was the brainchild of an Albanian minister.[18] The Albanian government has initiated several other projects to enhance cultural exchanges and improve trade relations with every Balkan country and has responded positively to similar proposals originating from other governments in the region.[19]

Albania's achievements have been noticed by some Western scholars. In the words of James Pettifer and Miranda Vickers:

> Albania has undergone a remarkable and unprecedented political, social and economic transformation since it emerged from the ruins of the harshest form of communism in 1991. Then an utterly poverty-stricken population was wholly dependent upon international food aid, and the state was in a condition of advanced disintegration. Within a year, however, Albania's international isolation had ended as the world's major powers hurried to establish their diplomatic missions in this impoverished but strategically important Balkan state. Despite chronic internal political unrest during the latter half of the 1990s, Albania gradually became a respected partner of the West in the region. During the Kosova crisis [in 1999] the country proved itself a worthy NATO ally, and following the 9/11 attacks on the USA, Albania has resolutely joined the 'War on Terror', by firmly monitoring the activities of radical Islamic individuals and groups in the country. Albania has also contributed soldiers to US-led coalitions in the wars in Afghanistan and Iraq.[20]

In spite of such positive developments, like other countries in the Balkans, Albania hits the headlines in the West, especially in the British media, mostly for the wrong reasons. Richard Hillman's conclusion, mentioned earlier in this essay, that media has sensationalised issues such as political corruption and instability, narcotics trafficking and immigration problems, overshadowing attempts to promote democracy, trade and development, tourism and regional co-operation, is valid not only for Latin America but also for Albania and the Balkans.

For many British journalists covering Albania, its identity and image are set in stone. Albania was and remains 'Europe's poorest and most isolated country'.[21] These are some of the titles of the articles about this country that have appeared in recent years in some of Britain's major newspapers and magazines such as *The Times*, *The Sunday Times Magazine*, *The Independent*, *The Observer* and *The Guardian*: 'The wild frontier', 'Rocks and hard places', 'Albanian gangs take control of Britain streets', 'Balkan criminals better organised than us: Blunkett', 'Shanty town in Albania built on toxic time bomb', 'Back home: the child of six sold to traffickers', 'Streets of despair', 'Welcome to Tirana, Europe's pollution capital', 'Partisan war at Albania's paradise bay', 'Secret Europe', 'The land that time forgot' and 'Travels through a midlife crisis'. From these titles it is not surprising that British citizens are strongly advised to think twice before taking the decision to visit Albania. The advice, several British reporters are keen to emphasise, comes mainly from the Foreign Office. This is how Esther Addley opens her article 'Welcome to camp Tirana', which appeared in *The Guardian* on 11 March 2003:

> Planning to visit Albania? If so the Foreign Office has a few tips. 'Public security has improved considerably in Albania…but crime and violence still represent a serious problem in some areas', its website cautions. 'Drink only bottled water and UHT milk. Medical facilities (including accident and emergency) are very poor. We do not recommend using dental facilities'.
>
> Of particular concerns, it warns, are hepatitis, rabies (due to 'the large number of stray dogs') and tick-borne encephalitis' ('we advice travellers to keep all areas of the body covered when close to shrubs, and to inspect themselves regularly for ticks'). In fact, it concludes, better safe than sorry: make sure your medical insurance covers evacuation by helicopter, just in case the worst should happen.[22]

The Foreign Office website is also mentioned in several other newspaper articles on Albania. In his piece 'Wish you were here', which was published in *The Guardian* on 11 August 2003, for instance, Tim Dowling notes that the Foreign Office draws attention to '"the widespread ownership of firearms", and strongly discourages travel in the north-east of the country'.[23] The information Dowling received about Albania from another source is hardly more encouraging:

> The Lonely Planet website warns of 'armed robberies, assaults, mobster assassinations, bombings and carjackings', exhorts visitors to 'avoid all large public gatherings' and says it is inadvisable to travel outside the main cities, or anywhere at night. This doom-laden paragraph is missing from the latest edition of its printed guide to eastern [sic] Europe, but the book does suggest that 'corrupt police may attempt to extort money from you' and the word 'banditry' is used in passing.[24]

Albania does not fare any better in other travel guide websites and some simply ignore this country altogether. On 13 July 2003, Andrew Muller wrote in *The Independent on Sunday* that Albania is not mentioned in the current *Rough Guide to Eastern Europe*, and *Fodor's Central & Eastern Europe* also gives it a swerve.[25] The lack of information on Albania and the frightening picture painted by the Home Office and the Lonely Planet websites are unlikely to entice foreigners to visit this country. No wonder some people in the West apparently share Muller's sentiment that '[y]ou'd no sooner go to Albania than you'd jump on the tail of a sleeping leopard, and nor would anybody else'.[26]

Cases are not rare when British reporters rely entirely on and accept uncritically the little available information on travel to Albania. They are also keen to refer in their articles, often inconsequentially, to some Albanian 'primitive' and 'bizarre' customs and traditions they have picked up from browsing hastily the 'exotic archive' on Albania mentioned earlier. Cases are not rare when British reporters write about Albania without consulting any scholarly book on the country's history. Indeed, many of them have no informed background to make a sensible assessment of the situation in Albania or the Balkans. British journalists who cover this region, as a rule, are commissioned at random for an occasional article, have never studied at any university in the Balkans, speak none of the Balkan languages and, perhaps more significantly, often write about the region without ever going there in person. This reminds me of the former British Minister for Europe Keith Vaz, who was also responsible for the Balkans. Shortly after the fall of Slobodan Milosevic, I attended a meeting with Mr Vaz in Birmingham, where I asked him why the British government was so eager to hail as a huge success the 'half-baked' Serbian revolution of October 2000, considering that Vojislav Kostunica, who succeeded Milosevic as president of Yugoslavia, was – and remains – as much of an ultra-nationalist as his predecessor when it comes to the issue of the independence of the Albanian territory of Kosova. To this the Minister replied: 'The Balkans, you know, is a very difficult region'. When Mr Vaz resigned in late 2001, it emerged that throughout his four years as a minister responsible for the Balkans, he had never visited the region.

It is unfortunate that some British journalists, who bring the world to the British public, seem to think that they can offer a realistic and impartial picture of a country like Albania by relying exclusively on outdated information coming from government departments, travel guides and sensationalist and biased travel writers. This kind of distance reporting, as was the case with Esther Addley's hurriedly written article 'Welcome to camp Tirana', is largely responsible for the perennial pauper image reserved for Albania in the British media.

Albania's image has hardly benefited in the UK even from British journalists who are 'brave' enough to take the challenge to visit this 'dangerous' country. The reputation of Albania as an 'unsafe' place often reaches a manic level in the UK. 'When I told my friends – educated, enlightened, citizens of the world – I was going to visit Albania', Andrew Muller wrote in the article mentioned earlier, 'their initial responses were instructive: "Wasn't Baghdad dangerous enough"; "Could I please have your flat?"; "Bring me back a, erm…cabbage?"'.[27]

The dispatches most British journalists send from Tirana or other parts of Albania often perpetuate the bad image this country and its people already have in Britain. Tim Dowling is right when he concludes that most information he consulted prior to his visit to Albania in August 2003 'seems designed to instil fear'.[28]

While many British reporters can be 'forgiven' for not writing sympathetically about Albania as they describe this country from their offices in London, Dowling chose to paint a very gloomy picture of the situation in Albania following his visit there. The article 'Wish you were here' quite often betrays Dowling's lack of objectivity and poor knowledge of the country. 'In Albania,' he claims, 'they worship Norman Wisdom as a cultural icon'. The myth about Wisdom's 'iconic status' among the Albanians is mentioned by most British reporters writing on Albania since the actor visited the country after the end of Communism.[29] Therefore, it stands to reason that an alleged bizarre obsession like this would not escape the attention of someone like Dowling who is obviously quite skilled in spotting cultural eccentricities, both real and invented. What Dowling has yet to learn is that in Albania, any foreigner who is anybody is given a red-carpet reception. Cases are not rare when this kind of special treatment is offered even to foreigners who are complete nonentities in their own countries.

As a reporter with a mission, it is not surprising that Dowling would spot and report other 'bizarre' things about the Albanians like their habit to 'shake their heads for yes and nod for no'. The remark which I like most in his article is the one testifying to his expertise as a linguist *par excellence*. The Albanians, he claims, 'speak two languages, Tosk and Gheg'.[30] This piece of information would give Western readers the erroneous impression that these are not two dialects of one and the same native tongue but two completely different languages.

Dowling is a typical sensationalist journalist who goes abroad not to write about real people with real problems, real achievements and real aspirations but only to look for potholes, concrete pillboxes, rubble, broken glass, twisted iron, and especially people 'walking cows as if they were dogs'.[31]

Either because he was not so confident in his ability to capture the 'seamy' side of Albania with absolute accuracy and authenticity, or because he felt that words are never enough to convince the British reader of what an 'appalling' place this corner of the Balkans is, he used the expertise of *The Guardian* photographer Dan Chung to document his historic visit.

The article is accompanied by three pictures. In the first one, Dowling sits smirking somewhere in the coastal town of Durrës in front of a concrete pillbox, a cow and lots of scattered rubbish. The poster-size picture takes the whole front-page of *The Guardian* and has a caption which reads: 'My holiday in Albania'. The second picture, this time in black and white, shows Dowling at the entrance of another concrete pillbox. In the last picture, which occupies more than half of the third page, Dowling sits quite smug at the edge of the beach showing mainly debris, mossy stones and, of course, more rubbish. This time the caption reads: 'Plenty of space by the water: "The beach in Durrës is composed almost entirely of hard-packed dust, concrete rubble, broken glass and twisted iron."'[32]

Any British reader who might have considered going to Albania for a bit of sun, sea and sand would have certainly been put off by Dowling's article and the pictures, especially the last one. To the unsuspecting British reader, the buildings shown in the background in the third shot seem to have no seafront worth passing by, let alone sunbathing or swimming facilities.

Like other holiday spots in Albania, Durrës has suffered as a result of pollution and a boom in construction work, often carried out without permission. The sorry picture Dowling and his photographer paint of Durrës, however, is hardly representative of this beautiful seaside resort famous for its golden sandy beaches that stretch for miles on end. It appears *The Guardian* duo did not go to Albania to discover it for themselves, but to hunt around for images that would fit perfectly with what they had heard about this country before arriving there.

In their journalistic mission to document only dirt in non-Western countries, reporters like Dowling often find zealous helpers among the locals who, either because of their naivety, their pathological inferiority complex towards any two-legged creature hailing from the West, or because of their legitimate frustration with rampant corruption, tell Western journalists what they want to hear.

vi. The Death of the Journalist

The Dowling-type journalism rarely offers imaginative reporting, and hence is hardly intellectually stimulating. Applying Derrida's deconstructionist approach to an intentionally derogatory and sensationalist newspaper text reveals some interesting, surprising and disheartening results. Once completed, a literary text, any text, no matter who pens it, can be plural in meaning and interpretation. The newspaper text, on the other hand, often seems stubbornly one-dimensional. The tone, the lexicon and the pictures accompanying it make for a pattern Western readers have been familiar with for at least a couple of centuries. As far as the British print media is concerned, Albania has always been and still is a 'backward', 'poor', 'enigmatic' country, just as the Balkans remains a 'powder keg', the local economies 'dysfunctional', the regional leaders 'political infants' and 'corrupt', and the whole peninsula a Pandora's box from where all evil things come to the West, especially Britain: drugs, human trafficking, money laundering, prostitution, contract killers, and the list goes on.

The newspaper 'text' says it all, allowing readers no opportunity to interpret it for themselves. Some British journalists, it appears are 'dead'. However, the demise of these authors is different from the death of the author as perceived by Roland Barthes. The journalist-author appears to be dead not only because the smearing article as a 'genre' predates him. Some reporters in the West seem to have a ghoulish existence also because their output is neither informative nor intellectually challenging. The journalist, to borrow Barthes cryptical line of argument, 'does not write' the 'text'. The newspaper 'text' does not need the 'author' or an 'author'. It already exists without him/her, and the 'author' is incapable of adding any new meaning to it.

The death of the Journalist-Author does not presuppose the birth of the independent reader, as Barthes had implied in the case of the literary Author.[33] In this case the reader is not given a chance to interpret the text in a new and imaginative way. The newspaper-text and newspaper-photo only reinforce what the reader has been fed on for years, decades and even centuries regarding the identity and standing of Albania and other 'lesser' countries. The reader is no longer served by a real journalist but by a phantom-writer who is incapable of breaking the mould and whose mission apparently is to keep on churning out scaremongering stories about 'footnote' peoples and countries.

vii. The price of biased journalism

This kind of biased, doom-and-gloom reporting is bound to harm the Albanian economy, especially the prospects of tourism, just as it gives ordinary people, investors and businessmen in the West the misleading impression that Albania has made no progress since the fall of Communism, and that the country is incapable of having a viable tourism industry.

The Albanian government has always been aware of the country's atrocious image in the West. It is only recently, however, that it has tried to do something to rectify the situation. On 23 February 2005, for instance, the Albanian daily *Biznesi* reported that the Albanian government had asked McKinsey & Company to contribute towards improving the country's image in order to attract more foreign investment. According to Ulrich Frincke, McKinsey's Regional Director for the South East European countries, the cooperation between his management consulting firm and Albania is expected to bring the country more than US$ 300 million a year.

The Albanian government's decision to seek advice from such a leading global strategic management consulting firm was met with derision by the reporter Robert Shrimsley. His article 'Tirana saw us', which appeared in the *Financial Times* on 3 March 2005, is rather long but I have quoted it in its entirety because I believe it reiterates some of the issues about biased, and in this case hostile, coverage that Albania often receives in the British press:

> The Albanian government has asked McKinsey to develop a strategy to improve the country's image and attractiveness to foreign investors.
>
> To: Albanian cabinet
>
> From: McKinsey, Zagreb Office
>
> Subject: Image refurbishment
>
> Further to our discussions last month we present our preliminary thoughts on upgrading Albania's image to overseas investors.
>
> You are already aware that structural changes are needed. Image makeovers rarely succeed if they are not underpinned by a genuine rethink. The bribery of tax and licensing officials may very well be a proud tradition in your country but it does rather cut against the reform and modernisation drive. You may be aware of the old German joke urging businessmen to 'fly to Albania; your car's already there'. Charming as this is, it is probably not the image you want to project. A requirement for all Mercedes to display a valid receipt in the window would work wonders.
>
> Once these measures are in place however, some cosmetic changes would go a long way towards signalling the birth of a new and modern Albania.
>
> For a start we recommend you consider a name change. Albania is so last century – it seems to date back to the year Zog. Something that suggests a more technologically advanced, even cool, nation. After consultations with branding experts, we recommend aPod. This conjures up a far more buzzing image, especially if U2 could

> be prevailed on to write your new national anthem.
>
> Finally we find nothing spurs on investors quite so much as a peaceful revolution, preferably one with a colour or material in it. The publicity value of one, if you could organise it, would be immense. Orange, rose, velvet and cedar have already gone but salmon pink is nice and has happy associations with business. Thanks to the widespread global ignorance of Albanian politics, there is probably no need even to oust the existing administration as long as it all takes place so suddenly as to sweep you into power before any foreign press can make it to Tirana. A new communications supremo would also help. Alastair Campbell will be available from May. He's a little brutal by Albanian standards but the great thing is his proven track record of securing such good coverage for reforms that it can be years before people realise they do not quite live up to expectations.

Asked if he would care to comment on the motives that made him write such a piece,[34] Shrimsley's response was: 'My article was primarily a bit of fun towards the end of a column based on the decision to invite McKinsey in.'[35] Shrimsley sees nothing wrong in the constant degradation that countries like Albania receive in the British press, because, as he puts it, '[i]n my experience countries bear their own responsibilities for the treatment they receive in the press.'

Shrimsley certainly has a point. It would be absurd to see countries like Albania, indeed any country that receives constant bad coverage in the British press, simply as a 'martyred' party. There is no denying that corruption is rife in Albania, that Albanian politicians have yet to understand the notion of a 'loyal opposition', that a lot needs to be done so that locals and foreigners feel safe across the country, that its infrastructure has a long way to go before it can match Western standards, and that quality health services are equally available to every citizen. Paul Brown is right to call Tirana 'Europe's pollution capital' in his article which appeared in *The Guardian* on 27 March 2004.

Albania, however, has made considerable achievements since its belated independence in 1912, especially since the end of Communist rule sixteen years ago. Trivialising the efforts of a small ancient nation to join the family of developed countries is not just 'a bit of fun'; it is fun in a bad taste. This fun *à la* Shrimsley has contributed significantly to sustaining the prevailing 'heart of darkness' image of Albania in the West.

Shrimsley, of course, is not the only self-professed 'funny' British journalist. Nor is he the only British reporter who fails to see why not everyone is bending over with laughter as they read such image-smearing articles that appear so often in the British press. A couple of years before the publication of Shrimsley's 'side-splitting' letter in the *Financial Times*, another British journalist, Charles Rae, was frustrated with '[a] few humourless killjoys' who 'did not see the funny side of *The Sun*'s Mr Men spoof',[36] which the tabloid ran on 21 January 2003. 'We invented seven characters in the style of kids' favourites Mr Men and Little Misses,' the self-appointed Mr Comedienne Rae explains, 'to reflect life in modern Britain.' Two of these 'favourites' are foreigners: Mr Asylum Seeker and Mr Albanian Gangster. This is how *The Sun* portrays the latter:

> Mr Albanian Gangster
>
> Mr Albania Gangster didn't like it in Albania so now he lives in Britain. He hangs out with Mr Drug Dealer and Mr Asylum Seeker. He often likes to do the same things as them. But Mr Albanian Gangster has a kind side – he invited all of his friends' sisters to stay. He even gave them

> a job. He put all his friends' sisters in a house together and then invited lots of men to come and see them so they would never get lonely. The men had such a good time they even paid Mr Albanian Gangster to visit the house. Unfortunately the poor girls saw none of the money. Mr Albanian Gangster pocketed the lot.[37]

Rae's and Shrimsley's 'harmless' mediatic 'fun' has been going on for far too long, and is largely responsible for the constant demonisation of some peoples, a demonisation which in capitalistic terms translates into a loss of revenue from potential investors understandably unwilling to take unnecessary risks in countries which are always portrayed as incorrigible. 'Let's do some word associations,' Andrew Mueller invites the readers of *The Independent on Sunday* at the start of his article 'Tirana's true colours', one of the rare pieces in the British press where there is no intention to denigrate the Albanians:

> I say 'Albanian', you say...Gangster? Asylum-seeker? Prostitute? There are viruses breeding in African rivers which have better public image than Albania. Indeed, in London schoolyards, the adjective 'Albanian' has passed into vernacular, descriptive of anything shoddy, unfashionable or criminal.[38]

The Albanian nation and the overwhelming majority of decent law-abiding Albanian citizens abroad have a lot to thank their criminal expatriates for this unjust collective punishment and humiliation in the West. Some irresponsible individuals, though, should not be seen as representing all the Albanians. Not all Western citizens behave themselves abroad. Yet when some British football hooligans, for instance, wreak havoc overseas, no British journalist sees them as the epitome of the whole British population. When it comes to some Albanian gangsters, however, Britain's 'hilarious' reporters are eager to resort to sensationalisation and tabloidisation of any scrap of evidence, genuine or fabricated, to brand all Albanians as criminals. This kind of reporting is intended not so much to inform and entertain the unsuspecting British readers, who are more sophisticated than some reporters and editors seem to believe, but to boost circulation figures.

As a rule Western journalists reporting on Albania and other former Communist countries see 'corruption' as an 'indigenous' problem. In addition to flagellating Albania's corrupt politicians and businessmen, some 'principled' British journalists and their Western colleagues would do poor Albania a huge favour if they named and shamed its corrupt leaders in the Western Media. And not only Albania. More importantly, such 'conscientious' reporters would benefit their own countries even more if they had both the courage and professional integrity to name and shame those Western politicians and business leaders who condone and even help directly corrupt politicians and entrepreneurs in countries like Albania. Corruption may be rife in Albania and across Eastern Europe, but it would not be a bad idea if Western journalists traced the source of the metastasises of corruption Westwards as much as Eastwards.

James Pettifer and Miranda Vickers identify other reasons why the British media portrayed the Albanians so negatively between 2001 and 2006. Having highlighted the decisive role of the Blair government in defeating Milosevic's ethnic cleansing of the Albanians in Kosova which culminated in their mass expulsion in 1999, Pettifer and Vickers note that the British bureaucracy still contains many people who have never broken with 'the British Yugoslavist psychology and tacit or active collaboration with Serb war crimes in the name of "opposing" Islam in the Balkans'.[39] The real worry for the British Serbophiles in the Foreign Office and secret intelligence service (MI6) is not Islam; they meddle in Balkan politics because they are keen 'to protect Serbian hegemony in the region'.[40] This is the reason why they are determined to sabotage Kosova's independence.

To achieve this 'open agenda' against Kosova and the Albanian nation, the British Yugophiles employed the British media, and so 'the anti-Albanian propaganda machine was cranked up in London in police and security circles, with stories fed to sympathetic journalists stressing the alleged and exclusive threat of the "Albanian mafia"'.[41] The employment of ex-Milosevic policemen as 'expert advisers' to international agencies such as Interpol meant that the demonization of the Albanians became a leitmotif also of the media in France, Greece, Italy and the USA.

This is not to say that all Western journalists were happy to besmirch the Albanians. Likewise, not all Western reporters were prepared to applaud 'the largely bogus "revolution" of October 2000 in Belgrade'.[42] Journalists who were likely to be critical of the West's interpretation of the Belgrade 'revolution' and of the handling of the issue of Kosova were left in no doubt that 'disobedience' would not be tolerated. This explains why they 'were as far as possible removed from reporting positions in the region' and replaced with 'pliable figures'.[43]

The direct involvement of some people from the Foreign Office, British army and MI6 in the media campaign against the Albanians after 2000 is a disturbing example of the back-stage censorship that goes unchecked in the British media. Unfortunately, this kind of censorship is a feature of the media across the Western world.

viii. The Media and double standards

The United Kingdom, it seems, is obsessed with political correctness and so is the British media. You cannot badmouth or vilify in Britain just any country. This 'preferential' treatment is reserved only for countries like Albania that have yet to produce a vigorous and independent media of their own and a scholarly elite to take on mediocre and ill-meaning Western journalists and biased scholars whose aim, one would argue, is to denigrate any 'other' that does not conform to Western 'norms' and is unable to protect its image.

More recently, the double standards of the British media regarding the treatment of different countries were noticeable in A. A. Gill's article on Albania 'The land that time forgot', that the *Sunday Times Magazine* ran on 23 July 2006. In Gill's view, Albania is 'funny…a punchline, a Gilbert and Sullivan country, a Ruritania of brigands and vendettas and pantomime royalty', and the Albanians are 'short and ferret-faced, with the unisex stumpy, slightly bowed legs of Shetland ponies'.[44] Like Dowling, Gill cannot help showing off what a linguistics expert he is. Different from Dowling, though, Gill does not pay attention to the Albanian dialects. What Gill finds unique about Albanian is that, in his view, this language is 'a ready-made code for criminals', and 'pathetically, phonetically funny'.

Gill's article outraged many Albanians and Westerners who wrote to the *Sunday Time Magazine* to complain. One of the Albanians who contacted the magazine was Lavdrim Terziu, editor of the London-based newspaper *Albanian Mail*. In his reply to Terziu, the editor of the *Sunday Time Magazine*, Robin Morgan, adopts a somewhat patronising tone, lecturing him and other 'unsophisticated' readers on the 'broad-brushstroke British wit', which, apparently, not everyone understands, especially if one is unlucky enough not to have been born British. No wonder Terziu and his fellow Albanians were not hugely impressed by, what they saw as, Morgan's arrogant attitude.[45]

Terziu also contacted the Press Complaints Commission (PCC) in London only to be told that:

> [Gill] was entitled to take a negative view of the place and to share it with the newspaper's readers, who would have been aware from the manner in which it was presented that the article represented his own subjective position rather than an indisputable statement of fact.[46]

To adopt the PCC's perverse logic in this case, a racist bigot like Hitler also was apparently 'entitled' to take a negative view of the Jews and share it with his supporters who, as history tells us, had no qualms in adopting his 'subjective position' as an 'indisputable statement of fact'. The verdict that 'the Commission was satisfied that the newspaper had demonstrated that the journalist had sufficient grounds on which to base his observations and conclusions about the country' will undoubtedly send the wrong message to other similar mediocre and racist British journalists like Gill that it is acceptable to write that what the Albanians do abroad 'is mostly illegal', and that except for Mother Teresa, the rest of them are internationally 'infamous'.[47]

British readers, of course, are not so easily duped by a second rate scribbler like Gill whose abrasive style of writing only a handful of editors like Morgan would consider the epitome of British wit. The issue here is would Gill and Morgan have dared to write and defend similar insulting articles against other peoples, especially among those that rank high in the 'hierarchy' of nations or against any other small country with more 'status' and 'weight' on the international stage than the 'insignificant' Albania? The answer to this question is provided by Noel Malcolm of All Souls College,

University of Oxford, one of the people who wrote to the *Sunday Times Magazine* to protest against Gill's article:

> Imagine if Gill had written the following: 'Jews are ugly, with big noses. Their history shows they are a complete joke — a bunch of losers. They believe in something called the Torah, which is a handbook on stoning people to death. Most Jews outside Israel are engaged in shady business practices and usury.' Would you have published it? Yet you published the direct equivalent about Albanians. Of course, your regular readers may understand that Gill is a self-publicist who thinks that insulting people en masse is a useful way to gain publicity.
>
> But there are many decent, hardworking Albanians, here and elsewhere, who do not know that, and will be deeply upset at seeing such a farrago of prejudice and misinformation.

Echoing Malcolm's last point, James Doherty does not mince words in his letter of complaint to the *Sunday Times Magazine*, when it comes to identifying some of the reasons why Albania does not deserve all the blame for the social ills ascribed to her:

> Albania has produced international figures ranging from philosophers, scholars, scientists, Popes (Clement XI) to Hollywood stars. The problem for Albania is that it sits between prostitute-producing and prostitute-consuming countries. If we in the West practised some of the decency we preach, Albania would not be a playground for prostitution-supporting networks ranging from the Italian mafia to the British consumer.
>
> I have worked in the Balkans for over 20 years and,

> excluding the criminal few, the Albanians are the most generous, faithful, hardworking and loving people in the Balkans.[48]

It appears that there are still writers and journalists in the West who seem to believe that civilisation is a virtue, a privilege, a God-given right and the destiny only of a select group of nations. As for countries like Albania, its neighbours and numerous small and large undeveloped nations around the world, the best they can do is vegetate and admire from a distance the achievements of the 'civilised' few, without any hope of ever joining them.

Some writers in the West apparently cannot even bear to contemplate the idea that 'a primitive' country like Albania could ever be civilised. The 'civilisation' of Albania, they seem to think, would be a loss to civilisation itself because without a 'rough', 'uncouth' and 'untamed' country like Albania, there would be no other way for Westerners to know what being 'uncivilised' means.

Travel writers of the muckraker type such as Simon Kuper, Tim Dowling, Jocasta Gardner, A. A. Gill and Mike Carter and unbiased reporters like *The Guardian* environmental correspondent Paul Brown and Andrew Mueller, are aware that Albania's integration in the European Union is no longer an unrealistic Albanian ambition. This is the reason why in most articles on this Balkan country that have surfaced in the British press over the last six years, readers are often urged to visit the place sooner rather than later. Should they delay going to Albania any further, they would have no one to blame but themselves. Even Tim Dowling can see the light at the end of his journey-to-hell article. 'If you want to see Albania,' he advises the unsuspecting *Guardian* readers, 'see it now. It won't be like this for long.'[49] More recently, the call to visit Albania in the British press was repeated by Duncan Campbell. In his article 'Secret Europe', which also appeared in *The Guardian* on 19 March 2005, Campbell's 'advice for anyone who has harboured any curiosity about Albania has to be – go now before it becomes like everywhere else'.

Until the moment arrives when Albania becomes 'like everywhere else' (read like the West), it seems unlikely that many British journalists would take an interest in Albania and the Balkans other than to keep alive their exotic image for as long as possible. Winston Churchill once remarked that the Balkans produced more history than they could digest. This is perhaps true. It is also true, however, that the Western media, especially the British press, appear to find it rather daunting to break free from a long tradition of employing a discourse that often betrays nuances of the Orwellian Newspeak when depicting the 'other', including the European 'other'. Edward Said maintains that identity is a process of continuous development and it must never remain static. The identity of countries and nations also is fluid but, unless this is reflected in the media, the outcome will be not just misinformation but, even worse, disinformation. By acting as moral agents, Western journalists can render their own inestimable contribution to make Europe whole.

Part Four: India

– 10 –

Oh! not Calcutta

Mother Teresa's impact on Calcutta has always been frowned upon by some Calcuttans in the West, who intensified their attacks on her after her death, seeing her as the main culprit for their city's bad image. In his book *Mother Teresa: The Final Verdict* (2003), Aroup Chatterjee holds her responsible for harming Calcutta's reputation irreparably.[1]

Many, however, are grateful to her for challenging taboos. The renowned academic and novelist Bharati Mukherjee, for example, has been familiar with Mother Teresa's work since 1951, and 50 years later, she still recalls how the tiny Albanian Catholic nun's leprosarium first puzzled, then led her and other non-Christians to marvel.[2]

I understand why some Calcuttans resent Mother Teresa. I myself come from Albania, a country long identified in the Western psyche as Europe's poorest place, and one that rarely receives realistic treatment in the Western media. Journalists often write about it mainly to dish the dirt. It is not uncommon for articles on Albania that appear in British papers to be illustrated with poster-size photos of bunkers and piles of rubbish. This kind of journalism explains why the perception of Albania in the West is that of a poverty-stricken country, a wasteland where banditry and human trafficking are rife.

Nor are Albania and the Balkans the only 'victims' of media misrepresentation. 'Every time one mentions Bangladesh in Britain,' a Bangladeshi intellectual in Birmingham told me recently, 'the first thing that comes to the people's mind are floods, famine and poverty. As if no one in Bangladesh lives a normal life.' Is it surprising that we are hostile to refugees and asylum seekers?

Places like the Balkans, Calcutta and Bangladesh are stigmatised in the West because we tend to pigeonhole, demean and patronise the 'lesser' Other. Mother Teresa did not victimise Calcutta; the real culprit is our culture of selective and biased information.

When Malcolm Muggeridge 'discovered' Mother Teresa in 1968, only the seamy side of Calcutta was deemed newsworthy. Her charitable work was – still is – often hijacked by religious, political and media circles for their own purposes.

But Mother Teresa did not invent the poverty of Calcutta. Nor did she hold the hands of the sick and the dying to promote a book or an album. She never saw Calcutta as the epitome of poverty. Whenever she spoke about her work there, she also mentioned similar work carried out by her followers elsewhere. She helped the destitute of Calcutta as much as those of Rome, London and New York.

It is in no one's interest, one would hope, to belittle or deny Mother Teresa's legacy. National pride should not stop us from acknowledging the truth, even when it hurts. We may not agree with the unfair pictures of our countries of origin that are circulated in the West, but nor should we deny the efforts of those well-meaning people who help their unfortunate fellow human beings, even when such benefactors come from the 'scheming' West. Mother Teresa was not part of any conspiracy against Calcutta; nor did she see herself as a tool of the West to purge its guilty conscience.

Her legacy will stand the test of time because it is that of a devoted Christian, a remarkable humane person who served the needy to the best of her ability and with the best of intentions. The Pope will soon declare her a saint, but to millions of non-Christians and secular-minded people, she is already a saint of mankind.

The twentieth century was one of the most violent in modern times, but also one enlightened by preachers of common sense like Gandhi, Martin Luther King, Nelson Mandela – and Mother Teresa. The people of Calcutta were privileged to share their lives with her for almost 70 years.

I only wish the peoples of the Balkans, the Middle East and other troubled regions had the same luck. Everyone, especially us in the West, should remember what she preached: 'We are all children of God'.

– 11 –

Media and celebrity culture – subjectivist, structuralist and post-structuralist approaches to Mother Teresa's celebrity status

There has never been a society without famous people and, as Thomas Carlyle once put it, '[t]he history of the world is but the biography of great men'.[1] In pre-industrialized societies 'fame' was usually inherited, but there were cases when 'commoners' also earned it as a result of achievements and heroic deeds that elevated them above the rest of the populace, thus legitimizing their rise to power and prominence. From the first half of the seventeenth century, the period which, in some West European countries, saw the emergence of newspapers as a novel means for disseminating the news, and especially after the mid-nineteenth century onwards, thanks to the development of other technologies – dry-plate photography, telephone, phonograph, the roll film, radio, motion picture, television, the Internet – that facilitated the continuous distribution of information at a much greater speed and to an ever-expanding audience, the notions of 'fame' and 'greatness' underwent significant denotative and connotative changes. Being famous in the industrialized world gradually came to mean mainly being in the public eye. Capitalism produced a new brand of famous people: the celebrity. In his acclaimed 1962 book *The Image: A Guide to Pseudo-Events in America*, Daniel J. Boorstin defined the modern hero-celebrity, as 'a person who is known for his well-knownness'.[2]

In true capitalistic fashion, the media industry manufactures celebrities by the bushel. So much so that it would be no exaggeration if we described them as constituting a social class of their own. Andrew Smith goes even further in his article 'All in a good cause?', which appeared in *The Observer* on 27 January 2002. In his view, Live Aid in 1985 demonstrated the truth that 'a new social world had been made, in which there were only two categories of people – the celebrity corps and what Liz Hurley would later notoriously characterise as "civilians", i.e. the rest of us'.[3]

In a media-saturated world where the attainment of celebrity status is seen as an end in itself and where, for better or for worse, celebrities are such influential role models for an ever-growing fandom, there is always the danger of either equating fake prominence with genuine greatness or ignoring some of our real heroes. Concentrating on the figure of Mother Teresa, this article identifies some of the approaches and flaws apparent in the contemporary celebrity discourse. Although she was a global 'celebrity', there are very few references in the academic debate about Mother Teresa to the nature of her celebrity status and her relationship with the media. This is even more surprising considering that most Mother Teresa experts approach her more or less in the same way as they would normally approach celebrities from the fields of cinema, politics, sport, television and music. Mother Teresa is yet another example of the extent to which celebrity culture has permeated every aspect of life. The celebrated nun's relationship with the media also reveals that, like any famous person, religious personalities often employ the press and every other medium of mass communication with dexterity and, at times, unscrupulously, to reach out to their intended audiences.

Mother Teresa was one of the most written about and publicized twentieth-century women. Except for Pope John Paul II, she was arguably also the most advertised religious celebrity of our time. During her lifetime as well as posthumously, Mother Teresa continues to generate a huge level of interest and heated debate from those who either praise or criticize her.

Different people approach Mother Teresa's celebrity status mainly from one of two differing perspectives: subjectivism or structuralism. The subjectivists and the structuralists often adopt a post-structuralist approach, which in itself indicates the complexity of the media icon called Mother Teresa and the 'liquid' nature of the notion of celebrity nowadays.

Subjectivists maintain that talent, which eventually leads to fame, is innate and God-given. In Mother Teresa's case, this attitude is apparent in the numerous books, un/authorized biographies, television programmes, films (documentary, feature and animated), plays, novels, poems, paintings, musicals and sculptures that often bear the signature of her friends, colleagues, admirers and supporters. In the media, this interpretation surfaced when she was first spotted by the Indian Catholic press in Calcutta shortly after she had set up the Missionaries of Charity order in 1950. Referring to this time, the reporter Desmond Doig, an Indian Catholic of Anglo-Irish origin, remembers how he was once advised by a colleague to watch the European nun because 'she's quite extraordinary. She's going to be a saint'.[4]

In the first instance, the myth about Mother Teresa's sainted status was apparently started by Mother Teresa herself. She always maintained that she received the first call from God to serve the poor some time in 1922, before her twelfth birthday.[5] A quarter of a century later she claimed she was the recipient of another call, which she would refer to as 'the call within a call'. On 10 September 1946, during a train journey, she professed to have heard God 'calling me. The message was clear. I must leave the convent to help the poor by living among them'.[6] This, Mother Teresa believed, 'was an order. To fail it would have been to break the faith'.[7]

Even when she became world famous, and was aware that her words were likely to be scrutinized by her friends and foes alike, Mother Teresa would not hesitate to express in public her belief that she was somehow in direct contact with God and the ancient Fathers of the Church. One of her preferred parables involving herself was the 'encounter' with Saint Peter at heaven's door. Peter had tried to keep her from going in, saying 'I'm sorry. We have no shacks in heaven.' Upset by the doorman saint's 'irreverence', the saint-to-be had responded: 'Very well! I will fill heaven with the people from the slums of the city, and then you will have no other choice than to let them in.'[8]

Mother Teresa accepts that the holy 'encounter' took place when she was delirious and suffering from very high fever. One does not have to be a psychoanalyst or an atheist to conclude that, like the second call in 1946, her 'audience' with Peter could have been triggered by her poor health and agitated state of mind. Unfortunately, we do not know much about the exact state of her health when she received the first call. Like most of her first eighteen years in Skopje, even this life-changing incident remains something of a mystery. What is widely known, though, is that throughout her childhood Mother Teresa was frequently sick.[9] Her poor health was always a major cause for concern for her parents, especially her mother, who thought 'she would lose her because of her fragile health'.[10] Mother Teresa's health hardly got any better in India. She was often sick, especially in 1946. This is what Sister Marie Thérèse recalls about that year: 'We were careful of her. I don't know whether she realized it, but we were....When it came to the work and the running around, our Superiors took extra care with her.'[11] She was apparently so sick that her friends feared she would be stricken with tuberculosis. As a precaution, she was asked to stay in bed for three hours every afternoon. Seeing no improvement, she was directed to go to the hill station of Darjeeling to recuperate. On the way there the sick and tired Mother Teresa allegedly had her second 'encounter' with God.

Seen in the context of the Holy Scriptures, Mother Teresa's paranormal experiences are similar to what many prophets, apostles, disciples and saints before her have apparently gone through. Mental anguish and poor health frequently seem to have paved the way to 'revelations'.

Different people approach and interpret 'holiness' in different ways. In the case of devout believers, a person's sanctity is measured not so much by their ability to perform miracles as by their absolute faith in the strange ways in which God works through some chosen individuals. This is one of the key themes in Saint Paul's first letter to the Corinthians:

> Now concerning spiritual gifts, brothers and sisters, I do not want you to be uninformed....Now there are varieties of gifts, but the same Spirit....To each is given the manifestation of the Spirit for the common good. To one is given through the Spirit the utterance of wisdom, and to another the utterance of knowledge according to the same Spirit, to another faith by the same Spirit, to another gifts of healing by the one Spirit, to another the working of miracles, to another prophecy, to another the discernment of spirits, to another various kinds of tongues, to another the interpretation of tongues. All these are acti-

> vated by one and the same Spirit, who allots to each one individually just as the Spirit chooses.[12]

Those who are not very religious, on the other hand, are eager to find some more down-to-earth explanations about Mother Teresa's 'audiences' with God or the Early Fathers of the Church. Failure to provide some rational accounts has shrouded the nun's figure in mysticism and mystery in the eyes of many secular beholders who respect her. While Mother Teresa's religious admirers consider her skill in 'paranormal' communication as an undeniable proof of her 'saintliness', others who are not religious and who do not necessarily object to her work and legacy could well perceive it as evidence of mental disturbance.

My intention here is not to approve or disapprove of the opposing interpretations of Mother Teresa's 'paranormal' abilities. Instead, I intend to offer a middle way which would hopefully be useful to approach her figure and legacy without preconceptions. It is my belief that the more details we know about the personal lives of influential people, especially if they are invested with 'supernatural' powers, the easier it will be to answer some of the puzzling questions about them in particular and human nature in general.

Considering how much Mother Teresa was immersed in literature (secular and religious) from a young age,[13] her strong ambition to become a writer, and the obvious creative flair she displayed in the poems she wrote in Skopje,[14] and in numerous letters she sent from India to her family and friends in the Balkans from 1929 onwards,[15] it is not difficult to see how the educated, enthusiastic and imaginative young woman, who turned into a devout nun, could at times, especially when she was suffering from recurring bouts of ill health, have blurred reality with fantasy.

A string of coincidences also seems to have strengthened

Mother Teresa's conviction that God intervened to help her in fulfilling her vocation as Jesus's special 'envoy' to alleviate the suffering of the poor. In her speeches, press conferences and books penned by her, or by her admirers on her behalf, she would often mention moments of crises when things had finally turned out to be all right out of the blue. Food, money, clothes and shelter were allegedly made available to Mother Teresa and her sisters and brothers when most needed and least expected. Mother Teresa never saw such occurrences as mere coincidences.[16] Neither did her supporters and admirers whose numbers grew as a result of her 'divine' ability to seek and always secure God's help.

As the news about Mother Teresa's extraordinary ability to secure God's intervention for the sake of the poor at the eleventh hour began to spread, she came to be seen as the modern personification of a shamanic figure *par excellence*. Likewise, her unique devotion to *care* for the sick was gradually but steadily perceived and interpreted as a miraculous power to *cure* them. Everything about Catholic saints – clothes, strands of hair, possessions, books, letters, vials of blood – is venerated and cherished dearly by their brethren after their death. In Mother Teresa's case, however, her sanctity took root and flourished during her lifetime. Rich and poor, intellectuals and uneducated people, believers and unbelievers, Catholics and followers of other faiths who had been in contact with her or had only heard about her were gradually falling under her spell.

Following the 1968 BBC interview in London, Mother Teresa's charisma also began to spread across the 'secular' and 'rational' Western Europe. Many people who met her in the late 1960s and early 1970s did not know what to make of her. There were some, however, who felt spellbound in her presence, and their numbers grew throughout the 1980s and 1990s.[17] Stories about Mother Teresa's positive impact on people's lives mushroomed not only among

Catholics but also among non-Catholics and the secular-minded.[18] The Mother Teresa 'fan-club', it appears, was and remains a very broad church.

Mother Teresa's opponents, on the other hand, find stories about her 'supernatural' abilities ridiculous and bizarre. They are particularly keen to make fun of the incident involving the controversial BBC journalist Malcolm Muggeridge who in 1969 went to Calcutta to prepare a documentary about Mother Teresa. Referring to the incident in his 1971 book *Something Beautiful for God: Mother Teresa of Calcutta*, Muggeridge explains that filming inside the Home for the Dying proved problematic because the place was dimly lit. Reluctantly, the cameraman Ken Macmillan eventually shot some footage inside. Confident that he would fail to record anything, however, he also shot some footage outside the building.

But the cameraman had obviously worried in vain. Much to his and Muggeridge's surprise, when the film was processed in London, they noticed that 'the part taken inside was bathed in a particularly beautiful soft light, whereas the part taken outside was rather dim and confused'.[19] Both Muggeridge and Macmillan were delighted with the unexpected result but not for the same reason. For Macmillan there was no mystery involved. He had taken delivery of some new film made by Kodak shortly before going to Calcutta. This is Macmillan's reaction to the pleasant surprise:

> 'That's amazing. That's extraordinary.' And I was going to go on to say, you know, three cheers for Kodak. I did not get a chance to say that though, because Malcolm, sitting in the front row, spun round and said: 'It's divine light! It's Mother Teresa. You'll find that it's divine light, old boy.' And three or four days later I found I was being phoned by journalists from London newspapers who were saying

> things like: 'We hear you've just come back from India with Malcolm Muggeridge and you were the witness of a miracle.'[20]

Muggeridge did his best to spread the news about the 'miracle'. He was so eager to tell people about his divine experience that it soon turned almost into an obsession. In his own words, 'I fear I talked and wrote about it to the point of tedium, and sometimes of irritation'.[21] But who can blame Muggeridge for being carried away? After all, miracles are not daily occurrences, not even for journalists. And since not many mortals were with him in Calcutta to witness the miraculous event for themselves, Muggeridge naturally saw it as his own sacred duty to describe the paranormal encounter as vividly and accurately as possible to humanity at large:

> I myself am absolutely convinced that the technically unaccountable light is, in fact, the Kindly Light [Cardinal] Newman refers to in his well-known exquisite hymn.... Mother Teresa's Home for the Dying is overflowing with love, as one senses immediately on entering it. This love is luminous, like the haloes artists have seen and made visible round the heads of the saints. I find it not at all surprising that the luminosity should register on a photographic film....I am personally persuaded that Ken recorded the first authentic photographic miracle.[22]

Muggeridge's interpretation of the 'miracle' and his unashamedly partisan portrayal of Mother Teresa's image and work in his 1969 television documentary, the 1971 book and numerous interviews undoubtedly heightened his 'celebrity' status. His career as a journalist was also given an unexpected boost. This was hardly surprising. After all, Muggeridge had scooped the 'miracle' story of the twentieth century. It is not often that a journalist has the chance to offer his contemporaries the opportunity to see with the naked eye what countless generations have hoped for in vain. Not many mortals have been blessed to witness a miracle since Moses parted the Red Sea, Jesus walked on water, and Mohammed ascended to and returned from heaven. Muggeridge must have really felt like the chosen one.

Muggeridge's 'miracle claim' and the noise he made about it caused some embarrassment to the Catholic Church. None the less, the story stuck. Muggeridge the journalist had paved the way for the elevation of Mother Teresa to the position of a 'living saint'. Four years after the publication of his saint-making book *Something Beautiful for God*, on 29 December 1975 *Time* magazine accompanied Mother Teresa's portrait on the front cover with the caption: 'Messengers of Love and Hope – Living Saints'.

The news about the miracle called Mother Teresa was music to the ears of a largely sceptical, but willing-to-be-deceived, secular Western audience. It is always good to know that we are not a God-forsaken race, that there is still hope for redemption, that we are being looked after by a divine power, that we have the means of finding proof about the existence of our heavenly Father and communicating with him, if not on a one-to-one basis, at least through the mediation of a nun called Mother Teresa.

'We need not be theologians,' Daniel J. Boorstin remarked in 1962, 'to see that we have shifted responsibility for making the world interesting from God to the newspaperman....If there were not many intriguing or startling occurrences, it was no fault of the reporter. He could not be expected to report what did not exist.'[23] In a way, the newspaperman has been reporting 'what did not exist' since the dawn of the modern press. Reporting the real and the unreal, or what Boorstin calls 'pseudo-events', was a seminal feature of the news industry from the start. Boorstin rightly laments that 'pseudo-events' seem to have taken over, but he apparently did not foresee the extraordinary length some journalists would go to and the sources and means they would employ to 'invent' them. In the case of the 'divine' light recorded in the Home for the Dying, we apparently discovered yet another potential of the media: the ability to produce miraculous pseudo-events. If God was indeed dead, thanks to modern technologies we could reincarnate him, and if he never existed in the first place, we could literally invent him. Apparently, we have not only the mental gift to imagine miracles but also the means to materialize them.

Technology obviously does not necessarily make myths distant and irrelevant. On the contrary, it manufactures them as commodities that are increasingly in demand. As Christopher Hitchens puts it, 'modern technology and communications have ensured...that rumour and myth can be transmitted with ever greater speed and efficiency to the eyes and ears of the credulous'.[24]

The fact that Mother Teresa herself was instrumental in creating the myth about her 'paranormal' abilities, something she later came to regret,[25] does not necessarily belittle the significance of her work in Calcutta. Nor does the endorsement of her saint-like status by devout Catholics and a 'sensationalist' journalist like Muggeridge make her lifetime devotion to the poor less appealing to millions of people who do not necessarily believe in miracles allegedly recorded by Kodak. If Mother Teresa's saintly nature is a matter for debate, her commitment to her vocation and to the poor remains exemplary.

This is one of the reasons why the Indian media, both Catholic and non-Catholic, were keen to support and advertise her work from the start. And not only the Indian media. From the 1950s onwards, many leaders in India and West Bengal were eager and willing to fully endorse and sponsor Mother Teresa's charity work. Politicians such as the Chief Minister of West Bengal, Dr Bidhan Chandra Roy, and Indian Prime Ministers like Jawaharlal Nehru and his daughter Indira Gandhi would often employ the Bengali and Indian press to put and keep Mother Teresa constantly in the spotlight. Thanks to numerous Indian leaders' direct interest in her, the Indian political establishment and the Indian media acknowledged Mother Teresa as a 'living saint' before she caught the lenses of the European and American media, even before the miracle-spotter Muggeridge. In July 1962 Mother Teresa made headlines in the Indian press thanks to her good friend Dr Roy. Interviewed on his eightieth birthday, Dr Roy surprised his fellow countrymen by the tribute he paid to the Catholic nun. 'As I climbed the steps of the Writers' Building', he told a Calcutta *Statesman* reporter, 'I was thinking of Mother Teresa who devotes her life to the service of the poor.' The same paper commented that 'Dr Roy felt that Mother Teresa was doing magnificent work. She served those who were most miserable and found no place in hospitals, and among them were lepers and cholera patients'.[26] Asked by a Christian audience in the late 1960s what he thought of Mother Teresa, Dr Zakir Husain, the Muslim president of India, replied: 'In your lexicon I believe this woman is a saint.'[27] This may explain why the Indians took to their hearts a foreigner and a Catholic missionary like Mother Teresa. They acknowledged and appreciated from the first her selflessness and devotion to the poor, the orphans, the old and the infirm who had been abandoned by their families and ignored by neighbours.

Indian politicians at local and national level were interested in ensuring that the 'saintly' Mother Teresa was widely known in Calcutta and throughout India. It was equally important that the news about her spread around the world. The leaders of India had their own agenda in presenting the nun as a 'saint' and they used the media very effectively to achieve their aims. Their efforts were soon to produce dividends. The Catholic nun proved very helpful to them in the wake of independence from Britain and separation from Pakistan in 1947, and the civil war that led to the creation of Bangladesh in 1971, to keep secularism alive and promote India abroad as a tolerant and welcoming nation. Likewise, successive Indian governments, backed by the Indian media, used Mother Teresa to push forward with their progressive reforms at home to better the lives of millions of citizens traditionally abandoned and shunned by the class-conscious and caste-ridden Indian society. Their message could not have been any clearer: if a white Western woman, a Roman Catholic nun, could show so much love and affection for India's abandoned children, lepers, untouchables, and the dying old, Indians too were surely capable of finding enough love, compassion and tolerance in their hearts to show the same noble sentiments. After all, Mother Teresa was hardly saying or doing something the Indians themselves had not heard or done before. With her charity work, she was rendering her contribution, small as it was, towards keeping alive a not-much-publicized Calcuttan and Indian tradition furthered by 'home-grown' humanists like the 1913 Nobel Prize laureate for literature Rabindranath Tagore, Mahatma Gandhi (another great twentieth century media icon), and several of her contemporaries such as Pandurang Shashtri Athavale and Acharya Shri Chandananji. In the words of an Indian journalist in the late 1970s, Mother Teresa and her Sisters:

> with their serene ways, their saris, their knowledge of local languages...have come to symbolise not only the best in Christian charity, but also the best in Indian culture and civilisation, from Buddha to Gandhi, the greatest saints,

> the seers, the great lovers of humanity with boundless compassion and consideration for the underprivileged: what Shakespeare called the 'quality of mercy'.[28]

In the late 1960s and throughout the 1970s Mother Teresa became the personification of human compassion not only in India but also throughout the world. Millions of people, irrespective of their colour, creed, nationality, social status, political beliefs and financial position, apparently saw in her work the answer to some of their problems. The nun, it appears, came to be regarded as a modern sage who had found a purpose in life which had nothing to do with materialistic values. Through her much publicized simple life, her strong faith in God, her belief in the goodness of human nature, her humanitarian work and her veneration for life, many people in India and especially in the West seemed to have discovered for themselves a new purpose in life. In a materialistic world, many apparently believed they had to be grateful to Mother Teresa for showing them a different and equally satisfying way of living. Western individualism and materialism were single-handedly challenged by a tiny and unpretentious nun who became an idol for the poor as well as for the rich, for believers as well as non-believers.

Mother Teresa was aware that she would not have had such a strong impact on so many people without the constant support of her friends in high places and, equally important, if she was not backed all the way by the Indian and the world media. Her relationship with the media, however, has not been a long and uninterrupted honeymoon. One of the earliest critical newspaper articles about her appeared in the *Boston Globe* on 16 October 1983. Sylvia Whitman, the author of the uncomplimentary feature, had spent a couple of months as a volunteer in Calcutta a year earlier. In her piece, Whitman takes issue, although indirectly, with the way the vulnerable people in the care of Mother Teresa and her sisters were treated. The media criticism of Mother Teresa began in earnest, however, only in the early 1990s. On 13 April 1992, for instance, *The Nation* ran Christopher Hitchens's article 'The Ghoul of Calcutta', which has set the tone for much of the criticism against the nun ever since.[29] In addition to reporters like Hitchens, the list of Mother Teresa's opponents includes theologians like Ken Matto, and academics such as the feminist scholar Germaine Greer. These and other critics of the nun find absolutely nothing positive in her work in India and throughout the world. Like other fierce adversaries, they also adopt an essentially structuralist approach when assessing Mother Teresa's celebrity status, as well as the scope, intentions and the consequences of her work.

Contrary to the subjectivists, the structuralists investigate celebrity 'as the expression of universal structural rules imbedded in culture',[30] arguing that well-known people are manufactured and expected to serve the powers that make them famous. In the case of Mother Teresa, her structuralist opponents argue, her role as a fabricated media icon was manifold: to legitimize the exploitation of the poor, spread Christianity in non-Christian lands, preach a fake Gospel, perpetuate the humiliation of third world countries, present as normal the subjugation of women by men, and help the West to ease its guilty conscience about its colonial legacy in India and other developing countries.

Structuralist interpretations of Mother Teresa's figure are often based on conspiracy theories. The Washington-based British journalist Christopher Hitchens, for instance, believes that she was essentially a fundraiser for the Vatican. This, he argues, is the reason why she was willing to be seen more often than not in the company of a dictator like 'Baby Doc' Duvalier of Haiti, an alleged fraudster like the American businessman Charles Keating, or a shady media mogul like Robert Maxwell. Hitchens is one of the first journalists to express concern, and perhaps not without reasons, about millions of dollars donated to Mother Teresa to help the poor and which allegedly remain still unaccounted for. The only 'reliable' information Hitchens uses in his 1995 book *The Missionary Position: Mother Teresa in Theory and Practice* comes from *In Mother's House*, the unpublished manuscript of Susan Shields, a former member of the Missionaries of Charity order.[31]

Hitchens's scathing criticism of Mother Teresa as a conspiratorial religious figure can be matched only by the vitriolic attacks against her by the Indian physician Dr Aroup Chatterjee. In contrast to Hitchens, Chatterjee occasionally gives Mother Teresa some credit for her charity work in Calcutta, especially before her first encounter with Muggeridge in 1968. All the same, Chatterjee's well-researched 2003 book *Mother Teresa: The Final Verdict* also abounds in conspiracy theories. Chatterjee argues that those who initially made Mother Teresa a public face in the West were very much part of a carefully crafted conspiracy against India and especially against his native West Bengal and its capital Calcutta. He singles out mainly three chief 'conspirators': the journalist Malcolm Muggeridge, the former American Secretary of Defence, who later became President of the World Bank, Robert Strange McNamara, and the French author and script-writer Dominique Lapierre.

Chatterjee is adamant that Muggeridge, McNamara and Lapierre bore strong personal grudges against the city of Calcutta and its people. In the case of Muggeridge, argues Chatterjee, he disliked the former imperial city for its independence movement, liberal humanism, emancipated and proud middle class women, and early attachment to Marxism. On a personal level, Muggeridge allegedly despised Calcutta and its people because he could never forgive the sophisticated Bengali intellectuals for patronizing him during the several years he was posted there as a journalist. As for McNamara, Chatterjee insists, the American politician-businessman never forgave the Calcuttans for the massive demonstrations they held to protest his visit to the city as Secretary of Defence during the Vietnam War. The third conspirator, Lapierre, argues Chatterjee, found it impossible to stomach the humiliation he had experienced in Calcutta when he was shooting on location the 'image-smearing' film *City of Joy* in 1991. In the words of the film's producer Jake Eberts, the cast and the crew were faced all the time with 'riots, firebombs, government protests, lawsuits and crowds marching in the streets'.[32] Calcuttans made it clear to Lapierre and his team that they would not tolerate easily their collective humiliation in the eyes of the world.

If one is to take seriously all the 'facts' recorded by Chatterjee, it is not very difficult to see how people like Muggeridge, McNamara, and Lapierre were allegedly intent on paying the Calcuttans back for the personal insults they had received there. Interestingly enough, notes Chatterjee, all the 'conspirators' were 'evangelical type Christians', or born-again Catholics who apparently have never thought highly of India and the Indians. Moreover, Chatterjee believes that these powerful, 'malicious' *sahibs* (his preferred term for the white 'enemies' of his city), discovered in Mother Teresa the ideal 'tool' and the perfect 'simpleton' to get even with Calcutta.

Chatterjee rightly argues that Muggeridge and McNamara were instrumental in securing the much-coveted Nobel Prize for Mother Teresa in 1979. It is very doubtful she would have ever been awarded the distinguished prize if these two allies had not been able to secure the energetic support of several American senators such as Pete Domenici, Mark O. Hatfield and Hubert Humphrey. By the time these and other influential political players supported her nomination for the Nobel Prize, initially in 1978 and then again in 1979, they had already been involved in fundraising activities for

Mother Teresa. It is interesting to note that it was around this time that Mother Teresa modified her stance on the sensitive issue of abortion to coincide completely with the views of Muggeridge and of his powerful American friends.

What Chatterjee fails to acknowledge, however, is that far from being a 'simpleton saint', Mother Teresa was a very shrewd practical woman. She played the game of her 'conspirator' backers from the fields of the media, politics and film for as long as they helped her to achieve her main goal in life: Mother Teresa went to India to serve Jesus.

Indian intellectuals like Aroup Chatterjee (2003), Krishna Dutta (2003) and Dhiru Shah (2003), who are critical of Mother Teresa, obviously believe she played a major role in creating and sustaining the unsavoury image of Calcutta in the West. While I do not hold Mother Teresa on her own responsible for Calcutta's negative media coverage, I fully understand Chatterjee's and his fellow Indians' consternation. The depiction of what was once one of the most fascinating cities of India as 'hell on earth' reveals some of the weakest aspects of the Western media: its partiality, sensationalism and tendency for selective information about those 'alien' parts of the world that we often tend to humiliate at worst and patronize at best. Calcutta, Bangladesh, Albania or Columbia become newsworthy in the West mainly for reasons related to floods, famine, epidemics, drugs, human trafficking, economic crises and political unrest.

In this context, Chatterjee and other Bengali intellectuals who are critical of Mother Teresa are right to be upset about the constant negative media coverage their city has been exposed to for so long. What they also should bear in mind, however, is that Mother Teresa did not have any hidden agenda against their city as such. In her interviews, speeches and books she never singled out Calcutta as being the poorest place on earth. Nor did she ever make any disparaging remarks against its people. On the contrary, she always commended them for their religious tolerance and generosity. More importantly, whenever she spoke about the poor of Calcutta she also referred to the poor in other countries, in both the developed and the undeveloped world.

By the time the world press focused its cameras on Mother Teresa of Calcutta in the late 1960s and throughout the 1970s, in spite of its unparalleled economic and cultural heritage in India and throughout the British Empire, her adopted city had already been stigmatized in the West. The writings of Rudyard Kipling (1865-1936) and Margaret Rumer Godden (1907-1998) make only a small part of the huge archive of unsympathetic literature about Calcutta. Western reporters have been drawing for decades upon this far from flattering literature to present this part of India as the epitome of poverty and human depravity. The situation has not changed for the better even today and it seems that the tabloidization and degradation of the city of Calcutta and of its proud citizens will continue to go unchecked for quite some time.

One could argue that Calcutta's 'unsavoury' reputation in the West was the price this corner of India and its people had to pay for the headaches they caused the British Empire from the eighteenth century onwards. Moreover, the intellectuals of Calcutta apparently did not do themselves any favours in the eyes of the West with their open sympathy for Marxism throughout the twentieth century. While all East European countries have been eager to wipe out any trace of their Communist legacy following the domino-effect collapse of their Communist governments in the late 1980s and early 1990s, Calcutta is one of the few places outside the former Soviet Union where you can still find statues of Marx, Engels, Lenin and Stalin.

Some Indian intellectuals believe that the West would not have been able to demean the city of Calcutta, to the extent that it obviously has, unless Western propaganda had found 'collaborators' from within India. The Atlanta-based Indian writer Dhiru Shah, for instance, blames the 'westernized'/'Anglo-Americanized' Indians, some of India's 'selfserving', 'greedy' and 'dishonest' politicians, some sections of the Indian press and 'the indifferent majority' for presenting Mother Teresa as the only person in India who '[was] engaged in caring for the poor and helpless folks'.[33] Aroup Chatterjee holds that his native Bengal and Calcutta have been stigmatized by the Indian political establishment because they envy the Bengalis for their pride, cultural heritage and achievements.[34] Chatterjee and other Indian scholar who hold this view are keen to mention the remark made by the Indian nationalist leader Gopal Krishna Gokhale: 'What Bengal thinks today, India will think tomorrow.'

Some of the conspiracy theories which attribute blame to Western countries, Western media, the Catholic Church, Indian politicians and the Indian media are certainly far-fetched. It is absurd to think that Mother Teresa could generate so much support because of a global conspiracy against India, the Bengalis or the city of Calcutta. The nun was not supported by the capitalist West to spite the Marxists of Calcutta. Mother Teresa was known to have been on good terms with many of the city's Communist officials. Nor was she deemed an ideal candidate for the Nobel Prize, as Chatterjee argues, because she was originally from Albania, which in the 1960s had officially adopted atheism. The fact of the matter is that, contrary to the version of events presented by the Enver Hoxha regime, throughout the Cold War, Albania on its own was never considered such an important member of the Communist block that it warranted the West's special attention.[35]

Considering the constant attention the Indian and world media paid to Mother Teresa's charity work in Calcutta after she was awarded the much publicized Nobel Prize in 1979, it was inevitable that the city's somewhat illusory image would suffer. This, however, does not justify the predominantly negative picture of Mother Teresa that Chatterjee and other Indian and Western critics depict relentlessly in their writings. While the 'divinity' of Mother Teresa is to some extent the outcome of Mother Teresa's own words about herself as well as the end-result of the efforts of many people, countries, institutions (political, religious, business, media) that apparently took a lasting and calculated interest in her persona and work, it would be unfair to brush aside as insignificant, and even worse as devious, the almost seven decades of her life she spent trying to help the poorest of the poor in person, through her Sisters, Brothers and Co-Workers, or by bringing them to the attention of those who have the power and the resources to do something to alleviate their hardships.

Mother Teresa's devout opponents are inclined to discredit not only her but also anyone who supported her. This is the reason why they dig deep into the private lives of anyone who helped the nun to become an international celebrity. The numerous derogatory comments that Hitchens and Chatterjee make in their books against Malcolm Muggeridge, Robert S. McNamara, Dominique Lapierre or Ronald Reagan are at times rather too personal and vindictive, and, as is often the case in Hitchens's writings, in bad taste, insulting and even banal. While both critics have raised some serious issues about the motives and nature of Mother Teresa's work in and outside India, their uncompromisingly hostile attitude towards her and those who supported her has undermined considerably the value of their criticism. Likewise, some Indian opponents of the 'Saint of the Gutters', as the Indian press often refers to Mother Teresa, have ended up producing, either on purpose or unwittingly, what one could consider 'muck-raking' criticism.

The personal attacks mounted on Mother Teresa's supporters are partly related to their allegedly chequered past as well as their not-so-holy intentions in financing, endorsing and promoting the work of this particular Christian missionary. One could interpret such attacks as an indication of the pent-up frustration and failure of Mother Teresa's committed opponents to uncover something embarrassing and humiliating about the nun herself. The unprecedented media attention Mother Teresa generated for almost fifty years in India and throughout the world was bound to expose many personal details about her. Being a celebrity, it was inevitable that her life would become 'public property', that people would want to know as much as possible about the woman behind the nun.

The vast literature on this religious celebrity, however, would disappoint anyone hoping to find there revealing details about the private Mother Teresa. Accounts of her personal life remain rather sketchy even in the best authorized and unauthorized biographies. Both her subjectivist admirers and her structuralist opponents have failed to produce a complete biography of Agnes Gonxhe Bojaxhiu, Mother Teresa's original name. As for those who approach her figure from a post-structuralist position, they too have been unable so far to 'uncover' the woman behind the missionary. While Mother Teresa was undoubtedly a 'media star', analysing her life along the straightforward post-structuralist lines employed when commenting on the lives of stars from the fields of the media, sport, music and cinema remains problematic.

The star discourse emerged for the first time in the United States in the early 1910s when interest in actors went beyond their screen roles. John Belton holds that: '[a]ctors develop a persona or portrait of themselves out of the personalities of the various characters they have played over the course of their careers and out of elements of their personal lives that have become public knowledge.'[36]

With the press becoming ever more inquisitive and intrusive, many famous actors found it impossible to keep details of their personal lives out of the public gaze. Media played a crucial role in the transformation of actors into stars. As Christine Gledhill notes, '[a]ctors become stars when their off-screen life-styles and personalities equal or surpass acting ability in importance'.[37] As a result of the information about the actors' personal lives made public by the media, the attention of many film fans shifted from the screen characters to the real people who portrayed them. This important shift was possible because of the emergence of, what Richard deCardova calls, the 'star scandal' discourse.[38]

The unprecedented interest the public started showing in the stars' intimate lives transformed not only the relationship between actors and their admirers, but also redefined the notion of fame for screen actors. The 'star scandal' thus became an irreplaceable stepping stone to fame (or infamy) and celebrity status not only in twentieth century America and other developed countries but also across the developing world.

The 'star scandal' has hardly played any significant role in the celebrity status of Mother Teresa. This does not mean that she was and remains immune from controversial stories. On the contrary, thanks to the relentless efforts of opponents like Hitchens and Chatterjee to reveal the 'real' Mother Teresa, the controversial has always been an important part in the often heated debates about her. Claims that Mother Teresa accepted preferential treatment in India and overseas, that she travelled in luxury, that she was treated in expensive clinics and mishandled millions of dollars are a familiar theme in the ever-growing critical literature about her. In spite of such sustained iconoclastic attacks on her figure, during her lifetime and after her death her image has hardly been dented seriously. So far her avowed opponents appear to have been unable to produce the 'killer' evidence that would irreparably damage Mother Teresa's reputation.

The main reason why Mother Teresa has apparently remained

immune for so long from the 'star scandal' is because, unlike most stars, she does not seem to have suffered from the tensions resulting from the dichotomy between the *public face* a celebrity has to promote all the time, and the *private self*, or what Chris Rojek calls, the 'veridical self',[39] which the star tries to protect fanatically but often without success. In Mother Teresa's case, the private and the public appear to have been one and the same thing. Although, like any other international 'star', she was constantly under media 'surveillance', throughout her long public life Mother Teresa never had to lash out at any photographer as the actor Johnny Depp did in London in 1999: 'I don't want to be what you want me to be tonight'.

It appears that Mother Teresa was unique among twentieth-century celebrities in that she could be in public what she was in private. This was quite an achievement for Mother Teresa and for those who supported and promoted her in a world that teems with paparazzi who are always scandal-hunting and thus undermining the careers of all sorts of famous people, including religious celebrities.[40]

As a seasoned public figure Mother Teresa apparently succeeded where many media stars usually fail. Not only did she seem able to establish very good contacts with journalists, but she also appeared to have cast a spell on them. For her devoted supporters, the reporters' veneration for Mother Teresa was, and remains, yet another proof of her 'saintliness'. Bob Geldof, however, found 'nothing other-worldly or divine about her'[41] when he met her in 1985. If Geldof found anything extraordinary about his 'saintly' fellow charity worker, it was her skilful handling of the media. She struck him as 'outrageously brilliant'[42] in the way she handled reporters: 'She made them laugh and she defined the terms of the questions they could ask her.' 'The way she spoke to the journalists,' concluded Geldof, 'showed her to be as deft a manipulator of the media as any high-powered American PR expert.'[43]

To a large extent, Mother Teresa's good relation with the media and her ability as a 'deft manipulator' were made possible and tolerated mainly because of the high moral ground she occupied as a result of her charity work and simple preaching for almost seventy years in India and throughout the world. No political, religious and business support would have kept her in the public eye for five successive decades, unless the propaganda machine and the news industry had paid exclusive attention to her humanitarian work. The nun's status as an exemplary media icon is likely to remain secured for as long as the media focus exclusively on her selflessness and devotion to 'human debris'. It is mainly thanks to the media that the celebrity Mother Teresa has entered the consciousness of our age as the epitome of compassion for humanity. Whether she deserves this status or not is something that would continue to divide her admirers and supporters in the years to come. What is certain, however, is that in our sceptical age nobody's sanctity can be taken for granted for too long, not even the sanctity of a media revered icon like Mother Teresa.

– 12 –

A review of Hiromi J. Kudo's book *Mother Teresa: A Saint from Skopje*

Dr Hiromi Josepha Kudo's monograph on Mother Teresa[1] is the latest work on the Albanian-born Roman Catholic nun who continues to attract the attention of scholars (religious as well as secular) from around the world now as much as when she was alive. *Mother Teresa: A Saint from Skopje* is the first book in English by a Japanese scholar on the famous missionary.

The work is structured in four chapters. In the first chapter 'Early Life in Skopje', the focus is on some formative moments in the life of Agnes Gonxhe Bojaxhiu (Mother Teresa's original name) during the 1910-1928 period. The author rightly emphasizes from the start the significance of studying Mother Teresa's childhood and youth to understand better the worldwide famous personality she became from the end of 1970s onwards.

In the second chapter 'Religious Life in India and Mother's Second Vocation', the focus of attention moves to some key moments in Sister Teresa's life as a cloistered nun and as head of the Missionaries of Charity congregation she set up in 1950. Of particular interest in this part of the book is the author's attempt to highlight what Mother Teresa had in common with social workers in general as well as what set this charitable nun apart. The author, however, could have paid more attention in this chapter, especially on pp. 83-90, to Mother Teresa's growing professionalism as a 'social worker', her determination not to be perceived as such as well as her original take on inculturation in post-independence India.

The third chapter 'Principal Activities', provides information on the strict daily routine and work of Mother Teresa and members of her congregation in the Mother House (headquarters of the Missionaries of Charity) and some of the charitable institutions run by Mother Teresa's sisters and brothers in and around Calcutta such as Shishu Bhavan (children's home), Prem Dan (institution for the mentally handicapped), the leprosy rehabilitation centres Shanti Nagar (place of peace) and Gandhiji Prem Nivas (Gandhi Centre of Love), and Shanti Dan (gift of peace), the centre for female drug addicts, mentally disabled women and 'jail girls'. The author is able to record such minute details thanks to her knowledge as an 'insider'. Dr Kudo first met Mother Teresa in 1988 and since then she has been doing voluntary work for and carrying out research on the Missionaries of Charity regularly. Having seen for myself some of these institutions during my visit to Calcutta in 2005, I believe the author is right to highlight the positive impact the sisters and brothers of Mother Teresa's order are having on the elderly, abandoned orphans, mentally handicapped patients and lepers in their care.

In the 'Concluding Chapter' the author identifies some of the reasons for Mother Teresa's popularity in India. In this section an interesting connection is made between Mother Teresa's appeal in India and the Indians', especially the Hindus', veneration for deities, mainly goddesses, and the mother figure.

Of the eight appendices included in the book, I found of particular interest Mother Teresa's letter to the Archbishop of Calcutta, Ferdinand Périer. In this letter, dated 13 January 1947, Mother Teresa explains very vividly why she wants to leave the Loreto order, and refers briefly and diplomatically to the ridiculing she had to put up with following her announcement that she wanted to start her own congregation. I understand this is the first time this important document appears in print.

This study, which is a mixture of biography, hagiography, diary and doctorial thesis, could have benefited from copyediting. The information in some footnotes and in the text itself is at times repetitive and even out of place. The author relies almost entirely on her own observations to draw conclusions on Mother Teresa's personality and work. She has obviously studied carefully several works written by some of Mother Teresa's fellow missionaries in India (such as Edward Le Joly) and Indian admirers (like Navin Chawla), but makes no mention of renowned Western biographers of Mother Teresa such as Kathryn Spink, Eileen Egan and Anne Sebba. Like most uncritical scholars of Mother Teresa, Kudo avoids referring to some of the nun's critics like Aroup Chatterjee and Germaine Greer and mentions only in passing Christopher Hitchens. The author also steers clear of controversial topics such as Mother Teresa's opposition to abortion.

The study sheds new light on some of the early influences in Mother Teresa's life, and especially on the people who helped her both in Skopje (to realise that she had a religious vocation) and Calcutta (to establish her congregation). The book identifies correctly the inestimable role Drane (Mother Teresa's mother), several Jesuits in Skopje and Calcutta (especially Father Celeste Van Exem, Father Julien Henry and Archbishop Périer), the spirituality of the Carmelite nuns, numerous Indian officials and Indian citizens (Christians, Hindus and followers of other faiths) played in the life and work of this twentieth century religious and media icon.

Like many other scholars who study celebrities, however, the author seems to ignore the fact that history makers like Mother

Teresa are essentially self-made individuals. There could have been no Mother Teresa if Mother Teresa herself had not been so focused, determined and such a visionary missionary.

Dr Kudo is one of the few Mother Teresa scholars to have visited Mother Teresa's birthplace. However, in Skopje she appears to have been almost exclusively in the company of Macedonian Slav scholars and religious people who have yet to admit that Mother Teresa was Albanian. Had Dr Kudo paid more attention to what Mother Teresa herself and her brother Lazar said and wrote repeatedly about their Albanian roots and their father's devotion to the Albanian national cause, she would not have drawn the wrong conclusion that the nun's father Nikollë was not Albanian.

In spite of the above-mentioned drawbacks, the book is a sincere attempt to study and understand Mother Teresa's charismatic personality, spirituality and, what Malcolm Muggeridge calls in his 1971 book *Something Beautiful for God*, 'love in action'. As Cyril Veliath, Professor of Indian Studies at Sophia University in Tokyo, Japan, emphasises in his foreword, Dr Kudo's study reflects her devotion to Mother Teresa and the people she loved. Dr Kudo may not have always provided the right answers but she frequently asks the right questions.

– 13 –

A note on Gëzim Alpion's book *Mother Teresa: Saint or Celebrity?*

By Gaston Roberge

Like Mother Teresa, Dr Gëzim Alpion is a teacher. As a teacher/writer he may have given a hint to readers, and more so to reviewers of his book[1] when he wrote:

> To research Mother Teresa I had to employ tools I had not used before as a researcher, and more importantly to trespass into fields of knowledge that I have no formal education in. The writer, literary critic and journalist in me had to quarrel and make peace with the sociologist, theologian, historian, anthropologist, psychologist, cultural studies expert and the political and media analyst whenever they tried to establish their supremacy over each other. My challenge was to let them be and keep them on the team (p. 231).

So, readers and reviewers, you know the challenge in front of you. But not to worry. Alpion provides a gentle pedagogy for dealing with human beings.

Indeed, a human person cannot be reduced to any of the categories Alpion mentions in the quotation above. And, therefore, one cannot hope to encompass the mystery of a person in a book – especially a book – on that person. We commune with people; we do not fully understand them. Should that sound strange to the reader, I would ask, 'Are you sure you understand yourself? And yet don't you know everything about yourself?' In the last few centuries, we have put such a premium on reason, on understanding, that we have let reality – especially personal reality – slip out of our enquiries. To explain a person is to explain that person away.

That is why Professor David Marsh so rightly wrote in his preface to the book:

> I urge you to read this book; you will find it interesting and rewarding. It will give you a new and more balanced insight into the identity and impact of one of the most prominent figures of the twentieth century (p. xiii).

Any writer who can give or foster such insight is a peacemaker who facilitates encounters with civilizations.

After *Mother Teresa: Saint or Celebrity?* scholarship about Mother Teresa will not be the same. Alpion covers and assesses the entire literature about Mother Teresa. Where he finds it lacking, he humbly formulates the questions yet to be raised and answered. He deals with his subject and with his sources with utmost respect.

He approaches Mother Teresa – 'saint' and 'celebrity' – from every possible angle, with astounding erudition – even in those fields where he has had no formal training. He is open to whatever is perceived as spiritual by Mother Teresa, but he remains a secular humanist.

In his unparalleled scholarly book, Alpion has presented a

multidimensional portrait of Mother Teresa. And she appears human as she rarely did in any discourse about her.

Gëzim Alpion is an Albanian who, in every part – not to write page – of his book loves, supports and defends his fellow Albanians, their culture, their history and their rights. I leave the question open as to whether that makes him a nationalist and a patriot, because of the political overtone these two words have acquired.

– 14 –

Mother Teresa, abortion and the media

By Gaston Roberge

Introduction: In praise of Mother Teresa

In this article, I explore three interrelated issues: Mother Teresa's thought about abortion, the way she talked about it, and the way the media reported her sayings about it. Abortion is a thorny subject. A taboo for most devotees of Mother Teresa. For, that subject readily invites criticism. And many admirers of Mother Teresa – of whatever religion – feel that she should not be criticized. Hindus, in particular, and generally many among the people who venerate Mother Teresa, believe that a saint, being established in God, can commit neither sin nor error. Many a Christian would consider it a lack of respect toward a saintly person like Mother Teresa to even entertain the possibility that she may have made mistakes.

Yet, Christians believe that God creates a saint in a person's frail humanity, without eliminating that humanity. When the Church declares that a person is a 'Blessed' or a 'Saint', she does not proclaim that the person had no defects or was sinless. The Church affirms that the person allowed God to be present in him or her and to do

His work in and through him or her. Mother Teresa once confessed that, when she went through the 'dark night of the soul', at times she wondered if she really believed in what she said. But she added that she could see that when she spoke of God or of joy, 'people were moved and responded to her words'.[1] God was in her and worked through her.

In examining, as I do here, whether Mother Teresa may have been wrong at times in the way she spoke about abortion, in giving the impression that she did not take into account those involved, I in no way question her sanctity. But in accepting that she may have been wrong, I acknowledge the limits of her humanity. And at the same time I acknowledge the power of God at work in her. In fact, I proclaim that I believe she is a saint. With regard to abortion, in particular, she heroically played the role of a prophet clamoring the truth to 'people who have ears but do not hear'.[2] At the same time, she lovingly came to the defense of the unborn child whose dignity she upheld.

I, for one, feel I owe it to Mother Teresa to examine her life critically in order to praise her for what she really was. In doing so, I glorify God Who, with her accord, made her what she was.

Part One: Mother Teresa's thought about abortion

Mother Teresa made it very clear in her statements and actions that she loved all people without distinction: the poor and the rich, the sinners and the virtuous, even if she had a preferential love for the poor and, among the poor, for the poorest. However, one notices a sharp difference between her talks about poverty and her talks about abortion. When she spoke about the poor, she never castigated the causes – still less, the persons – responsible for their poverty.

In other words, she never took a moral stand, except for affirming in words and examples that it is a duty to succor the poor.

But when she talked about the unborn child, she took a firm moral stand. She castigated those who commit abortion. She singled out the mother as the main culprit, calling her a killer and a murderer. For instance, she said in her Nobel Prize lecture: 'I feel the greatest destroyer of peace today is abortion, because it is a direct war, a direct killing, a direct *murder* by the mother herself.' (emphasis added)[3]

Here, the word 'murder', especially as an act performed with malice, is perhaps an unwarranted generalization. But one must bear in mind that Mother Teresa had a limited command of English. Yet, for Mother Teresa, to say that a hapless mother directly kills her child is to speak a language quite different from the one she uses when she speaks about the poor.

The difference in approaches is problematic. It is too easy to say that abortion and destitution are two different matters; that abortion is an action, and poverty is a condition. Talks on abortion focus on agents, talks on poverty focus on victims. As we shall see, things are not that simple: abortion has its victims, poverty has its causes. There is a lot of confusion in the field.

The first area of confusion has to do with the idea – and the fact – of poverty. All forms of poverty are often lumped together in one group. Poverty, understood as freedom from inordinate attachment to the goods of this world, or as a feeling of satisfaction with even the basic necessities of life, may be a virtue. But demeaning poverty or destitution, often described as living 'below the poverty line', is inhuman, and certainly a destroyer of peace. One hears it said, 'Poverty must be eradicated'. But what has to be eradicated is destitution, not poverty. To eradicate destitution would require a collective effort to transform the way we live. Not so easy. On the other hand, 'consumerism' destroys the virtue of poverty, a virtue that is essential for justice and peace in the world. As a virtue, poverty is freedom from greed, and wisdom in the management of the world's resources. That too is not so easy.

Mother Teresa herself may have added to the confusion between the two subjects of destitution and abortion. For, it was she who linked them up in her acceptance speech, when she was awarded the Nobel Prize for Peace. She was given the prize for her work among the poor. Her work was seen as fostering respect for the human person, and thus fostering peace. But then, she declared that the greatest destroyer of peace was abortion. That may be true, but the statement comes as a surprise to those who legitimize abortion, and those who do not see any link between working for the poor and fighting abortion.

Mother Teresa was not a theoretician, but a servant of the poor. And, for her, the link between abortion and poverty was obvious. It was born out of her practice. She fought abortion not only by adoption, as she put it, but by spreading among the poor a natural approach to family planning, an approach that called for mutual respect and love. The latter is essential to foster justice and peace.

Personally or through her sisters and volunteers, Mother Teresa dealt vigorously with family planning. In her Nobel lecture, she declared:

> We are teaching our beggars, our leprosy patients, our slum dwellers, our people of the street, natural family planning. And in Calcutta alone in six years – it is all in Calcutta – we have had 61,273[4] babies less from the families who would have had them, because they practice this natural way of abstaining, of self-control, out of love for each other. We teach them the temperature method which is very beautiful, very simple. And our poor peo-

> ple understand. And you know what they have told me? 'Our family is healthy, our family is united, and we can have a baby whenever we want.'[5]

Mother Teresa must have had to face cases when the poor failed to use the so-called natural method properly, and when the hapless parents were led to contemplate abortion. Some such parents who rejected the option of abortion and lovingly accepted the coming child as a gift of God must have edified her. As for those who finally committed abortion, she may have seen them as killers. But however heinous was their action, Mother Teresa would not reject them.

Abortion, in itself, is an evil act, committed in each instance by a person or a group of persons. But destitution is a condition. A human agent does not always cause it. Although, it is clear that all those who benefit from the wealth of the earth and wantonly 'consume' it are, to an extent, responsible for the destitution of the poor. It is also clear that the destitute people often are the victims of willful exploitation. But that exploitation is often institutionalized, thus masking individual responsibility.

When poverty is ill defined, when the focus is on the agent with regard to abortion, when the causes of destitution are not considered, then anyone active in society, including Mother Teresa, may be excused if one appears to be or simply is confused. In particular, the fact that Mother Teresa spoke in different ways, or to be more precise, the fact that she seemed to have an exclusively moral approach with regard to abortion and an exclusively compassionate approach with regard to destitution, can be understood, if not fully accepted.[6]

Another aspect of Mother Teresa's thought on abortion is problematic. That is, her calling the mother who commits abortion a 'killer'. It may be true in some cases that a mother kills her own unborn child, but in India – in particular – it often happens that other family members are involved, and the pregnant mother is helpless. Moreover, there is no allusion in Mother Teresa's Nobel lecture about why a mother kills, as she says, her unborn child. For, the question arises. For instance, in some milieus of India, there is a strong preference for having a baby boy for the sake of maintaining the patriarchal line, and in the hope that the boy will take care of his parents when they grow old. There is also the idea, vigorously spread throughout India, that a family cannot afford more than two children. And hence, in such an environment, is it fair to call the mother 'a killer, a murderer' of the child?

Entire social groups have internalized these two imperatives. Yet, when Mother Teresa speaks of abortion, she seems to assume that parents who perform an abortion just do it thoughtlessly, and without there being some reasons for them to commit these crimes. And the mother is singled out as the killer.

Mother Teresa's stand on abortion was at first moral, and independent of the involved persons' situation and needs. But, as we shall see later in this article, there has been an evolution on her part in this respect. The moral stand remained firm, but her concern for the persons involved became more and more apparent. On the other hand, when she spoke of or dealt with the poor there was no moral judgment, only compassion and service, giving an impression that she was unaware that destitution, alas, has causes.

In her Nobel lecture, she continued:

> Our children, we want them, we love them. But what of the other millions? Many people are very, very concerned with the children of India, with the children of Africa where quite a number die, maybe of malnutrition, of hunger and so on, but *millions are dying deliberately*

> *by the will of the mother*. And this is what is the greatest destroyer of peace today. Because *if a mother can kill her own child, what is left for me to kill you and you to kill me? There is nothing between*. (emphasis added)[7]

Can feticide be equated with every possible case of killing? Surely not. That is not to say that killing can be justified, but that some 'killers' experience situations that call for compassion as much as moral judgment. Given her remarkable compassion for the poor, her detached, moral approach to abortion is problematic.

There is yet another difference in Mother Teresa's work for the poor and for the unborn child. Her concern for the poor brings her to the lowest rank of society; her concern for abortion brings her to the highest rank of society. Though, at times, because of her fame, her work for the poor caused her to relate with people like Princess Diana, Charles Keating and Jean-Claude Duvalier. But then she does not fight with them. On the other hand, when she addressed the United States President Bill Clinton on the issue of abortion on 3 February 1994, she confronted him. No less.

Here is her message for America and President Clinton:

> If we remember that God loves us, and that we can love others as He loves us, then America can become a sign of peace for the world. From here, *a sign of care for the weakest of the weak – the unborn child* – must go out to the world. If you become a burning light of justice and peace in the world, then really you will be true to what the founders of this country stood for. (emphasis added)[8]

This difference in her approach is well exemplified graphically by an image of her holding a child when, in 1982, she persuaded Israelis and Palestinians to stop shooting long enough for her to rescue

37 retarded children from a hospital in besieged Beirut. Then she did not condemn war, she saved children.[9] On the other hand, her anti-abortion work consisted mainly of speeches, although, as she herself put it in her Nobel lecture, she fought abortion by adoption.

Mother Teresa was not a social worker, caring for particular groups of poor people. She did everything in the name of Jesus. Like Jesus, Mother Teresa did not discriminate among rich and poor. She was sensitive as much to the spiritual poverty of some of the rich as she was to material poverty surrounding her. She wanted the rich to experience the freedom of spiritual poverty by helping the poor.

Some time in 1993, on the occasion of the 25th anniversary of the Papal Encyclical Letter *Humanae Vitae*, Mother Teresa was invited to address the participants of a pro-life congress in Oklahoma, US. Since she could not go to Oklahoma, she sent a recorded message. The message was of some five minutes only. Before starting the recording, she made the sign of the cross and prayed for a few seconds. The speech was entirely written and Mother Teresa read it. At one point, she said: 'And today the greatest destroyer of peace is abortion.'[10]

On the other hand, when she cared for the victims of poverty, although she did not indict anyone, she showed through her action and words that poverty also is a destroyer of peace.

When, on 3 February 1994, Mother Teresa delivered an address at the National Prayer Breakfast, she repeated almost word for word extensive parts of her Nobel lecture of 1979 – fifteen years earlier! Has there not been any change? Yes. The change consists in a more explicit concern for the persons involved in abortions. For instance, in her message to America just quoted, she called the unborn child 'the weakest of the weak'.

Shortly after that address Mother Teresa presented a brief *amicus curia*[11] urging the Supreme Court to hear favorably the petition of a man who had been accused of attempting to prevent his *fiancée* from having an abortion. Here she talks in terms of the persons involved in abortions. Her petition contains these passages – presumably prompted by her advisers, but nonetheless signed by her as representing her own views:

> America needs no words from me to see how your decision in Roe v. Wade has deformed a great nation…Human rights are not a privilege conferred by government…The Constitutional Court of the Federal Republic of Germany recently ruled: '*The unborn child is entitled to its right to life independently of its acceptance by its mother*; this is an elementary and inalienable right which emanates from the dignity of the human being.' Americans may feel justly proud that Germany in 1993 was able to recognize the sanctity of human life. *You must weep that your own government, at present, seems blind to this truth.* (emphasis added)[12]

Through her repeated and strong condemnations of abortion, and – seen in the light of abortion – of contraception, Mother Teresa lent herself to recuperation by the pro-life movement, but she did not 'belong' to any such groups.

Part Two: How Mother Teresa talked about abortion

For Mother Teresa, any abortion was a rejection of the gift of life. And since, in her view, abortion was the termination of the life of an unborn human being, it was unquestionably tantamount to killing.

a. *A prophetic approach*

Speaking of abortion, Mother Teresa was hard hitting, even harsh. She showed concern for the unborn child, but in her words, though not in her action, she did not express the same concern for the parents of the child. One might argue that Mother Teresa was speaking as and like a prophet. In fact, in her Nobel lecture she makes an important reference to prophet Isaiah. Perhaps Mother Teresa felt herself called to speak like a prophet. Most religions have prophets. And, as far as the Hebrew prophets are concerned, they were direct, often harsh, addressing thorny issues, but always loving. Most of them met with stiff opposition; some paid with their lives. Just hear Jesus speaking to the Pharisees:

> Then Pharisees and scribes from Jerusalem came to Jesus and said, 'Why do your disciples break away from the tradition of the elders? They eat without washing their hands.' He answered, 'And why do you break away from the commandment of God for the sake of your tradition?....Hypocrites! How rightly Isaiah prophesied about you when he said: "This people honors me only with lip services…the lessons they teach are nothing but human commandments."'[13]

Even if we grant that Mother Teresa played a prophetic role, how do we reconcile the fact that regarding poverty, she never blamed anybody for the situation of the poor? In other words, she did not take a moral stand. That made her a-political. But with regard to abortion, she took the strongest moral stand. And that brought her close to the realm of politics.

However, it should be emphasized here that prophets are primarily concerned with the moral aspect of an act or a situation.

And they must be absolutely clear about it. For them to bring in considerations of pity, concern and sympathy for the guilty might blur the precision of their statements. When Jesus told the Pharisees that with regard to the observance of their man-made laws they were 'hypocrites', he did not mitigate his statement by going into the plausible causes of their stand regarding the Jewish law. Similarly, Mother Teresa unambiguously condemned abortion in all circumstances, but, on the other hand, she would not refuse to care for a mother who terminated her pregnancy. In words, she condemned; in action, she comforted.

She was so concerned about the spreading evil of abortion that she felt compelled to mention it during the ceremony when she was awarded the Nobel Prize. And this brings us to another problematic issue, namely the confusion regarding the two allocutions Mother Teresa delivered on the occasion of her receiving the Nobel Prize.

b. The Nobel Prize for Peace: acceptance speech and Nobel lecture

Mother Teresa received her Prize during a very solemn ceremony on 10 December 1979. On that occasion, there was the traditional introduction speech by a representative of the Nobel Foundation, explaining why she was given the Prize. Then Mother Teresa gave a short acceptance speech. The next day, that is, on 11 December, she gave the so-called Nobel lecture.

It is important to distinguish the two addresses, because they have different functions and are delivered on different occasions. The acceptance speech is part of a ceremony, and is called for by the awarding of the Prize. The Nobel lecture is an occasion given to the laureate to express views of his or her choice.

Several websites[14] give the full text of the Nobel lecture but some of them introduce it as the 'acceptance' speech. On the other hand, it was reported by the press that in her acceptance speech Mother Teresa: i.) accepted the Nobel Prize on behalf of the poor; and ii.) condemned abortions. However, most websites reproduce only a short excerpt of her acceptance speech, quoting her words about accepting the Prize on behalf of the poor and leaving out her condemnation of abortion.

By speaking against abortion in her acceptance speech, Mother Teresa gave the impression that, since she herself construed her anti-abortion work as a work for peace, the Nobel Prize was given her for her work among the poor as well as for her anti-abortion work. I believe that is not at all the case, though. If the Nobel Foundation had wanted to reward a 'pro-life' stalwart, would they not have said so?

In his presentation speech at the award ceremony on 10 December 1979, Professor John Sanness, who chaired the committee that selected Mother Teresa as the recipient of that year's Prize for Peace, did not say a word about her stand on abortion. Rather, he said:

> She sees Christ in every human being, and this in her eyes makes man sacred. The hallmark of her work has been respect for the individual and the individual's worth and dignity. The loneliest and the most wretched, the dying destitute, the abandoned lepers, have been received by her and her Sisters with warm compassion devoid of condescension, based on this reverence for Christ in Man....With her message she is able to reach through to something innate in every human mind – if for no other purpose than to create a potential, a seed for good.[15]

Steering away from 'controversial' issues (like that of abortion) that often mask real issues, Professor Sanness went straight to the heart of the matter; namely that Mother Teresa saw Jesus in the poor, indeed in every one.

It is widely believed that Mother Teresa herself wrote the 4,500-word Nobel lecture, which was made available in advance to the Nobel Foundation and the Press. But, regarding her 'acceptance' speech, Mother Teresa once told me that up to a few minutes before the award ceremony, she was not clear as to what she would say. She added that she was praying intensely.[16]

It can be inferred that she did not write her acceptance speech. She is known to have often spoken without a text. It may be concluded that the aforementioned excerpt from her acceptance speech comes solely from press reports. As pointed out above, according to these reports, in her acceptance speech Mother Teresa: i.) accepted the Prize on behalf of the poor; and ii.) condemned abortion.

Unfortunately, the entire acceptance speech does not seem to have been recorded. However, in the absence of authoritative testimonies, it may be suggested as an hypothesis that, after praying over the issue, Mother Teresa felt that she should accept the Prize on behalf of the poor, since the Prize was given her because her work for the poor contributes to establish the basis for peace, namely, a recognition of the human person's dignity. But at the same time she felt she should mention that, for her, abortion was an obstacle to peace greater than poverty, because in performing an abortion one directly denies the unborn child – the weakest of the weak – his/her right to dignity. Besides, the rich countries practicing abortion show their spiritual poverty, a form of poverty that is the most difficult to redress.

Even if one accepts this hypothesis as plausible, the fact remains that since Mother Teresa had apparently intended to use the entire Nobel lecture as an opportunity to proclaim what amounts to an anti-abortion manifesto, it may be argued that it was unnecessary, perhaps even improper, for her to bring in the subject in her 'acceptance' speech.

When one considers the evil of abortion, the offence to Jesus seen in the killing of the unborn child, the havoc abortion is bringing in certain milieus, especially with regard to gender bias and to gender ratio,[17] would not a consideration of proprieties here be somewhat factitious, and similar to the objections raised by the Pharisees, and for which Jesus called them 'hypocrites'? They gave more importance to their man-made laws than to God's command.

Mother Teresa attended at least two other functions, in addition to the award ceremony (10 December) and the Nobel lecture (11 December). The sequence of functions is as follows:

> 8th December – Mother Teresa arrives in Oslo. Reception on her honor by the Indian Ambassador to Norway.
>
> 9th December – morning service at St Olaf's Cathedral, afternoon Mass in the chapel of St Joseph's Institute, evening ecumenical service at the Lutheran Domkirche, and a torchlight procession through the streets of Oslo.
>
> 10th December – Nobel Prize award ceremony. Acceptance speech.
>
> 11th December – Nobel lecture in Oslo.

Part Three: How the media reported Mother Teresa's statements about abortion

The rather unexpected condemnation of abortion by Mother Teresa during her acceptance speech may explain partly why, in Kolkata, *The Statesman* emphasized this particular fact in the caption of its report on the ceremony. It may also partly explain why some websites do not quote her anti-abortion words when they give an excerpt from her acceptance speech. So, by bringing the issue of abortion in her acceptance speech, Mother Teresa may well have created the confusion between her two allocutions.

But there is more. The book in which the Nobel lectures are reproduced, contains a footnote by the editor stating:

> [a]pparently Mother Teresa had planned to begin her Nobel lecture on the following day (11 December) with a prayer ['Make me a channel of your peace,' attributed to St Francis of Assisi], as is indicated in her prepared text, which is what was submitted for publication in *Les Prix Nobel*....In the newspaper reports of the ceremonies, however, it is clear that she included the prayer in her acceptance speech on 10 December and did not refer to it in her lecture the next day.[18]

Similarly, her reference to abortion in her acceptance speech, though not exactly in the same words, 'apparently' was prompted by the lecture she gave the next day.

a. The Nobel Prize for Peace

Here is how *The Statesman* (Kolkata) of 11 December 1979, reports on the award ceremony of the previous day, and thus on her acceptance speech:

Abortions criticized by Mother Teresa

OSLO. Dec. 10. Mother Teresa today received the 1979 Nobel Peace Prize and in her speech of acceptance condemned abortion as the greatest destroyer of man in the world today, reports Reuter.

Mother Teresa, awarded the prize for her work among the world's destitutes, said: 'To me the nations who have legalized abortion are the poorest nations. They are afraid of the unborn child and the child must die.'

In her speech, made before King Olav and invited guests in the Nobel ceremony Mother Teresa called upon the king and the audience to pray for and to stand by the unborn child.

She said she accepted the Nobel Prize on behalf of the unwanted, poorest of the poor and the unhappy of the world.

Professor John Sanness handed Mother Teresa the Nobel insignia, the gold medal and diploma on behalf of the Nobel Committee. The prize money of 800,000 Swedish crowns (about Rs. 15.28 lakhs) was given to her at a private meeting earlier today.

Professor Sanness said there was no better way of explaining why Mother Teresa was chosen for this year's award than the comment of the World Bank President, Mr. Robert McNamara, who said: 'Mother Teresa deserves the Nobel Peace Prize because she promotes peace in the most fundamental manner by her confirmation of the inviolability of human dignity.'

Professor Sanness said that with her message Mother

> Teresa was able to reach through to something innate in every human mind – to create the seed for good. If this were not the case the world would be deprived of hope and work for peace would have little meaning, he said.[19]

This news item is confirmed by reports appearing in three London based papers: *The Times*, *The Telegraph* and *The Guardian*. They quote the words: 'Those countries which legalized abortion are the poorest countries in the world. They are afraid of the unborn child and the child must die.' But these papers also quote these words: 'Holiness is not the luxury of the few but the duty of all.'[20] The Kolkata-based *The Statesman* also mentions that Mother Teresa 'said she accepted the Nobel Prize on behalf of the unwanted, poorest of the poor and the unhappy of the world'.

It is striking that *The Statesman* gives a heading that emphasizes Mother Teresa's condemnation of abortions. Would it not have been normal to caption the report as 'Mother Teresa is awarded the Nobel Prize for Peace'? Was not the award the main point of the news? On the other hand, a few websites quote Mother Teresa's words accepting the Prize on behalf of the poor, but they do not quote her words about abortion.[21] And here you have an example of how the media inflect their reports in ways of their own choosing.

b. A feature film on Mother Teresa

Dominique Lapierre's film, *Mother Teresa: In the Name of God's Poor*, was released in 1997, at the time of Mother Teresa's death. The film's story ends in 1979, with Mother being awarded the Nobel Prize for Peace. This means that the film does not cover the last eighteen years of Mother Teresa's life. To end the film at that point was wise because an additional eighteen years of the eventful and increasingly controversial life of Mother Teresa would have required another film. Moreover, a mention of the Nobel Prize award ceremony was a fitting ending for the thirty-two years the film deals with. People who have known Mother Teresa very well, including two Roman Catholic Archbishops, have declared that the film presents an image of Mother Teresa that comes as close as possible to the Mother Teresa they have known.

Yet, by alluding to the Nobel Prize Award Ceremony, Lapierre created a tough dilemma for himself. The acceptance speech of Mother Teresa included a condemnation of abortions. Lapierre's film ends in an apotheosis, with Mother Teresa accepting the Prize on behalf of the poor. There is no mention of abortion in the entire film.

Obviously, the condemnation of abortion would come as a jarring note at the end of Lapierre's film, since there is not a word or scene in the entire film about abortion or family planning, notwithstanding the fact that reliable persons vouched for the documentary value of the film. In fact, that part of her acceptance speech that appeared in some of the media reports in 1979 did come as a jarring note to many people. But, strikingly, the 'excerpt' from her acceptance speech that one can find in a few websites, does not quote the condemnation of abortion. So, to put Mother Teresa's anti-abortion statement at the culminating point of the film would have required an explanation very difficult to provide, especially at the very end of the film.

Still, one could argue that the spectator, who does not know what Mother Teresa said in her acceptance speech in Oslo in 1979, is to an extent misled by the ending of Lapierre's film, as well as by the 'excerpt' reproduced by some websites. And this instance shows how difficult Mother Teresa's relationship with the media was. I leave aside the cases of the websites presenting a truncated excerpt from the acceptance speech. In the case of Lapierre, one can say that here is a filmmaker who always showed utmost respect for Mother Teresa, and would not willfully distort the events of her life.

But what about those who are 'against' her? If Mother Teresa used the media to propagate her views, other people too used the same media to criticize her.

Mother Teresa was well aware of a possible manipulative use of her statements. In her Nobel lecture, she makes this rather unexpected confession, issuing from the depth of her experience: 'If I don't go to heaven for anything else I will be going to heaven for all the publicity because it has purified me and sacrificed me and made me really ready to go to heaven.'

Mother Teresa repeated the same statement in her address to the National Prayer Breakfast in 1994. She surely meant it. But at the time of the Nobel lecture (1979) Mother Teresa had no idea of how much she would have to suffer on the occasion of Lapierre's film project – for no fault of Lapierre, I hasten to add. Mother Teresa was in full sympathy with the project, and, at his request, she gave Lapierre her unconditional permission to make the film, although no permission was required. She understood that the film would make her work and her sisters' work known in a correct perspective. Moreover, those who supported the film project felt that any film on Mother Teresa's life made while she was alive would record true facts, and thus would prevent undue mythologizing of the Mother Teresa phenomenon. But – again, for no fault of Lapierre – she withdrew her permission. She gave it three times and withdrew it three times, until she could no more cope with the issue. She suffered for over ten years, and so did the film's makers.

Whereas *The Statesman* emphasized Mother Teresa's condemnation of abortions, Dominique Lapierre chose to omit it. An example of the somewhat unpredictable manner in which the media reported Mother Teresa's statements. Yet, it must be noted that Mother Teresa's 'wavering' regarding the Lapierre film was not due specifically to the fact that Lapierre chose not to mention her condemnation of abortion.

The difficulties encountered by Mother Teresa in her relationship with the media were not caused solely by the media, and, as the case of the film by Lapierre shows, at times some people close to her apparently did not necessarily make things easier for her.

Conclusion: The logic behind Mother Teresa's concern about abortion

There is logic in Mother Teresa's concern about abortion. Her decision to leave her convent and work among the poor was prompted by her love for human beings and her respect for their dignity. Life, she thought, is a gift from God. It should be received gratefully, and lived with dignity. Hence, she cared for the dying destitute, especially those who lacked loving care. She also cared for the abandoned children. And then, she cared for those suffering from leprosy, and, as a consequence of the social stigma attached to the disease, from neglect and lack of loving care. She cared for those living with AIDS. Finally, she cared for the unborn children and their mothers. Moreover, as mentioned earlier, Mother Teresa saw Jesus in all human beings, especially in the poor.

There is yet another aspect of Mother Teresa's action that has logic and coherence: Mother Teresa was a radical in all aspects of her life, action and thought. For instance, she thought, the poor have no fans in their houses, so her nuns have no fans; the poor cannot easily invite them to tea, so they accept tea from no one; the dying destitute lie abandoned on the streets, they pick them up (whether directly as in the early days, or, later, through the Kolkata Municipality's cooperation); the same thing for the abandoned children. And finally, unborn children are threatened with death, Mother Teresa's nuns fight abortion with adoption; 'don't kill the child, give the child to us', she said in her Nobel lecture. Her response to human needs was unconditional, immediate and practical. For Mother Teresa, compassion meant solidarity with the poor, sharing their life conditions.

She was concerned for the unborn babies, but she did not express an equal concern for the other people involved in abortion. She emphasized the moral aspect of the issue. Her concern was strengthened by the fact that her statements or actions against abortion met with the strong approval of the pro-life coalition. Her moral concern was also strengthened by the awareness that her position was that of the Roman Catholic Church and, particularly, of the Pope.

Nearly twenty-five years after Mother Teresa was awarded the Nobel Prize, Pope John Paul II added Mother Teresa's name to the Roll of the Blessed. In the sermon he delivered during the beatification ceremony, on 19 October 2003, he praised her for being the 'servant of all', especially 'the least', and for being 'an icon of the Good Samaritan'. Moreover, the Pope praised her for her courage. He said: '[e]very now and then she would come and tell me about her experiences in her service to the Gospel values. I remember, for example, her pro-life and anti-abortion interventions, even when she was awarded the Nobel Prize for peace.'[22] It is striking that in his encyclical letter, *Deus caritas est*, Pope Benedict XVI mentions Mother Teresa three times (paragraphs 18, 36 and 40).[23]

Mother Teresa surely knew that she had the full support of Pope John Paul II, and she would have been comforted by the words of Benedict XVI. Yet, she derived her clarity of thought and strength in action from her relationship with God, and from no human source. It is possible that she felt certain that she had a special call to do what she was doing. This may be suggested if not confirmed by the fact that before delivering her acceptance speech, when she received the Nobel Prize for Peace, on 10 December 1979, she did not know what to say, and she was praying intensely. Mother Teresa was a celebrity and a saint.

Envoi: ‘No’ to social closure

– 15 –

Brain down the drain – an *exposé* of social closure in Western academia

i. Introduction

Towards the end of the twentieth century, there was a significant increase in the number of asylum seekers and refugees coming to the West from Central, South-East and Eastern Europe. The increase was due to the collapse of Communism in the late 1980s and early 1990s and the disintegration of the former Yugoslavia throughout the 1990s. For many such immigrants the move to the West appears to be an ongoing depressing experience, especially for those who are highly educated. This explains why some of the most disappointed migrants are found among scientists, academics and artists whose hopes to continue or further their careers have often been dampened in the United Kingdom and across the Western world.

This article aims to address three issues: provide some information about the extent to which brain drain has affected most countries in Central, South-East and Eastern Europe, especially Albania, Bulgaria and Romania; identify some of the reasons why 'brain drain' has turned into an as yet not fully acknowledged 'brain waste'; and explore some of the causes – historical, cultural, political, economic and media-related – behind the alleged discrimination against foreign scholars in Western academia.

The article is also intended to draw attention to patterns of prejudice apparent in employment procedures in several Western countries (and elsewhere in the world) and to the lack of adequate research on the marginalization of foreign scholars in the West, especially those coming from South-East Europe.

ii. The modern workhouse

If one believes the British tabloids, the United Kingdom is in imminent danger of being swamped with refugees and asylum seekers. Recent polls reveal that a large number of people in Britain believe that the UK has up to twenty-three percent of the world's refugees. According to Home Office statistics, however, the real figure is below two percent. Prior to the European Union enlargement on 1 May 2004, 2.8 million foreign nationals were living legally in the UK and, of these, 1.44 million were in employment.

With its often hostile representation of foreigners, fuelled by uneducated guesses about the real number of migrants coming to work in Britain and their impact on the British economy, it could be argued that the tabloid press is largely responsible for the reported and unreported racial tensions flaring across the UK over the past few years. Considering that many tabloid readers rarely read anything else, it is not surprising that they feel threatened by the ever growing 'army' of alien 'spongers', 'scroungers' and 'cheats', as foreigners are labelled at times in some British papers.

Britain does not seem to have a clear policy on immigration and especially on the employment of economic migrants, in spite of the fact that this is one of the most sensitive issues in contemporary British politics. While politicians often claim that immigrants are needed to sustain the country's workforce and population growth, thus far there seems to be no properly thought-out plans for attracting and recruiting qualified workers from overseas.

Many asylum seekers arriving in the UK have left their own countries to escape torture and persecution. A considerable number of them, however, especially those from countries in South-East Europe that are not EU members, have come to Britain mainly in search of better living conditions. Since most EU countries, including the UK, apparently lack a proper recruitment policy, these economic migrants have no option but to invent all kinds of excuses to enter Western Europe. It is estimated that since May 2004, migrants could use over 80 different routes to move to the European Economic Area, which includes the European Union as well as Norway, Iceland and Liechtenstein.

The unregulated immigration policy in the UK is one of the reasons why a considerable number of foreigners arriving here are uneducated or unskilled. These migrants are often hired as 'seasonal workers' and are usually paid less than unskilled British workers doing similar jobs. Whether they are staying legally or illegally in the UK, these contingent workers are generally considered as cheap labour. In most cases they are not issued contracts; nor are they insured by their employers although they are often required to carry out dangerous construction work.[1]

The illegal employment practices, the often unsuitable working conditions and the low wages immigrants receive across Western Europe indicate that 'slavery' has reappeared in Europe some twenty-one centuries after Spartacus's call for an end to it.[2] The difference between Rome's slaves and our 'slaves' is that the latter seem to have entered into this humiliating bondage of their own accord. Western democracies are rightly condemning violations of human rights and enslaving practices in other parts of the world but they should do more to protect vulnerable people in their own backyard.

While immigration has been for quite some time one of the most topical issues in the Western media, the unfair treatment of vulnerable migrants in Western Europe rarely attracts the attention of the news industry. In the UK, for instance, migrant workers become newsworthy usually in the event of a tragic accident, like the drowning of 21 Chinese cockle pickers in Morecambe Bay on 5 February 2004. In spite of the wide media publicity this and other similar high profile cases have attracted, Western governments do not seem to take the ongoing exploitation of immigrants very seriously.

The West is an affluent 'workhouse' that also relies on skilled foreign workers. Since the early 1990s, for instance, a large number of highly educated and skilled migrants from Central, South-East and Eastern Europe have been doing low-skill, low-status and low-wage jobs in the UK and other countries in the West. This is one of the conclusions that Bridget Anderson *et al* draw in their 2006 paper 'Fair enough? Central and East European migrants in low-wage employment in the UK', which is part of the research project *Changing Status, Changing Lives? The Socioeconomic Impact of EU Enlargement on Low-Wage Migrant Labour in the UK.*

Although the authors of this research project occasionally refer to migrants with postgraduate degrees doing manual work,[3] drawing attention to the trade-offs they and other high-skill migrants make 'consciously, if reluctantly',[4] their main purpose is to explore the employment of migrants from East and Central Europe in low-wage occupations – agriculture, construction, hospitality and *au pair* work – and what determines employer demand for migration labour in these sectors.

Unlike the above-mentioned research project and other similar studies, this article focuses primarily on foreign scholars and artists in the West. The study has two main aims: firstly, to explore how foreign scholars and artists fare in the job market in the UK and other Western countries, especially those coming from countries outside the EU such as Albania, Romania and Bulgaria,[5] and secondly, to draw attention to the fact that they are one of the most under-researched groups of migrants.

Most of the South-East European graduates interviewed for this study admit that their main aim in coming to the UK is to further their academic and artistic careers. Many of them have worked for years in their native countries as medical doctors, researchers, lecturers and engineers. Their graduate and postgraduate degrees and work experience, however, have not always been very useful to them in Britain for reasons which will be identified shortly.

A large number of these highly educated migrants have ended up doing various low paid manual jobs for years.[6] Referring to statistics made available from the Council for Assisting Refugee Academics (CARA), based at London South Bank University, Nick Pandya wrote in *The Guardian* in April 2005 that:

> there are at least 1,500 doctors, dentists and other health service professionals and around 2,000 academics who are skilled in the sciences, engineering and ICT in the UK but only a handful of these refugees are employed at the same level as they were in their country of origin.[7]

Referring to the same issue, Frances O'Grady, Deputy General Secretary of the British Trade Union Congress (TUC), argues that:

> [i]n the current high temperature debate around asylum and immigration, the issue of skilled academics and pro-

> fessionals has been missed. We need to separate this issue from the hyperbole and urgently reassess how we treat the thousands of skilled refugees in this country who are forced in to jobs way below their ability.[8]

One way the Home Office can help these academics is by offering them grants similar to those already awarded by CARA to several refugee academics. This would enable many hospitals and schools in Britain to secure the human resources they badly need at the moment.

iii. Brain drain: a new chapter of an old story

Brain drain is hardly a recent phenomenon in the history of mankind. The term itself may have been coined initially in 1963,[9] but brain migration has been constantly occurring since the dawn of civilisation. Brain drain is triggered by several factors and accelerates especially as a result of and in the wake of major social and political upheavals. Brain drain became a major issue across Central, South-East and Eastern Europe immediately after the end of Communism in the late 1980s and as a result of the disintegration of the former Yugoslavia throughout the 1990s.

No advanced society has ever been built relying entirely on its own 'indigenous' human resources. Brain drain has been instrumental in laying and consolidating the foundations of every civilization. One of the reasons why Ancient Mesopotamia and Egypt flourished was because they attracted and promoted many bright foreigners to leading positions. The ancient scribes of 'Genesis' record that at the age of thirty Joseph 'gained authority over the land of Egypt', because, as the Pharaoh apparently told him:

> 'there is no one so discerning and wise as you. You shall be over my house, and all my people shall order themselves as you command; only with regard to the throne will I be greater than you.' And Pharaoh said to Joseph, 'See, I have set you over all the land of Egypt.' Removing his signet ring from his hand, Pharaoh put it on Joseph's hand; he arrayed him in garments of fine linen, and put a gold chain around his neck. He had him ride in the chariot of his second-in-command; and they cried out in front of him, 'Bow the knee!' Thus he set him over all the land of Egypt. Moreover Pharaoh said to Joseph, 'I am Pharaoh, and without your consent no one shall lift up hand or foot in all the land of Egypt.'[10]

It appears the Pharaoh did not think highly of Joseph only because of his ability to interpret dreams. The ruler of Ancient Egypt decided to put a stranger in charge of the economy mainly because Joseph the seer was also a very capable official, an ingenious economist and a very tough administrator when necessary. An important factor that seems to have contributed towards the almost unparalleled longevity of the 'otherworldly' Pharaonic civilisation was the Egyptian rulers' farsightedness to welcome and benefit from talented earthly 'aliens'.

This old-fashioned spirit of welcoming and promoting bright foreigners was also apparent in Ancient Greece and Rome. Contrary to widespread and long-held erroneous perceptions about the so-called predominantly obscurantist nature of the Ottoman Empire, its long reign and outstanding cultural and architectural heritage can also be attributed to the Sublime Porte's tendency to attract foreign scholars and artists and create all the conditions needed for them to flourish in their chosen professions. Many ambitious and talented South-East Europeans took full advantage of the generosity of the sultans and other powerful patrons of science and arts in Constantinople and across the breadth of the vast empire.

A large number of such European beneficiaries came originally from Albania. Except for the 1945-1989 period, in the last two thousand years, bright and ambitious Albanians have usually built their careers either in Rome or in Constantinople. Numerous Albanians have been successful abroad from the time their country was defeated by the Romans towards the end of the second century BC, up until the end of the Turkish yoke at the start of the twentieth century. It is believed that an impressive number of Roman emperors, Catholic popes and saints, and Ottoman *grand viziers* (prime ministers) and architects were Albanian or of Albanian descent.[11]

Like Ancient Egypt and the Ottoman Empire, the West has a long tradition in welcoming talented foreigners. It is largely due to 'outsiders' from across the world that several countries in Western Europe as well as the United States of America, Canada and Australia gradually emerged as centres of great economic, scientific and cultural importance. The West appears to have been particularly welcoming to 'aliens' up until the early decades of the twentieth century.

There are many reasons why the West was inclined to receive foreign scholars and artists more readily in the past. The study of 'alien' literatures on many occasions seems to have played an important role in presenting unfamiliar cultures and civilisations in a sympathetic light. In his 1946 book *Mimesis*, Erich Auerbach highlights what Edward W. Said calls 'the diversity and concreteness of the reality represented in Western literature from Homer to Virginia Woolf'.[12] European scholars like Auerbach kept alive throughout the first half of the twentieth century the ideals of many outstanding Italian, French and German thinkers who during the eighteenth and nineteenth centuries were interested in knowing other peoples and other times for their own sakes and 'for purposes of co-existence and humanistic enlargement of horizons'.[13] Said considers especially Goethe's ideas about *Weltliteratur* as one of the reasons why at that time Europe tended to view other cultures and people with 'generosity' and 'hospitality'.[14]

This appreciative attitude towards and the desire to learn from strangers were reflected in the amiable treatment of ambitious foreign scientists and artists. Thanks to this generosity and hospitality, Polish born Marie Curie (*née* Marya Sklodowska) and several other scientists and artists from Central, South-East and Eastern Europe excelled in their fields and acquired recognition in their host countries and beyond. France is so proud of Curie that on 21 April 1995, thanks to President François Mitterrand's direct intervention, her ashes were transferred to the *Panthéon*, the final resting place for some of the nation's most noted citizens.

iv. Dictatorship and intellectual exodus

The West European tendency in the eighteenth and nineteenth centuries to study other cultures 'for their own sakes' and welcome foreigners was seriously undermined at the start of the twentieth century. The Russian Revolution of 1917 marked the gradual setting apart of the West not only from the now 'alien' Communist Russia but also from many other countries in Central, South-East and Eastern Europe. The already lukewarm relations between the West and the 'other' Europe throughout the 1920s and 1930s turned rather cold in the wake of World War II in the late 1940s and reached 'freezing point' during the Cold War.

The rise of Nazism in the 1930s had a detrimental impact on

the lives of numerous scholars, scientists and artists, especially those who were Jewish or of Jewish descent. Many brilliant minds (Auerbach being one of them) were forced to leave Germany and the territories occupied by the Nazi army, and a large number of them eventually settled in the United States.

At the end of World War II, scientists, scholars and artists in many West European countries could finally breathe a sigh of relief. They were no longer to suffer from the censorship that had affected their lives for over a decade. Their colleagues across Central, South-East and Eastern Europe, however, were not that lucky. For them Nazi censorship and persecution would soon be replaced by equally repressive measures. Scholars, scientists and artists were among the most persecuted and prosecuted people in countries ruled by Communist governments.

Up until 1989, the year when the Berlin Wall was finally demolished, brain drain was not an issue for most Communist countries. Scholars and artists from the East were not allowed by their governments to move to the West. There were 'escapees' but their number was insignificant. The only former Communist country known to have suffered considerably from brain drain during the Cold War was East Germany. It is estimated that 36,759 engineers, technicians, doctors, teachers and university lecturers as well as 11,705 students moved from East Germany to West Germany between 1954 and 1960.[15] This 'brain drain', it appears, was not spontaneous. In an article published in *The Guardian* on 27 October 1999, Rob Gowland argues that the massive departure of educated people and experts from the German Democratic Republic was orchestrated by West Germany to undermine the attempts of its other Communist half to industrialise and rebuild the economy of the eastern region:

> If the GDR [German Democratic Republic] Government announced plans to develop ship-building or chemical industries, specialists in those industries would soon receive letters, notes under doors, visits from 'friends', offering extremely well-paid positions in the West, complete with large flat and flash car.
>
> Times were tough and many took these offers, as they were meant to.
>
> They simply crossed over into west Berlin and went to the addresses they'd been given and that was that. *A well-organised brain drain was bleeding the GDR's economy* through an open wound called the border with west Berlin.
>
> The decision to close the open border between East and West Berlin was made at 4 pm on August 12, 1961. It was put into effect without any announcement, at midnight the following Sunday.
>
> The West was caught flat-footed...From the day the Wall was erected the economy of the GDR never looked back. It developed steadily to become the tenth leading industrialised country in the world. (emphasis added)

v. Between myth and reality

The publicised preferential treatment of East German scientists in West Germany during the Cold War sowed in the Communist countries the seeds of the myth about the West as a welcoming place for migrating scholars. Fed up with economic hardships and the pervasive control exerted by the state over education and research institutions, many educated people from Central, South-East and Eastern Europe rushed to the West after the collapse of the Communist regimes. It seems some of them were expecting to find in the West the *El Dorado* enjoyed by many East German intellectuals who had defected to West Germany before the phantom appearance of the Berlin Wall.

Brain drain affected virtually all former Communist countries in Europe, although not to the same extent. The countries that were hit the hardest were Albania, Romania, Poland, Estonia, Bulgaria and Slovakia. The following figures indicate the estimated percentage of the total number of scientists these countries lost as a result of brain drain during the 1989-1995 period: Albania 40%,[16] Romania 20%, Poland 15%, Estonia 13.8%, Bulgaria 11.5% and Slovakia 11.3%.[17]

The departure of so many scholars, scientists and artists continues to have a negative impact on these countries because they leave behind a vacuum unlikely to be filled in the near future. Brain drain has affected schools, universities and research institutions as well as social, cultural and political life. In most cases those who migrate are ambitious researchers and artists who are obviously prepared to take risks to enhance their careers, mainly in the West.

Poland is one of the former Communist countries where brain drain has been studied for years because the country suffered from the departure of qualified people before the collapse of Communism. Over the last ten years, several former Communist countries in Europe have made serious efforts to assess the negative consequences of this intellectual exodus. In 1997, for instance, a joint study involving ten Central and East European countries was carried out.[18] In spite of these praiseworthy efforts, there is room for more studies in this area.

Recent studies show that the emigration of academics and artists from Central, South-East and Eastern Europe to the West is much lower now compared to the years immediately after the fall of Communism. There are countries like Albania, though, where brain drain remains a serious problem. It is estimated that some 3,000 Albanian students leave the country every year to continue their studies abroad, mainly in the West. This represents 30% of the annual overall number of Albanians going to university. According to surveys carried out in 2000 and 2004 almost 50% of the Albanian students abroad had no intention of returning to Albania immediately after their graduation.[19]

The intention of so many educated Albanians to stay abroad is surprising since according to recent statistics their job prospects in the West are not very encouraging. Referring to different surveys, Myqerem Tafaj concludes that a high percentage of them 'do not work in their areas of specialisation. This is different according to countries: 74% in Greece, 70% in USA, 67% in Italy, 58% in Austria, 47% in Germany, and 19% in France'.[20]

Most of the studies carried out so far regarding countries affected by brain drain concentrate on the number of specialists who have migrated and their destinations in the West. In many cases, though, the figures provided do not reveal the full picture, and the information and conclusions are often hypothetical.

More importantly, so far not many countries affected by brain drain appear to have carried out thorough studies about the kind of jobs these migrant scholars and artists end up doing in the West, and how they are being treated in their adopted countries. While it is acknowledged that not all researchers who emigrate intend to continue their scientific careers abroad, not enough research has been carried out on those who are committed to pursue their academic life but fail to do so for reasons beyond their control. Studying this particular group would reveal some of the reasons why and the extent to which 'brain drain' turns into 'brain waste'.

The collapse of Communism heralded a new chapter in the West's and especially Western Europe's relationship with Central,

South-East and Eastern Europe. Serious efforts have been made over the last two decades to bring the peoples of the long divided continent together. In spite of some considerable achievements, it would be unrealistic as yet to talk about a pan European or Western revival of the humanistic ideas preached by Vico, Goethe and Auerbach. The frost that covered Europe for most of the twentieth century has not yet thawed completely. The expansion of the European Union is a welcome development. But it would take more than some cosmetic changes in the political map of the continent to make Western Europe a place where the 'indigenous' European feels at ease with the European 'other'.

While it is true that some researchers and artists from former Communist countries are employed in their fields in the West, many are those who have stopped working in their professions not because of choice but because they are unable and in some cases not allowed to do so. For many of them the reality they encounter in the West is often very different from what they had imagined back home.

Foreign scholars and artists in the West are faced with an imposed identity. Since the fall of Communism in the late 1980s, the West has failed to differentiate between scientists and economic immigrants. Like many unfortunate asylum seekers, foreign researchers and artists are often looked down upon. This is hardly surprising considering the yardstick the West has been using for quite some time to measure the worth of foreigners, especially those hailing from poor countries. Throughout the second half of the twentieth century, the West has normally employed a fiscal scale to define, appreciate or demean 'outsiders'. Even the definitions of 'brain drain', provided by some respectable publications, betray signs of this prevailing materialistic approach applied when assessing strangers. The term is often defined as a 'departure of educated and professional people from one country, economic sector, or field for another usually *for better pay or living conditions*' (emphasis added),[21] or as 'a migration of professional people (as scientists, professors, or physicians) from one country to another usu[ally] *for higher salaries or better living conditions*' (emphasis added).[22]

It is obvious that both definitions and other dictionary entries of the same term tend to concentrate primarily on the materialistic expectations of the educated migrants. The authors of such definitions appear to ignore the aspirations that migrating professionals have career-wise. Of course, the financial incentive plays a crucial role in many immigrants' difficult decision to uproot themselves from their *patria* to an unknown and, at times, unwelcoming country. Seeing their move only in financial terms, however, is degrading, especially considering the idealistic hope many talented people have before leaving their own countries. The feeling that they would have a better chance to fulfil their potential as scientists, scholars and artists, that they would be part of a welcoming scientific and artistic community, that their inventions, books, fiction, films or music would enlighten and entertain complete strangers, and that they would play a part, however modest, in enriching the world surely must outweigh any anticipated financial gain.

The two aforementioned definitions of 'brain drain' are part of the disturbing West-centric discourse that tends to view anyone from poor countries arriving in the developed world primarily in materialistic terms. Established and aspiring scientists, scholars and artists from undeveloped countries are usually lumped more or less into the same category as uneducated immigrants who come to the West only for 'better living conditions'. More importantly, these and other similar definitions of 'brain drain' seem to ignore the fact that such aspiring talented migrants have both the potential and the will to render an inestimable contribution to the development of science, technology, art and culture in their adopted countries.

If brain drain appears to have been one of the reasons why Berlin was split into two cities for over thirty years, notwithstanding the negative impact the migration of scholars has had on the former Communist countries, the same phenomenon could play a crucial role in bringing the people of Europe closer together. So far, however, European governments, both in the East and the West, have failed to benefit from the educated migrants they have lost or gained.

When the Berlin Wall, the epitome of what Churchill called the 'iron curtain', fell in 1989, many scholars from Central, South-East and Eastern Europe arriving in the West soon realised that they were up against a more impassable wall. Like some of their colleagues from Africa, these 'estranged' Europeans could see that they were judged in the West not on their individual merits but on the preconceived and often unfair impressions about their countries of origin. Misperceptions regarding and flimsy knowledge of places such as Albania, Romania and Bulgaria explain to some extent why scientists and artists from these countries often find it difficult to further their careers in Western Europe.

Foreign scholars and artists in the West realise that it is important for them to go through a period of training and probation in order to familiarise themselves with new education systems, update their knowledge, and acquire a high command of the foreign language in which they are required to speak and write. They are quite disheartened, however, when Western employers underestimate and, at times, simply disregard the degrees for which they have worked so hard in their own countries.

Some migrant academics in the UK, Germany and other EU countries, whose original degrees are not recognised, have no option but to unnecessarily attend undergraduate and postgraduate courses to keep alive the hope of having an academic career in the West. A considerable number of foreign academics apparently find themselves in the same Catch-22 situation also in the US and, according to Ian Roth, in Canada:

> Of course there is racism, there is the dubious job market that seems impenetrable to even the highest educated and most established citizens, not to mention the toils of having to learn a new language and understand a new culture. What people perhaps do not know is how many professionals are allowed to immigrate into Canada – often on the basis of their profession – and then are told once they arrive that their credentials are not sufficient to practice in Canada.[23]

Those foreign scholars who have their degrees accredited or obtain new ones in the West do not always fare much better. For many of them, even for those with degrees from first-rate Western universities, finding a full-time permanent lectureship or a researchship often remains an elusive dream.[24] Many such hopefuls spend years searching in vain for a post befitting their academic credentials, publications record and work experience. Their job applications often appear to go unnoticed, and even in those cases when a few make it to the short list, the posts almost always go to 'home' applicants. It appears that the politically correct 'equal opportunities in employment' statement, that many employers are keen to bedeck their newspaper advertisements with, in many cases is nothing more than empty rhetoric. Like many colleagues from Africa, Asia and Latin America in the West, a considerable number of scholars from Central, South-East and Eastern Europe often find themselves victims of malpractices in recruitment.

That such malpractices occur in British universities, for instance, is acknowledged by several officials involved in the recruitment process.[25] These malpractices affect not only foreign but also home applicants. Those who suffer most from such irregularities, however, are foreign scholars, although as British citizens they should not be treated any differently than 'home' applicants. When it comes to employment opportunities, foreign scholars in Britain and elsewhere in the West have realised on numerous occasions that they are as equal as the creatures in Orwell's imaginary farm. The motto that 'All animals are equal, but some animals are more equal than others' takes a whole new meaning for those educated foreigners whose hopes of finding a post are repeatedly dashed in many universities, colleges and research institutions in the UK and across the Western world.

In several cases unsuccessful foreign applicants suffer severe bouts of depression.[26] Some of them find it difficult to accept that their chances of employment in Western academia will always remain slim. Failure to secure a post means an early end to their professional careers for which they have worked hard and invested for many years in their native and adopted countries. This is also quite a blow to their self-esteem and some of them are often reluctant to talk about their 'failure' in public. Most of the foreign scholars interviewed for this article needed some persuasion to recount their experiences in the West, and all of them, without exception, asked not to be identified.[27]

Some scholars from Central, South-East and Eastern Europe and other parts of the world manage to find positions in teaching and research institutions in Western Europe through personal contacts with Western academics they initially come across in their native countries. However, even these lucky few are not always treated fairly by their employers. Their contracts are usually fractional and rarely permanent. This often puts them in a precarious position. The renewal and upgrading of their contracts often depend on the whims of employers some of whom admit openly that British born colleagues always come first, even if they are less experienced or qualified.[28]

In some cases Western employers see foreign academics as cheap labour. As for those foreigners who are employed full-time, they are often offered the lowest pay scale. The reason for this is because employers compare salaries in the West with what these academics would normally earn in their own countries.[29] Some employers in the UK, for instance, just cannot see how Albanian, Romanian or Bulgarian scholars could ask to be paid the same salaries as those paid to their British colleagues for similar work when the average monthly wage in their countries at the moment is around £350.[30]

A considerable number of foreign academics in the UK are employed as hourly paid lecturers for years on end, although they are fully qualified and experienced enough to carry out responsibilities that come with a full-time post. The performance of these 'seasonal workers' is often as good as, and in some cases even better than that of some of their British colleagues who hold full-time permanent posts. All the same, many of them are stuck for years in part-time jobs. Employers are interested in this cheap but highly qualified and very reliable workforce, and are not prepared to offer them full-time permanent positions.

The discrimination against foreign academics in the West is likely to continue as long as their universities and research institutions back home cannot offer them a better deal. This is the reason why many frustrated foreign academics have no choice but to put up with the ongoing blackmail they allegedly encounter in Western academia.

To add insult to injury, 'embarrassed' by their own unfair treatment of such dedicated part-time staff members, some colleges and universities in the UK acknowledge their contribution by awarding them honorary fellowships.[31] Such fellowships, which bring no money to the recipients, remind academics from Central, South-East and Eastern Europe of similar reward methods employed by Communist governments.

vi. An Italian and Japanese affair

Brain drain does not affect only the developing world. Many Western countries are affected by the departure of scholars just as well. In 2003, for instance, it was estimated that 75% of EU citizens who obtained doctorates in the US from 1991 to 2000 'have no specific plans to return to the EU'.[32]

Likewise, it would be wrong to assume that only foreign scholars arriving in the West are mistreated. Western academics pursuing their careers abroad are also not exempt from discrimination. Some Western scholars have been voicing their concerns for years about discriminatory practices and racist attitudes they claim to have encountered in several countries in and outside Europe. Of particular interest is the growing number of complaints about the alleged unfair treatment foreign lecturers and students receive in some Italian universities. A British professor, quoted in *The Guardian* on 25 March 1997, for instance, finds the Italian system 'rotten, in need of revolution and recasting, shamelessly exploitative, discriminatory and corrupt'. Other British academics and many 'angry and disappointed' students from Austria, Belgium, UK, Netherlands, France, Germany, Norway and Spain, who have expressed their frustration openly on several occasions, apparently share the same view. The situation appears to be particularly bad for 'foreign language lecturers'. So much so, that their 'blatant discrimination' has attracted the attention of several Members of the European Parliament who are exerting pressure on the Italian government to look into the issue.[33] In his letter of 29 September 1998 to Luigi Berlinguer, Minister of Italian Universities, regarding the alleged mistreatment of a Canadian scholar by the University of Calabria, the President of the Canadian Association of University Teachers (CAUT), mentions that by then Italy had apparently been brought before the European Court of Justice a record three times over its treatment of visiting scholars.[34]

Foreign language lecturers in Italy appear to be in the same predicament as their expatriates in Japan. Over the last twenty years many foreign lecturers (known in Japan as *gaikokujin kyoshi*) have made a series of complaints about 'a pattern of unfair treatment' they have allegedly encountered at several Japanese universities. Some Western lecturers hold that their Japanese employers often discriminate against them simply for being foreigners. They claim that they are not given long-term or permanent contracts, are refused promotion and, if they start complaining, they are simply sacked.[35] On 4 April 1995, for instance, a group of frustrated American, German and British academics working in Japan wrote an open letter to the US Ambassador Walter Mondale stressing that there was 'evidence of a systematic and officially approved discrimination on the basis of nationality (as well as age)'.[36] The signatories were outraged at being treated as 'disposable objects', and for 'being forced to sign one- or two-year final contracts as the only alternative to the threat of the thirty-day termination clause'.

vii. The long journey home

Western academics working abroad mostly have the support of their respective governments. This rarely occurs, however, in the case of scholars from Africa, Asia, South-East Europe or Latin America. At the moment, no one in the West seems to be protecting the many vulnerable foreign scholars, especially those coming from South-East and Eastern Europe. For almost two decades many educated migrants from Albania, Bulgaria and Romania, for instance, have been at the mercy of Western employers whose discriminatory employment practices seem to go unnoticed.

All South-East European governments should do more to protect the rights of their scholars, scientists and artists abroad. In doing so they would simply fulfil their duty towards their fellow citizens. Moreover, such institutional care would enable migrant scholars and artists to develop more positive relationships with their native countries and be an asset abroad.

Most governments whose countries have been seriously affected by brain drain acknowledge the need for the highly educated migrants to return home because of the important role they could play in the academic, social and political life. Except for Taiwan, South Korea and to some extent India,[37] however, few countries have been able to trigger a significant return of their expatriate specialists. Several governments have called on their educated nationals to return home in the name of patriotism, a method that so far has failed to work. It is unlikely that the patriotic card alone will induce academics and artists to return home. Unless the call for home-coming is accompanied by contracts and salaries of Western standards, a great number of scholars and artists will choose to stay abroad, especially those who have secured posts.

viii. Defining the 'ethnic'

Some foreign scholars interviewed for this article feel that they have been abandoned not only by their own governments but also by their Western colleagues. There have been cases when Western scientists, scholars and artists have voiced their concerns to their employers over alleged unfair treatment meted out to their foreign colleagues.[38] It is important, however, that more Western scholars show similar interest in the plight of these 'outsiders within' and be more generous with professional advice on how to increase their chances of employment and get their work published in a tough and often unfair academic publication market.

Racism in academia is a familiar theme in cultural and sociological studies especially in the UK. Like a large number of people in the UK, however, some British social scientists seem to have a rather narrow and unrealistic notion as to what constitutes 'racism' and who 'qualifies' to be included in the category of the 'unfairly discriminated' citizens in Britain. The politically correct discourse employed at times by some politicians, academics and the media, seems to indicate that 'ethnic communities' consist exclusively of people from Pakistan, India, Bangladesh, the West Indies and other former British colonies in Africa.[39]

While it is true that most of the people considered as 'ethnic minorities' in Britain originate from former British colonies, it would be wrong and irresponsible to ignore and sideline the tens of thousands of British citizens who come from corners of the world that Britain happened not to have conquered when she ruled the waves. Over the last two decades numerous immigrants from Albania, Bulgaria, Romania, Croatia, Serbia, Poland, North and other parts of Africa, China and many other countries have made the UK their home and are working hard to contribute positively to British society. Not all of them feel at home in Britain however, especially those scholars and artists who encounter racist and discriminatory attitudes similar to those faced by their colleagues from the acknowledged 'ethnic communities'.

The tendency to ignore the unfair treatment of foreign academics and artists who are not from the more widely recognized 'ethnic communities' is revealed in several studies about racism in British academia. In their 2000 study 'Ethnicity and Academia: Closure Models, Racism Models and Market Models',[40] for instance, Steve Fenton, John Carter and Tariq Modood assess the extent to which non-British academics feel sidelined as students and employees. By 'non-British', however, they mean mainly non-white British citizens. Even in those cases when reference is made to white non-British employees, the authors do not seem to have in mind scholars from Central, South-East or Eastern Europe. For the time being, this category of 'outsiders' continues to escape the attention of British sociologists and cultural theorists who have yet to acknowledge that their unfair treatment in institutions across the UK warrants serious study.

The British press often follows the same approach when addressing the issue of racism in academia. In 'All white at the top', which appeared in *The Guardian* on 25 May 2004, for instance, Stephen Hoare rightly points out that of the UK's 400-plus colleges there are just five ethnic minority principals. Like many journalists tackling the issue of race, however, Hoare seems to equate the notion of 'ethnic community' with 'non-white community'. This is one of the reasons why perhaps his recommendations are similar to those recently offered to and adopted by the National Health Service and the police force in Britain.

It seems as if the NHS, the police and now some higher education institutions across the UK see positive discrimination as the best policy to address the sensitive issue of racism in their ranks. No one should be discriminated because of their colour, race, religion or native culture. If applied sensibly, positive discrimination could bring some positive results. It would be wrong, however, to see this way of addressing racism and discrimination as the only long term solution. Positive discrimination could result in underestimating the real achievements of hard-working and talented high-flyers from ethnic communities as well as in ignoring members of other marginalised groups who are also discriminated against because of their ethnic origin and other 'peculiarities' that set them apart from the 'norm'.[41] Positive discrimination could also be abused both by those who apply it as well as its 'beneficiaries'. More importantly, this way of dealing with racism and discrimination could result in the creation of pockets of society perceived as being incapable *ad infinitum* of achieving success unless they receive preferential treatment. Finally, positive discrimination legitimises patronising which is yet another form of racism.

An increase in the number of non-white teachers, policemen, lecturers and college principals would certainly indicate a welcome change in the way citizens from 'ethnic communities' are treated but we should not rely only on statistics to address the issue of racism. Institutions may employ a certain number of non-white people and still do nothing substantive to counter racism. Some departments, colleges and universities in the UK are already successfully implementing positive discrimination. In some cases, however, it is alleged that this is more of a PR stunt than a serious attempt to do away with racial discrimination in the education sector.[42]

The British press often runs stories about the difficulties foreign academics and artists encounter in the UK. Some British journalists have a shrewd understanding of the sensitive and complex race issues in the UK. Gargi Bhattacharyya, for instance, offers a realistic picture of the unfair treatment of foreign academics in Britain in her *Guardian* article of 10 July 2003 'Welcome with closed arms'. Having acknowledged the important contribution of overseas scholars to British academia, Bhattacharyya rightly concludes that:

> Britain has not yet learned how to live with its migrants, however skilled they may be. More than half of university staff are employed on short-term contracts. Those requiring work permits have no right to stay in the country once the contract expires. On the whole, getting another contract is dependent on your relationship with your project manager.
>
> It is hard to imagine a more effective way of keeping your workforce passive and afraid. For at least one unlucky applicant this has meant pursuing an employment tribunal from half way around the world. The research that exists suggests that overseas staff in universities remain vulnerable – to racist harassment, to workplace exploitation, to exclusion from the processes of promotion and progression.

Bhattacharyya does not mention where these badly treated 'vulnerable employees' hail from, however. As for reporters like Stephen Hoare (2004) and Polly Curtis (2005) who do, they tend to find such victims almost exclusively among the black and ethnic-minority staff. In such cases, 'ethnic-minority' does not seem to include those coming from Central, South-East and Eastern Europe.

It is about time that British academia becomes more open to scrutiny from the media and relevant government departments to ensure that we do not continue to make in this country the same mistakes which are endemic in some countries. An open, well-informed and mature debate about a sensitive issue such as racism would ensure that no one in British academia suffers from what Max Weber called 'social closure'.[43] Many may disagree with Margaret Thatcher's statement that 'there is no such thing as society'. Few can deny, however, that to build an integrated and caring society, or rather for an 'imagined community' to become real and functional no one should be treated as a 'disposable object'. The Italian system does not seem to be the only one in the West that at times, to quote David Petrie, Chairman of the Association of Foreign Lecturers in Italy, appears to select its teaching staff 'on the basis of recommendation rather than one of honest merit'.[44]

Notes

Foreword

1 Rabindranath Tagore (1861-1941) delivered his lecture '*Sabhyatar Sankat*' (Crisis in Civilization) on his last birthday on 14 April 1941. He died three months later. The lecture was first published as a pamphlet in May 1941. A revised edition appeared in September 1950 (Calcutta: Visva-Bharati Publishing Department, pp. 11-23). Referring to this work, Amartya Sen, 1998 Prize Winner in Economics, remarked in his lecture 'Tagore and His India' on 28 August 2001: 'Even in his powerful indictment of British rule in India in 1941...[Tagore] strains hard to maintain the distinction between opposing Western imperialism and rejecting Western civilization.' <http://nobelprize.org/nobel_prizes/literature/articles/sen/index.html> (accessed 21 December 2006).

2 The etymology of the word *Bharat* is not very clear. Some believe that this name of India comes from that of a mythological king.

3 The other five people who have been made Honorary Citizens of the United States of America are: Winston Churchill (British Prime Minister during World War II; awarded in 1963); Raoul Wallenberg (Swedish diplomat and Holocaust hero; awarded in 1981); William Penn (17th and 18th century proprietor and governor of the American colony of Pennsylvania; awarded in 1984); Hannah Callowhill Penn (second wife of William Penn and administrator of Pennsylvania; awarded in 1984); Marquis de la Fayette (French supporter of the American Revolution; awarded in 2002). Only Winston Churchill and Mother Teresa received this honor during their lifetime.

4 The documentary *Mother of the Century* was produced by the Films Division of the Government of India and exists in two versions. The longer version was shown by Doordarshan, the Indian national television, on 5 May 2001, and the shorter one on 23 August 2002. Mr Bhattacharya, the film's Director, held a special screening of the film for Dr Alpion in the studio of Doordarshan on 28 June 2005 when Dr Alpion was visiting Kolkata.

5 A. Sen, *The Argumentative Indian: Writings on Indian History, Culture and Identity*, London: Penguin, 2005, p. 15. Sen gives the following reference for the quote included in his book: P. Green, *Alexander of Macedon, 356-323 B.C.: A Historical Biography*, Berkeley: University of California Press, 1992, p. 428.

6 Personal correspondence, 25 September 2005.

7 The origin of Visva-Bharati goes back to 1901, when Rabindranath Tagore founded a simple school on a seven-acre plot, where in 1863 his father, Debendranath, had built a small retreat for meditation. Tagore expanded the school after he received the Nobel Prize for Literature in 1913. Visva-Bharati University was inaugurated on 23 December 1921.

8 'Kosova' is the Albanian spelling of this region whose population consists of over 90% Albanians and less than 10% Serbs and other ethnic groups. The Serbs spell the name of the region as 'Kosovo'.

9 For more information see G. Roberge, 'Images of Calcutta: From Black Hole to Black Box', in J. Racine (ed.) *Calcutta 1981*, New Delhi: Concept Publishing Company, 1990, pp. 15-27 (Roberge's article is based on the lecture he gave at a seminar on Calcutta at the French Cultural Centre in Calcutta in November 1979. *Calcutta 1981* was published in French in 1986); and G. Roberge, 'Images of Calcutta: Mirages of Development', in *India International Center Quarterly*, New Delhi, Spring-Summer 1993, pp. 225-42.

10 Trouille painted a naked woman reclining on a couch, and seen from her back. The caption read: 'Oh, Calcutta!' ('*Oh, quel cul t'as*!' or 'Oh, what a lovely arsehole you have!')

11 G. Alpion, *Mother Teresa: Saint or Celebrity?*, London and New York: Routledge, 2007.

12 From discussions with Dr Alpion in Kolkata, and from his correspondence with me, it is obvious that he feels twice a foreigner. He told me in Kolkata: 'At times I feel I am a foreigner even in Albania although I love the country dearly'. In a letter to me of 17 September 2005, Dr Alpion wrote:

> As a wandering scholar and writer, I have tried for almost 20 years to define what 'my country' is or means. The best definition in my case would be: My country is my childhood. Such an approach has helped me considerably to feel at home 'abroad' and at times 'a stranger' in my own country. I believe that thanks to this early conscious 'weaning' from my roots, I have become more critical and appreciative of my Albanian heritage and at the same time see myself as *a citizen of the world.*
>
> Our countries of origin determine very much who we are and certainly how we are perceived by others but as scholars and writers it is essential that we ourselves develop a critical appreciation of our roots. This is an effective way for us to act as bridge-builders between countries, regions, religions, cultures and civilizations. I was born in Albania and I will always love my country dearly but the whole world is my *pátria*, and my foreigner-status would never prevent me from expressing my views openly even when they are deemed 'politically incorrect' by the 'indigenous' people. (emphasis added)

13 Tagore, 1950, op. cit.

Part One: Albania

1. An interview with the Ghost of Mohammed Ali, former ruler of Egypt

Initially a shorter version of this piece entitled 'An interview with Mohammed Ali's ghost' was published in the *Middle East Times* (MET)

(Cairo, Egypt, 4-14 June 1993, p. 12), when Gëzim Alpion was doing postgraduate studies at the University of Cairo. In those days, MET, founded in 1983, was the only independent English-language weekly in Egypt. Translated into Albanian by Dashi Alpion, this initial version was published in *Alternativa SD* (Tirana, Albania, 51: 350, 4 August 1995, p. 6). The version included in *Encounters with Civilizations* was first published in Gëzim Alpion's *Foreigner Complex: Essays and Fiction about Egypt*, Birmingham, UK: CPS University of Birmingham, 2002, pp. 22-32. The title of the piece has been changed to 'An interview with the ghost of Mohammed Ali, former ruler of Egypt' at the suggestion of Professor Gaston Roberge so that Indian readers will not mix Egypt's Albanian born ruler Mohammed Ali Pasha (c. 1769-1849) with the African American boxer Mohammed Ali (1942-) (born Cassius Marcellus Clay, Jr, himself not to be misidentified with the American abolitionist of that same name (1810-1903)), or the Lollywood star Mohammed Ali (1935-2006), who appeared in nearly 300 films, mostly in Urdu and produced in Lahore, the 'Hollywood' of Pakistan.

2. Kosova – a corner of Europe still waiting for peace

This feature was first published in the UK in the broadsheet *The Birmingham Post* (10 December 2003, p. 10) as two articles: 'A corner of Europe still waiting for peace' and 'A rich land where poverty is the norm'. *The Birmingham Post* was launched in 1857 as the *Birmingham Daily Post*.

Gëzim Alpion was a visiting professor at the University of Prishtina, Kosova, from October 27-31 where he gave two lectures: 'American literature and American identity' and 'Mother Teresa and the Western media'.

Part Two: Egypt

3. Foreigner complex

This article first appeared serially in nine consecutive issues in the

Middle East Times (Cairo, Egypt): 'When in Rome', 20-26 July 1993, p. 12; 'Back to the army', 27 July - 2 August 1993, p. 12; 'Enslaved by the slaves', 3-9 August 1993, p. 16; 'Complete apathy', 10-16 August 1993, p. 12; 'Cultural invasion', 17-23 August 1993, p. 13; 'Cracked but not broken', 24-30 August 1993, p. 12; 'Becoming foreign to become Egyptian', 31 August - 6 September 1993, p. 12; 'Power returns to the people: the making of Egypt's politicians', 7-13 September 1993, p. 19; and 'Egypt for the Egyptians', 14-20 September 1993, p. 12. In its present form (excluding the subtitles) the article was first published in Gëzim Alpion's book *Foreigner Complex: Essays and Fiction about Egypt*, Birmingham, UK: CPS University of Birmingham, 2002, pp. 1-21.

4. Egyptian coffee shops

A short version of this article entitled 'The genesis of Egyptian coffee shops' first appeared in the *Middle East Times* (Cairo, Egypt, 23-29 May 1994, p. 6). In its present form (excluding subtitles) the article was first published in Gëzim Alpion's book *Foreigner Complex: Essays and Fiction about Egypt*, Birmingham, UK: CPS University of Birmingham, 2002, pp. 42-55.

5. The Bride of *Hapi* – female sacrifice and cosmic order

This essay has its origin in the article 'The Bride of *Hapi*', which Gëzim Alpion first published in the *Middle East Times* (Egypt, Cairo, 31 August - 6 September 1993, pp. 1, 3). A year later, a longer four-part version appeared in England, UK, in the University of Durham *On Magazine*: 'The genesis of Miss Universe', 8.1 May 1994, p. 8 (reprinted as 'The Bride of *Hapi*' also in *On Magazine*, 8 Fresher's Issue, October 1994, p. 6); 'The Nilotic *arousa*', 8 Fresher's Issue, October 1994, p. 7; 'The drowning of the rite', 8.3 November 1994, p. 10; and 'The resurrection of the rite', 8.3 November 1994, p. 11. In its present form (excluding the subtitles) the article was published as 'The Bride of *Hapi*' in Gëzim Alpion's book *Foreigner Complex: Essays and Fiction about Egypt*, Birmingham, UK: CPS University of Birmingham, 2002, pp. 56-65.

6. A parade of porters

This article first appeared in four consecutive issues in the *Middle East Times* (Cairo, Egypt): 'The Nubian doorman', 15-21 June 1993, p. 12; 'The peasant *bowab*', 22-28 June 1993, p. 12; 'The *simsars* in their prime', 29 June - 5 July 1993, p. 13; and 'Today's *bowab*', 6-12 July 1993, p. 12). In its present form (excluding the subtitles) the article was first published in Gëzim Alpion's book *Foreigner Complex: Essays and Fiction about Egypt*, Birmingham, UK: CPS University of Birmingham, 2002, pp. 33-41.

1 This is an excerpt from Nicolas Pelham's preface to Gëzim Alpion's book *Foreigner Complex: Essays and Fiction about Egypt*, Birmingham, UK: CPS University of Birmingham, 2002, pp. xiii-xvii (pp. xvi-xvii).
2 The phrase 'these days' refers to the early 1990s.

Part Three: The United Kingdom

8. Images of Albania and Albanians in English literature – from Edith Durham's *High Albania* to J. K. Rowling's *Harry Potter*

This article is part of the paper Gëzim Alpion presented at the Institute for Advanced Research in Arts and Social Sciences (IARASS) at the University of Birmingham, UK, on 12 February 2002. Alpion was appointed Fellow of IARASS in 2000. The paper was first published in *BESA Journal* (Truro, UK), Vol. 6, No. 2, Spring 2002, pp. 30-4.

1 E. Durham, *High Albania*, London: Virago, 1985, p. 131.
2 Gëzim Alpion explored the nature of Nopcsa's interest in Albania in the paper 'Baron Franz Nopcsa and his ambition for the Albanian throne', which he presented at the School of Slavonic and East European Studies, University College London, UK, on 9 January 2002.
3 Lekë Dukagjini (1410-1481) was an Albanian prince who fought, often alongside Skanderbeg, against the invading Ottomans. He is

believed to have devised a set of laws, known as *The Canon of Lekë Dukagjini*, which some Albanians, especially in the North of the country, apparently adhere to to this day. Gëzim Alpion addressed the significance of this 'legal document' in the talk 'Albania and Albanians through Western eyes from early twentieth century to the present: the search for a half-forgotten mythology', he gave at the Albanian Youth Action (AYA), London, UK, on 4 December 2001.

4 Durham, op. cit., p. 118.

5 Ibid., p. 119.

6 Ibid., p. 344.

7 Ibid., p. 123.

8 Ibid., p. 128.

9 Ibid., p. 140.

10 Ibid., p. 197.

11 Ibid., p. 175.

12 Ibid., p. 1.

13 In an attempt to discourage economic immigrants from seeking asylum in the United Kingdom, in 1999 the British government introduced the vouchers scheme, according to which asylum seekers and refugees were given vouchers worth £35 a week towards their cost of living. This degrading cashless system, which outraged human right groups, was criticised by Gëzim Alpion in his 2001 controversial play *Vouchers* (Birmingham, UK: University of Birmingham CPS). Directed by Serbian-born dramaturg Dr Duška Radosavljević Heaney, the play received its first performed rehearsed reading in the UK at the Festival of Contemporary European Plays in Huddersfield on 16 March 2002. The Home Office scrapped the voucher system in 2001.

14 G. Orwell, 'Boys' Weeklies', in J. Giles and T. Middleton (eds), *Writing Englishness: 1900-1950 – An Introductory Sourcebook on National Identity*, London: Routledge, 1995 (pp. 177-85) p. 178.

15 See Ibid., p. 183.

16 Ibid.

17 Ibid., p. 185.

18 J. K. Rowling, *Harry Potter and the Chamber of Secrets*, London:

Bloomsbury, 1998, p. 242.

19 J. K. Rowling, *Harry Potter and the Goblet of Fire*, London: Bloomsbury, 2000, p. 58.

20 Ibid., pp. 292-3.

21 Ibid., p 388.

22 Ibid., pp. 567-9.

23 Ibid., p. 597. J. K. Rowling mentions Albania also in her 2007 *Harry Potter and the Deathly Hallows*, London: Bloomsbury (see pp. 237, 496).

24 Orwell, op. cit., p. 182.

9. Western media and the European 'other' – images of Albania in the British press

This is an updated version of the article entitled 'Western media and the European "other": images of Albania in the British press in the new millennium', which was first published in *Albanian Journal of Politics: 2005* (AJP), Vol. 1, Chapel Hill, NC: Globic Press, 2006, pp. 7-27. AJP is edited from the USA with an international scope.

1 E. W. Said, *Orientalism*, London: Penguin, 2003, p. 27.

2 Ibid., p. xii.

3 Ibid., p. 27.

4 For more information on the denigration of Ancient Egypt by Rome see in this book 'Foreigner Complex'.

5 Said, op. cit., p. 26.

6 R. S. Hillman (ed.) *Understanding Contemporary Latin America*, London: Lynne Rienner Publishers, 2001, p. xiii.

7 O. Halecki, *Borderlands of Western Civilisation: A History of East Central Europe*, New York: Ronald, 1952, p. 3. For more information on the negative image of the Balkans in the West see L. Wolff, *Inventing Eastern Europe: The Map of Civilization on the Mind of the Enlightenment*, Stanford, California: Stanford University Press, 1994; M. Todorova, *Imagining the Balkans*, New York and Oxford: Oxford University Press, 1997; V. Goldsworthy, *Inventing Rurita-*

nia: The Imperialism of the Imagination, New Haven and London: Yale University Press, 1998; and G. Alpion, *Mother Teresa: Saint or Celebrity?*, London and New York: Routledge, 2007; New Delhi: Routledge India, 2008; Rome: Salerno Editrice, 2008.

8 See D. Dauti and E. Robelli, 'Një gjeneral mban peng Kroacinë', *Shekulli*, 4 April 2005.

9 B. Gallagher, 'Will Croatia join a Balkan NATO?', *Hrvatski Vjesnik*, No. 927, *The New Generation English Supplement*, 26 July 2002.

10 Ibid.

11 For more information on J. K. Rowling's references to Albania as a country harbouring the evil 'Dark Lord' and his followers see in this book 'Images of Albania and Albanians in English literature – from Edith Durham's *High Albania* to J. K. Rowling's *Harry Potter*'.

12 See K. E. Fleming, '*Orientalism*, the Balkans, and the Balkan Historiography', *The American Historical Review*, Vol. 105, Issue 4, October 2000, pp. 1218-33, <http://www. historycooperative.org> (accessed 7 November 2004).

13 See in this book 'Images of Albania and Albanians in English literature', op. cit., and 'Oh! not Calcutta'; and G. Alpion, 'Baron Franz Nopcsa and his ambition for the Albanian throne', *BESA Journal*, Vol. 6, No. 3, Summer 2003, pp. 25-32.

14 E. Durham, *High Albania*, London: Virago, 1985, p. 118.

15 S. Capen, 'Interview with Paul Theroux', aired on the Futurist Radio Hour in the San Francisco Bay Area, 27 November 1995, <http://www.worldmind.com> (accessed 7 April 2004).

16 J. Llupo, 'Shqiptarët kursyen 49 miliardë lekë për 2004-n', *Shekulli*, 4 April 2005.

17 See B. Hoxha, 'Turizmi, shqiptarët prishën 560 milionë $ jashtë', *Korrieri*, 22 March 2005; A. Korkuti, 'Shqiptarët, 560 milionë dollarë jashtë vendit në 2004', *Shekulli*, 22 March 2005; and J. Llupo, 'Shqiptarët, 583 milionë euro për pushime jashtë', *Shekulli*, 28 January 2007.

18 A. Mile, 'Evropa Juglindore, nje këshill ministrash për kulturën', *Shekulli*, 2 April 2005.

19 *Korrieri*, 'Projekte që shkrijnë kufijtë', 6 April 2005.

20 J. Pettifer and M. Vickers, *The Albanian Question: Reshaping the Balkans*, London and New York: I. B. Tauris, 2007, p. 257.
21 T. Dowling, 'Wish you were here', *The Guardian G2*, 11 August 2003, p. 2.
22 E. Addley, 'Welcome to camp Tirana', *The Guardian*, 11 March 2003, p. 7.
23 Dowling, op. cit., p. 2.
24 Ibid.
25 A. Mueller, 'Tirana's true colours', *The Independent on Sunday*, 13 July 2003, p. 17.
26 Ibid.
27 Ibid.
28 Dowling, op. cit., p. 2.
29 See R. Williamson, 'Interview with Gëzim Alpion – Fallen hero: how the clown prince of Albania got right up the nose of his greatest fans', *Sunday Mercury*, 9 September 2001, pp. 45, 46; and A. A. Gill, 'The land that time forgot', *The Sunday Times Magazine*, 23 July 2006.
30 Dowling, op. cit., p. 2.
31 Ibid.
32 Ibdi., p. 3.
33 R. Barthes, 'The Death of the Author', in R. Barthes, *Image, Music, Text*, Trans. S. Heath, London: Fontana Press, 1990, p. 148.
34 The author wrote to Robert Shrimsley on 6 April 2005.
35 Robert Shrimsley's e-mail to the author of 8 March 2005.
36 C. Rae, 'Mr Moaner and pals rap *Sun*'s spoof', 22 January 2003, p. 7.
37 Ibid.
38 Mueller, op. cit., p. 17.
39 Pettifer and Vickers, op. cit., pp. 246-7.
40 Ibid., p. 247.
41 Ibid.
42 Ibid.
43 Ibid.
44 Gill, op. cit.
45 See A. Lalaj, '*The Times* fiton të drejtën për të ofenduar – Vendimi i PCC – thikë me dy presa', *Albanian Mail*, 23 October 2006.

46 See 'Press Complaints Commission Report: 73 Adjudication', 22 September 2006, <http://www.pcc.org.uk/news/index.html?article=NDE1MQ==> (accessed 23 October 2006).
47 See Gill, op. cit.
48 N. Malcolm's and J. Doherty's letters were published in the *Sunday Times Magazine* on 30 July 2006.
49 Dowling, op. cit., p. 3.

Part Four: India

10. Oh! not Calcutta

This article first appeared in the Saturday 'Face to Faith' column in *The Guardian*, 6 September 2003, p. 25. *The Guardian* is one of Britain's most influential quality newspapers known for its long history of editorial and political independence. Founded in 1821 as the weekly *Manchester Guardian*, it became a daily in 1855. 'Manchester' was dropped from the name in 1959; by then the paper had become a national daily with an international reputation.

1 A. Chatterjee, *Mother Teresa: The Final Verdict*, Kolkata, India: Meteor Books, 2003.
2 B. Mukherjee, 'The Saint Mother Teresa', *Time*, 14 June 1999.

11. Media and celebrity culture – subjectivist, structuralist and post-structuralist approaches to Mother Teresa's celebrity status

This article was initially published in the referred publication *Continuum: Journal of Media & Cultural Studies*, Vol. 20, No. 4, December 2006, pp. 541-57. *Continuum* is edited from Australia with an international scope, and is published by Routledge. The journal is affiliated with the Cultural Studies Association of Australia.

1 T. Carlyle, *On Heroes, Hero-Worship and the Heroic in History*, C.

Niemeyer (ed.), Lincoln and London: University of Nebraska Press, 1966, p. 29.

2 D. J. Boorstin, *The Image: A Guide to Pseudo-Events in America*, New York: Vintage Books, 1992, p. 57.

3 A. Smith, 'All in a good cause?', *The Observer*, 27 January 2002, (pp. 45-7), p. 45.

4 E. Johnson, *Mother Teresa: From Teacher to 'Living Saint'*, London & Sydney: Franklin Watts, 2003, p. 51.

5 L. Gjergji, *Nëna e Dashurisë/Mother of Love*, Prishtinë, Kosova: Academy of Sciences and Arts of Kosova, p. 64.

6 Johnson, op. cit., p. 38.

7 K. Spink, *Mother Teresa: An Authorized Biography*, London: Fount, 1998, p. 22.

8 J. L. Gonzáles-Balado (ed.) *Mother Teresa: In My Own Words*, London: Hodder & Stoughton, 1997, p. 87.

9 For accounts of Mother Teresa's poor health throughout the period 1910-1928 see D. Porter, *Mother Teresa: The Early Years*, Oxford and New York: ISIS Large Print, 1986, pp. 12, 24; L. Gjergji, *Nëna Jonë Tereze/Our Mother Teresa*, Ferizaj, Kosova: Drita, 1990, pp. 11, 15; Spink, op. cit., p. 9; A. Sebba, *Mother Teresa: Beyond the Image*, London: Orion, 1997, p. 17; Gjergji, 2000, op. cit., pp. 47, 54, 70; and Johnson, op. cit., p. 6.

10 Porter, op. cit., p. 27.

11 Spink, op. cit., p. 22.

12 Corinthians 12: 1-11, in *The Holy Bible, Containing the Old and New Testaments with Apocryphal/Deuterocanonical Books*, New Revised Standard Version, New York and Oxford: Oxford University Press, 1989, p. 182.

13 For Mother Teresa's interest in reading as a child and as a young woman in Skopje during the period 1910-1928 see Gjergji, 1990, op. cit., pp. 21, 22; and Gjergji, 2000, op. cit., pp. 47, 58, 63.

14 Gjergji, 1990, op. cit., p. 20.

15 Porter, op. cit., pp. 35-8; 40-1.

16 For the importance that Mother Teresa and her admirers attached to coincidences see E. Egan, *Such a Vision of the Street: Mother*

Teresa – The Spirit and the Work, Complete and Unabridged, New York and London: Doubleday, 1986, pp. 362-3; E. Egan and K. Egan (eds), *Living the Word: A New Adventure in Prayer Involving Scripture, Mother Teresa, and You*, London: Collins, 1990, pp. 64-5; and N. Chawla, *Mother Teresa*, London: Vega, 2002, p. 182.

17 While writing this article the author received several e-mails and letters from Catholic and non-Catholic admirers of Mother Teresa professing the huge impact she had apparently made on them when they first met her. They explain Mother Teresa's charismatic appeal to them with her profound faith which enabled her to help people in a way that others could not.

18 Author's interviews with several individuals who met Mother Teresa in the 1990s. The interviewees, who do not wish to be identified, were contacted between 2003 and 2005.

19 M. Muggeridge, *Something Beautiful for God: Mother Teresa of Calcutta*, London: Collins, 1971, p.41.

20 Quoted in C. Hitchens, *The Missionary Position: Mother Teresa in Theory and Practice*, London and New York: Verso, 1995, pp. 26-7.

21 Muggeridge, op. cit., p. 45.

22 Ibid., pp. 41, 44.

23 Boorstin, op. cit., p. 8.

24 Hitchens, op. cit., p. 27.

25 Referring to Mother Teresa's first call at the age of twelve, Kathryn Spink notes in her *Mother Teresa: An Authorised Biography* (1998) that this was 'an intensely personal experience on which she would not elaborate, other than to say that it did not take the form of any supernatural or prophetic apparition'. In Mother Teresa's own words, what she had experienced at twelve was 'a private matter. It was not a vision. I've never had a vision' (p. 8).

26 Egan, op. cit., p. 359.

27 Spink, op. cit., p. 159.

28 K. Spink, *For the Brotherhood of Man under the Fatherhood of God: Mother Teresa of Calcutta, her Missionaries of Charity and her Co-Workers*, Surrey, UK: Colour Library Information, 1981, p. 227.

29 For more information on C. Hitchens's critical stance on Mother Tere-

sa see the following interviews he gave to: S. Capen, *Worldguide* (Palo Alto, CA), 24 December 1995; M. Cherry, 'Christopher Hitchens on Mother Teresa', *Free Inquiry* (New York), Vol. 16, No. 4, Fall 1996; and D. Postel, 'The Missionary Position: Mother Teresa's Crimes Against Humanity', *LiP Magazine* (Oakland, CA), 15 September, 1998.

30 C. Rojek, *Celebrity*, London: Reaktion Books, 2001, p. 33.

31 See Hitchens, *Missionary Position*, pp. 43-8.

32 J. Eberts, R. Joffé and M. Medoff, *City of Joy: The Illustrated Story of the Film*, New York: Newmarket Press, 1992, p. 20.

33 D. Shah, 'Mother Teresa's Hidden Mission in India: Conversion to Christianity', 2003, <http://www.indiastar.com/DhiruShah.htm> (accessed 16 August 2004).

34 Aroup Chatterjee's letter to the author of 26 January 2005.

35 See A. Lalaj, 'Shqipëria, asnjëherë faktor i rëndësishëm', *Korrieri*, 29 June 2004, <http://www.korrieri.com> (accessed 20 December 2004).

36 J. Belton, *American Cinema/American Culture*, 2nd edn, Boston: McGraw-Hill, 2005, p. 98.

37 G. Gledhill, 'Introduction', in C. Gledhill (ed.), *Stardom: Industry of Desire*, London and New York: Routledge, 2003, (pp. xiii-xx), p. xiv.

38 R. deCardova, 'The Emergence of the Star System in America', in C. Gledhill (ed.) *Stardom: Industry of Desire*, London and New York: Routledge, 2003, pp. 17-29. See especially pp. 26-8.

39 C. Rojek, *Celebrity*, London: Reaktion Books, 2001, p. 11.

40 For more information on how Mother Teresa and those who supported her managed to keep away from the media any 'controversial' detail about her personal life that could put her 'saintly' image in jeopardy see G. Alpion, 'Media, ethnicity and patriotism – the Balkans "unholy war" for the appropriation of Mother Teresa', *Journal of Southern Europe and the Balkans*, Vol. 6, No. 3, December 2004, (pp. 227-43), pp. 240-1.

41 C. Gray, *Mother Teresa: The Nun Whose 'Mission of Love' Has Helped Millions of the World's Poorest People*, Herts, UK: Exley, 1990, p. 51.

42 Ibid., p. 49.

43 Ibid., p. 51.

12. A review of Hiromi J. Kudo's book *Mother Teresa: A Saint from Skopje*

This book review was first published in the peer-reviewed academic publication *Albanian Journal of Politics:2006* (AJP), Vol. 2, Chapel Hill, NC: Globic Press 2007, pp. 120-2. AJP is edited from the USA with an international scope.

1 H. J. Kudo, *Mother Teresa: A Saint from Skopje*, Gujarat, India: Gujarat Sahitya Prakash, Anand, 2006 (xxx + 216 pp, hb Indian Rs 250.00, US$ 25.00, ISBN 81 89317 09 1).

13. A note on Gëzim Alpion's book *Mother Teresa: Saint or Celebrity?*

Gaston Roberge wrote the note on Gëzim Alpion's *Mother Teresa: Saint or Celebrity?* (Routledge: London and New York, 2007) on 31 October 2006, the day the book was launched at the University College London, UK. Entitled 'A new book that asks: Is she a saint or just a celebrity?', the note was initially published in *The New Leader*, Chennai, India, combined issue of December 1-15 and 16-31, 2006, p. 51. *The New Leader*, founded in the 1880s, is a leading national Catholic magazine in India.

1 G. Alpion, *Mother Teresa: Saint or Celebrity?*, London & New York: Routledge, 2007; New Delhi: Routledge India, 2008; Rome: Salerno Editrice, 2008.

14. Mother Teresa, abortion and the media

This is the first time this article appears in print. The author is thankful to Father Pierre Jacob SJ, Father Lawrence Abello SJ and Mr Brian McDonough for their valuable comments and suggestions during the writing of this essay.

1 A. Huart, 'Mother Teresa: Joy in the Night', *Review for Religious*,

September-October 2001, pp. 494-502. See also C. Zaleski's article, 'The Dark Night of Mother Teresa', *First Things,* No. 133, May 2003, pp. 24-7. Zaleski based her discussion on four articles by Father Brian Kolodiejchuk, MC, *The Soul of Mother Teresa: Hidden Aspects of Her Interior Life,* ZENIT News Agency, Rome, Italy, November-December 2002, <http://print.firstthings.com/ftissues/ft0305/articles/zaleski.html> (accessed 11 November 2006).

2 The phrase is used, in particular, by thundering prophets like Jeremiah (Jer. 5:21) and Ezekiel (Ez. 12:2).

3 M. Teresa, 'Nobel Lecture', 11 December 1979. The lecture is often wrongly introduced as the 'acceptance' speech, as is the case in the following website: <http://www.dadalos.org/int/Vorbilder/vorbilder/Theresa/nobelpreis.htm> (accessed 11 November 2006). On the other hand, the Nobel Foundation clearly distinguishes the two speeches. See <http://nobelprize.org/peace/laureates/1979/teresa-lecture.html> (accessed 11 November 2006).

4 One wonders how this figure is arrived at.

5 Teresa, 11 December 1979, op. cit. This is how the Natural Family Planning is described by the NGO Northwest Family Services <http://www.nwfs.org/home.htm> on their website <http://www.nwfs.org/nfp.htm> (both sites accessed 11 November 2006):

> Natural Family Planning (NFP) is an effective, scientifically based method of family planning that treats fertility as a normal, healthy process. Northwest Family Services teaches the Sympto-Thermal Method which is based on changes in a woman's cervical mucus, waking or resting temperature, and cervix. These observable signs change in response to the hormones of the menstrual cycle. It only takes seconds a day for a woman to track her fertility; then the couple interprets the chart and makes a decision based on their family planning intention. NFP works through periodic abstinence during the method-defined fertile time for couples who are avoiding a pregnancy. NFP can be used effectively throughout a woman's entire reproductive life. Regular cycles are NOT required. NFP is NOT Calendar Rhythm.

However, the matter may not be that simple. Some scientists believe that the NFP may be a destroyer of embryos. See for instance the following website: <http://www.newscientist.com/article/dn9219-rhythm-method-criticised-as-a-killer-of-embryos-.html> (accessed 11 November 2006).

6 Mother Teresa, as mentioned earlier in this essay, was not a scholar. Nor did she have the time to read about all aspects of both destitution and abortion. With her practical sense, she went to the most urgent: the poor need to be helped, and abortion has to stop. On these two counts, she did pretty well.

7 Teresa, 11 December 1979, op. cit.

8 An address at the National Prayer Breakfast, 3 February 1994, Eternal Word Television Network (Global Catholic Network), <http://www.ewtn.com/New_library/breakfast.htm> (accessed 11 November 2006).

9 Source: *The Associated Press, 1997*, <http://www.cnn.com/WORLD/9709/mother.teresa/chronology/index.html> (accessed 11 November 2006).

10 The original videotaped address is kept at the Educational Media Research Center of St Xavier's College, Kolkata, India, where the talk was recorded.

11 *amicus curiae* (Latin for 'friend of the court', i.e. a party that is not involved in a litigation but is allowed by the court to advice it on the case).

12 'Mother Teresa takes pro-life message to Supreme Court', *Arlington Catholic Herald*, 4 February 1994, <http://www.ewtn.com/library/ISSUES/MTERSPCT.HTM> (accessed 11 November 2006). In the 'Roe v. Wade' case, 1973, the United States Supreme Court held that most laws regarding abortion violate a constitutional right to privacy. That was one of the most controversial decisions of the US Supreme Court.

13 Matthew 15: 1-9. *The New Jerusalem Bible*, Standard Edition, Bombay, India: Darton, Longman & Todd Ltd and Bombay Saint Paul Society, 1985.

14 The same excerpt from the acceptance speech (10 December 1979),

without any mention of abortion, appears, among others, on the following websites: <http://almaz.com/nobel/peace/1979a.html>; <http://www.cyberindian.com/mother-teresa/quotations.php>; <http://www.sapphyr.net/women/motherteresa.htm>; and <http://members.tripod.com/~DreamMatchMaker/mothert.htm>.

Mother Teresa's Nobel lecture presented as her 'acceptance speech', and dated 11 December 2006, appears, among others, on the following websites: <http://www.quoteworld.org/speeches/mother-teresa-nobel-prize-acceptance>; <http://www.writespirit.net/inspirational_talks/spiritual/mother_teresa_talks/oslo_1979>; <http://www.quotedb.com/speeches/mother-teresa-nobel-prize-acceptance>; and <http://www.catholiceducation.org/articles/social_justice/sj0004.html>. All the above websites were accessed on 3 December 2006.

Mother Teresa's Nobel Prize lecture, 11 December 1979, is introduced as 'lecture' on the following website: <http://nobelprize.org/nobel_prizes/peace/laureates/1979/teresa-lecture.html> (accessed 11 November 2006).

15 J. Sanness, 'Speech delivered on the occasion of the award of the Nobel Prize to Mother Teresa', Oslo, Norway, 10 December 1979, <http://www.dassk.org/contents.php?id=72> (accessed 23 February 2006).

16 While Mother Teresa's information is vivid in my memory, regretfully, I do not recall the exact day or the circumstances in which she gave it to me. For, I met her on numerous occasions.

17 For instance, in some districts of India, the gender ratio has come to 800 girls for 1000 boys.

18 T. Frängsmyr and I. Abrams (eds), *Nobel Lectures, Peace: 1971-1980*, Singapore: World Scientific Publishing, 1997, <http: http://nobelprize.org/peace/laureates/1979/teresa-lecture.html> (accessed 11 November 2006).

19 *The Statesman*, 'Abortion criticized by Mother Teresa', Kolkata, India, 11 December 1979.

20 I am grateful to Dr Aroup Chatterjee for drawing my attention to this information. A. Chatterjee. E-mail (11 December 2005).

21 See, for instance, <http://www.almaz.com/nobel/peace/1979a.html> (accessed 23 February 2006).

22 'On Sunday, 19 October 2003, the Holy Father raised Mother Teresa of Calcutta to the honours of the altar, presiding at the Mass for her beatification in St Peter's Square, with an estimated 300,000 faithful participating. In his Homily the Pope praised this diminutive woman of Albanian descent (1910-1997), who founded the Missionaries of Charity to help "the poorest of the poor" in whose broken bodies she saw Our Lord Jesus Christ.' <http://www.ewtn.com/library/PAPALDOC/JP2BTMTR.htm> (accessed 3 December 2006).

23 Pope Benedict XVI, 'Encyclical Letter: "On Christian Love"', Rome, 25 December, 2005, <http://www.vatican.va/holy_father/benedict_xvi/encyclicals/documents/hf_ben-xvi_enc_20051225_deus-caritas-est_en.html> (accessed 11 November 2006).

Envoi: 'No' to social closure

15. Brain down the drain – an *exposé* of social closure in Western academia

This essay has its origin in the talk 'Brain Down the Drain – East European Academics in Western Europe', which Gëzim Alpion gave at the 'Hope and Disappointment' seminar on immigration hosted by the *Deutsch-Albanische Freundschaftsgesellschaft* and the *Auslandsgesellschaft Nordrhein-Westfalen* in Dortmund, Germany, on 24 April 2004. In its present form the article will be published in the *Albanian Journal of Politics* (AJP), Vol. 4, Chapel Hill, NC: Globic Press, 2008. AJP is edited from the USA with an international scope.

1 Interviews with uneducated and unskilled migrants from South East Europe in London, UK, 24 March 2004.

2 Spartacus (c. 120 BC - c. 70 BC) was a gladiator slave who is believed to have led an unsuccessful uprising against the Roman Republic.

3 B. Anderson, et al., 'Fair enough? Central and East European migrants in low-wage employment in the UK', 1 May 2006, pp. 37-8,

<http://www.compas.ox.ac.uk> (accessed 2 May 2006).

4 Ibid., p. 103.

5 This article, completed in December 2006, refers to Bulgaria and Romania before their accession to the European Union on 1 January 2007.

6 Interviews with highly educated migrants from South-East Europe in the UK throughout 2003 and 2004. The interviewees have requested not to be identified. The same request was made by other people interviewed for this article: African scholars, personnel managers, heads of departments and successful 'home' applicants in the UK.

7 N. Pandya, 'Refugees are wasting their skills', *The Guardian*, 23 April 2005, p. 25.

8 Ibid.

9 See *Webster's Ninth New Collegiate Dictionary*, Springfield, MA: Merriam-Webster Inc., Publishers, 1987, p. 174.

10 Genesis 41: 39-44. *The Holy Bible containing the Old and New Testaments with the Apocryphal/ Deuterocanonical Books*, New Revised Standard Version, New York and Oxford: Oxford University Press, 1989, p. 42.

11 For more information on successful Albanians from Roman times to the present see Gëzim Alpion, *Mother Teresa: Saint or Celebrity?* London and New York: Routledge, 2007, pp. 34-7.

12 E. W. Said, *Orientalism*, London: Penguin, 2003, p. xix.

13 Ibid., p. xiv.

14 Ibid., p. xix.

15 For more information on the extent to which brain drain affected East Germany see 'Why the Berlin Wall was built', <http://www.guillotine.net>.

16 In Albania's case the figure 40% applies to the 1990-1999 period, and is based on the findings of the *Albanian Human Development Report*, Y. Cabiri *et al.*, United Nations Development Program (UNDP), 2000, <http://www.al.undp.org>. For information on the extent to which brain drain has affected Albania from 1990 to 2006 see M. Tafaj, 'Considerations about massive brain drain from

Albania and strategies attracting high-qualified scientists', <http://www.see-educoop.net> (accessed 16 April 2004); 'Albanian Brain Drain: Turning the Tide', Albanian Institute for International Studies, Tirana, 2005, <http://www.aiis-albania.org/Brain-drain_engl.pdf> (accessed 12 January 2007); and 'From Brain Drain to Brain Gain: Mobilising Albania's Skilled Diaspora', A policy paper for the Government of Albania, Prepared by the Centre for Social and Economic Studies, in collaboration with the Development Research Centre on Migration, Globalisation and Poverty, University of Sussex, UK, Tirana, April 2006, <http://www.migrationdrc.org/publications/other_publications/Brain_Gain_Policy_Paper_english_FINAL.pdf> (accessed 12 January 2007).

17 For more information on the extent to which brain drain has affected countries like Romania, Poland, Estonia and Bulgaria see D. Bobeva, 'Synthesis Report,' in R. Gerold *et al.*, *Brain Drain from Central and Eastern Europe: A Study Undertaken on Scientific and Technical Staff in Ten Countries of Central and Eastern Europe*, April 1997, pp. 4-31, <http://www.csd.bg> (accessed 10 February 2004).

18 See Gerold *et al.*, op. cit.

19 See 'From Brain Drain to Brain Gain: Mobilising Albania's Skilled Diaspora', op. cit., p. 9.

20 See Tafaj, op. cit. For more information on the same issue see 'From Brain Drain to Brain Gain: Mobilising Albania's Skilled Diaspora', op. cit., p. 11.

21 This definition from *Encyclopaedia Britannica* appears in S. Mahroum, 'Europe and the Challenge of the Brain Drain,' the Institute for Prospective Technological Studies (IPTS) Report, No. 29, November 1998, <http://www.jrc.es> (accessed 17 February 2004).

22 See *Webster's Ninth New Collegiate Dictionary*, op. cit., p. 174.

23 I. Roth, 'Strict degrees of accreditation,' *The Varsity* (University of Toronto's Student Newspaper), October 1997, <http://varsity.utoronto.ca> (accessed 26 May 2004).

24 Interviews with African and South-East European applicants in the UK.

25 Interviews with personnel managers, heads of departments and

successful 'home' applicants in several universities and colleges of higher education in the UK.

26 Interview with a Romanian scholar in the UK.

27 The interviewed scholars who declined to be identified in this article were from several countries in South-East Europe and Africa.

28 Interviews with British, South-East European and African scholars in the UK.

29 Recently, an East European graduate in the UK was repeatedly asked by an interview panel at a university about her salary in her native country. The interviewee explained to the panel that there was no point in comparing salaries in the two countries. The applicant was eventually offered the job. The pay package, however, was allegedly the lowest possible and not in accordance with her qualifications and work experience.

30 Interviews with South-East European lecturers in the UK.

31 Interview with a Romanian scholar in the UK.

32 N. Stafford, 'Brain drain? What brain drain? – Not all German scientists agree there's a problem with researchers abandoning Europe,' *The Scientists*, 23 December 2003. For more information about the extent to which brain drain is currently affecting several West European countries see L. Segal, 'The brain drain,' *The Guardian*, 17 May 2002; N. Nelson, 'Brain drain,' *The People*, 25 January 2004; and M. Brindley, 'Lecturer brain drain fears,' *The Western Mail*, 10 February 2004.

33 For more information on the concerns expressed by some Members of the European Parliament about the treatment of foreign academics at Italian universities see D. Pacitti and J. Meikle, 'Unfair exchange,' *The Guardian*, 25 March 1997. Pacitti addresses the issue of the alleged discrimination of non-Italian lecturers also in the following *Guardian* articles: 'In search of justice: Italy is embroiled in a bitter diplomatic row over its *lettori*,' 7 March 2000; 'Governments side with Italy's foreign teachers,' 20 April 2000; and 'Fourth court case for Italy's *lettori*,' 18 December 2000.

34 The text of the letter is available online at: <http://list.cineca.it>.

35 For information on the alleged discrimination of Western academ-

ics at Japanese universities see T. Laszlo, 'Learning a lesson: the uncertain future of foreign academics in Japan', *American Chamber of Commerce in Japan Journal* (ACCJ), August 1996, <http://www.issho.org> (accessed 16 April 2004); I. Hall, 'Academic Apartheid at Japan's National Universities', a publication of the Japanese Policy Research Institute (JPRI), Working Paper No. 3, October 1994, and 'Academic Apartheid Revisited,' JPRI, Working Paper No. 9, May 1995.

36 I. Hall and Six *Gaikokujin Kyoshi* (Foreign Teachers), 'Open Letter to Ambassador Mondale', 4 April 1995, <http://www.debito.org> (accessed 24 May 2004).

37 For more information on the positive measures taken by some countries affected by brain drain to promote and facilitate temporary, 'virtual' or permanent return of highly qualified migrant specialists see W. J. Tettey, 'Africa's brain drain: exploring possibilities for its positive utilization through networked communities,' *Mots Pluriels*, No. 20, February 2002; and 'From Brain Drain to Brain Gain: Mobilising Albania's Skilled Diaspora', op. cit., pp. 21-6.

38 Interviews with British academics in May and September 2002 and April 2003.

39 Gëzim Alpion deals at length with the issue of the narrow definition of 'ethnic community' in the UK in his article 'Racism of a different hue', *The Birmingham Post*, 5 July 2003, p. 9.

40 S. Fenton, J. Carter, and T. Modood, 'Ethnicity and academia: closure models, racism models and market models', *Sociological Research Online*, Vol. 5, No. 2, 2000, <http://www.socresonline.org.uk> (assessed 16 April 2004).

41 For more information on different views about the issue of positive discrimination in British academia see P. Curtis, 'Segregation, 2006 style', *The Guardian*, 3 January 2006, and 'John hits the web in search of student guidance', *The Guardian*, 6 January 2006.

42 A non-white academic from overseas was insulted recently at seeing his photo included in the publicity literature of another department at his British university. In his view, his picture was used because none of the employees in the other department were non-white. Interview with an overseas scholar in the UK.

43 For more information on the Weberian notion of 'social closure' see M. Weber, *Economy and Society: An Outline of Interpretive Sociology*, Vol. I, Eds. G. Roth and C. Wittich, Berkeley, CA: University of California Press, 1978, pp. 341-3.

44 D. Petrie's words about the alleged discrimination of foreign lecturers in Italy are included in Pacitti and Meikle, 1997, op. cit.

Select bibliography

Addley, E., 'Welcome to camp Tirana', *The Guardian*, 11 March 2003, p. 7.

'Albanian Brain Drain: Turning the Tide', Albanian Institute for International Studies, Tirana, 2005, <http://www.aiis-albania.org/Brain-drain_engl.pdf> (accessed 12 January 2007).

Alpion, G., *Vouchers*, Birmingham, UK: University of Birmingham CPS, 2001.

— 'Albania and Albanians through Western eyes: the quest for a half-forgotten mythology', Paper presented at the Albanian Youth Action (AYA), London, UK, 4 December 2001.

— *Foreigner Complex: Essays and Fiction about Egypt*, Birmingham, UK: University of Birmingham CPS, 2002.

— 'Images of Albania and Albanians in English literature', *BESA Journal*, Vol. 6, No. 2, Spring 2002, pp. 30-4.

— 'Baron Franz Nopcsa and his ambition for the Albanian throne', *BESA Journal*, Vol. 6, No. 3, Summer 2002, pp. 25-32.

— 'Racism of a different hue', *The Birmingham Post*, 5 July 2003, p. 9.

— 'Oh! not Calcutta', *The Guardian*, 6 September 2003, p. 25.

— Review of *The Search for Greater Albania*, by Paulin Kola, London: Hurst, 2003, in *Islam and Christian-Muslim Relations Journal*, Vol. 15, No. 3, July 2004, pp. 413-14.

— 'Media, ethnicity and patriotism – the Balkans "unholy war" for the appropriation of Mother Teresa', *Journal of Southern Europe and the Balkans*, Vol. 6, No. 3, December 2004, pp. 227-43.

— 'Western media and the European "other": images of Albania in the British press in the new millennium', *Albanian Journal of Politics*, Vol. 1, Issue 1, 2005, Chapel Hill, NC, USA: Globic Press, 2006, pp. 7-27.

— Review of *Between Morality and the Law: Corruption, Anthropology and Comparative Society*. Ed. Italo Pardo, Aldershot, UK & Burlington, USA: Ashgate, in *The Journal of the Royal Anthropological Institute*, Vol. 12, Issue 1, March 2006, pp. 231-2.

— Review of *Mother Teresa: A Saint from Skopje*, by Hiromi Josepha Kudo, Gujarat, India: GSP Anand, 2006, in *Albanian Journal of Politics*, Vol. 2, Issue 2, December 2006, Chapel Hill, NC, USA: Globic Press, 2006, pp. 120-122.

— 'Media and celebrity culture – subjectivist, structuralist and post-structuralist approaches to Mother Teresa's celebrity status', *Continuum: Journal of Media & Cultural Studies*, Vol. 20, No. 4, December 2006, pp. 541-57.

— Review of *The Albanian Question: Reshaping the Balkans*, by James Pettifer and Miranda Vickers, London and New York: I. B. Tauris, 2007, in *Journal of Southern Europe and the Balkans*, Vol. 9, No. 2, August 2007, pp. 204-6.

— *Mother Teresa: Saint or Celebrity?*, London and New York: Routledge, 2007; New Delhi: Routledge India, 2008; Rome: Salerno Editrice, 2008.

— *If Only the Dead Could Listen*, Chapel Hill, NC, USA: Globic Press, 2008.

— 'Brain down the drain: an *exposé* of social closure in Western academia', *Albanian Journal of Politics*, Vol. 4, Issue 1, June 2008, pp. 41-63.

Anderson, B., *et al.*, 'Fair enough? Central and East European migrants in low-wage employment in the UK', 1 May 2006, pp. 37-8, <http://www.compas.ox.ac.uk> (accessed 2 May 2006).

Andreae, H., 'Gill in new racism row over "ferret-faced" Albanians jibe', 3 August 2006, <http://www.pressgazette.co.uk/article/030806/gill_ferret_face_albanian_jibe> (accessed 10 August 2006).

Auerbach, E., *Mimesis: The Representation of Reality in Western Literature*, Trans. W. R. Trask, Princeton, NJ: Princeton University Press, 2003.

Barthes, R., 'The Death of the Author', in R. Barthes, *Image, Music, Text*, Trans. S. Heath, London: Fontana Press, 1990, pp. 142-8.

Belton, J., *American Cinema/American Culture*, 2nd edn, Boston: McGraw-Hill, 2005.

Benedict XVI, Pope, 'Encyclical Letter: On Christian Love', Rome, 25 December, 2005, <http://www.vatican.va/holy_father/benedict_xvi/encyclicals/documents/hf_ben-xvi_enc_20051225_deus-caritas-est_en.html> (accessed 11 November 2006).

Bhattacharya, Amar Kr. (dir.), *Mother of the Century*, India, 2001; shorter version 2003.

Bhattacharyya, G., 'Welcomed with closed arms', *The Guardian*, 10 July 2004.

Boorstin, D. J., *The Image: A Guide to Pseudo-Events in America*, New York: Vintage Books, 1992.

Bradbury, M., *Doctor Criminale*, London: Secker & Warburg, 1992.

Brindley, M., 'Lecturer brain drain fears', *The Western Mail*, 10 February 2004.

Brontë, C., *Jane Eyre*, London: Penguin, 1994.

Brown, P., 'email Paul Brown @ Tirana', *The Guardian*, 7 May 2001.

— 'Albania bids to boost tourism', *The Guardian*, 21 June 2003.

— 'Welcome to Tirana, Europe's pollution capital', *The Guardian*, 27 March 2004.

Burke, S., *Authorship: From Plato to the Postmodern, A Reader*, Edinburgh: Edinburgh University Press, 2004.

— *The Death and Return of the Author: Criticism and Subjectivity in Barthes, Foucault and Derrida*, Edinburgh: Edinburgh University Press, 2004.

Cabiri, Y., *et al.*, *Albanian Human Development Report*, United Nations Development Program (UNDP), 2000, <http://www.al.undp.org>.

Campbell, D., 'Partisan war at Albania's paradise bay', *The Guardian*, 12 March 2005.

— 'Secret Europe', *The Guardian*, 19 March 2005.

Canagarajah, A. S., *A Geopolitics of Academic Writing*, Pittsburgh: University of Pittsburgh Press, 2002.

Capen, S., 'Interview with Paul Theroux', Aired on the Futurist Radio Hour in the San Francisco Bay Area, 27 November 1995, <http://www.worldmind.com> (accessed 7 April 2004).

Carlyle, T., *On Heroes, Hero-Worship and the Heroic in History*, C. Niemeyer (ed.), Lincoln and London: University of Nebraska Press, 1966.

Carter, M., 'Travels through a midlife crisis', *The Observer*, 22 October 2006.

Carver, R., *The Accursed Mountains: Journeys in Albania*, London: HarperCollins, 1999.

Chatterjee, A., *Mother Teresa: The Final Verdict*, Kolkata, India: Meteor Books, 2003.

Chawla, N., *Mother Teresa*, London: Vega, 2002.

Christie, A., *The Secret of Chimneys*, New York: HarperCollins, 2001.

Collins, W., *The Moonstone*, London: Penguin, 1998.

Curran, J., *Media and Power*, London and New York: Routledge, 2005.

Curtis, P., 'Jobs for the white boys: Who gets promotion? A new report shows ethnic minority academics are not getting promotions to higher grades', *The Guardian*, 22 November 2005.

— 'Segregation, 2006 style', *The Guardian*, 3 January 2006.

— 'John hits the web in search of student guidance', *The Guardian*, 6 January 2006.

deCardova, R., 'The Emergence of the Star System in America', in C. Gledhill (ed.), *Stardom: Industry of Desire*, London and New York: Routledge, 2003, pp. 17-29.

Derrida, J., *Dissemination*, Trans. B. Johnson., Chicago IL: University of Chicago Press, 1981.

— *Of Grammatology*, Trans. G. C. Spivak, Baltimore, MD: The John Hopkins University Press, 1998.

— *Writing and Difference*, Trans. A. Bass, London: Routledge, 2001.

Dowling, T., 'Wish you were here', *The Guardian G2*, 11 August 2003, pp. 2-3.

Durham, E., *Twenty Years of Balkan Tangle*, London: George Allen & Unwin, 1920.

— *High Albania*, London: Virago, 1985.

Durham, M. G., and D. M. Kellner (eds), *Media and Cultural Studies: Key Works*, Oxford: Blackwell, 2001.

Dutta, K., 'Saint of the gutters with friends in high places', *Times Higher Education Supplement*, 16 May 2003, p. 29.

Dyer, R. *Stars*, New Ed., London: British Film Institute (BFI), 2004.

Eberts, J., R. Joffé and M. Medoff, *City of Joy: The Illustrated Story of the Film*, New York: Newmarket Press, 1992.

Egan, E., *Such a Vision of the Street: Mother Teresa – The Spirit and the Work*, Complete and Unabridged, New York: Doubleday, 1986.

Egan E., and K. Egan (eds), *Living the Word: A New Adventure in Prayer Involving Scripture, Mother Teresa, and You*, London: Collins, 1990.

Eldridge, J., J. Kitzinger and K. Williams, *The Mass Media and Power in Modern Britain*, Oxford: Oxford University Press, 1997.

Eliot, G., *Silas Marner: The Weaver of Raveloe*, London: Penguin, 1994.

Elsie, R. (ed.), *Kosovo: In the Heart of the Powder Keg*, Boulder, CO: East European Monographs, 1997.

Fenton, S., J. Carter, and T. Modood, 'Ethnicity and academia: closure models, racism models and market models', *Sociological Research Online*, Vol. 5, No. 2, 2000, <http://www.socresonline.org.uk> (assessed 16 April 2004).

Fleming, D. (ed.), *Formations: A 21st-century media studies textbook*, Manchester and New York: Manchester University Press, 2000.

Fleming, K. E., '*Orientalism*, the Balkans, and the Balkan Historiography', *The American Historical Review*, Vol. 105, Issue 4, October 2000, pp. 1218-33, <http://www. historycooperative.org> (accessed 7 November 2004).

Frängsmyr T., and I. Abrams (eds), *Nobel Lectures, Peace: 1971-1980*, Singapore: World Scientific Publishing, 1997, <http://nobelprize.org/peace/laureates/ 1979/teresa-lecture.html> (accessed 11 November 2006).

Freundlich, F., *Albania's Golgotha*, Trans. S. S. Juka, New York: Juka Publishing Co. Inc., 1998, <http://www.alb-net.com/juka1.htm> (accessed 30 July 2003).

'From Brain Drain to Brain Gain: Mobilising Albania's Skilled Diaspora', A policy paper for the Government of Albania, Prepared by the Centre for Social and Economic Studies, in collaboration with the Development Research Centre on Migration, Globalisation and Poverty, University of Sussex, UK, Tirana, April 2006, <http://www.migrationdrc.org/publications/other_publications/Brain_Gain_Policy_Paper_english_FINAL.pdf> (accessed 12 January 2007).

Gallagher, B., 'Will Croatia join a Balkan NATO?', *Hrvatski Vjesnik*, No. 927, *The New Generation English Supplement*, 26 July 2002.

Gardner, J., 'One light bulb and an illuminating year', *The Times Higher Education Supplement*, 29 August 2003. p. 21.

Gerold R., *et al.*, *Brain Drain from Central and Eastern Europe: A Study Undertaken on Scientific and Technical Staff in Ten Countries of Central and Eastern Europe*, April 1997, pp. 4-31, <http://www.csd.bg> (accessed 10 February 2004).

Gjeçov, S., and L. Fox (eds), *Kanuni i Lekë Dukagjinit/The Code of Lekë Dukagjini*, New York: Gjonlekaj, 1989.

Gjergji, L., *Nëna Jonë Tereze/Our Mother Teresa*, Ferizaj, Kosova: Drita, 1990.

— *Nëna e Dashurisë/Mother of Love*, Prishtinë, Kosova: Academy of Sciences and Arts of Kosova, 2000.

Giles, J., and T. Middleton (eds), *Writing Englishness: 1900-1950 – An Introductory Sourcebook on National Identity*, London: Routledge, 1995.

Gill, A. A., 'The land that time forgot', *The Sunday Times Magazine*, 23 July 2006.

Gledhill, G., 'Introduction', in C. Gledhill (ed.), *Stardom: Industry of Desire*, London and New York: Routledge, 2003, pp. xiii-xx.

Goldsworthy, V., *Inventing Ruritania: The Imperialism of the Imagination*, New Haven and London: Yale University Press, 1998.

Gonzáles-Balado, J. L. (ed.), *Mother Teresa: In My Own Words*, London: Hodder & Stoughton, 1997.

Gowland, R., 'Culture and Life: Thoughts on the anniversary of the "fall of the Wall"', *The Guardian*, 27 October 1999.

Gray, C., *Mother Teresa: The Nun Whose 'Mission of Love' Has Helped Millions of the World's Poorest People*, Herts, UK: Exley, 1990.

Green, P., *Alexander of Macedon, 356-323 B.C.: A Historical Biography*, Berkeley: University of California Press, 1992.

Greer, G., 'Greer versus a saint', *The Melbourne Age*, 6 October 1990.

Halecki, O., *Borderlands of Western Civilisation: A History of East Central Europe*, New York: Ronald, 1952.

Hall, I., 'Academic Apartheid at Japan's National Universities' (a publication of the Japanese Policy Research Institute (JPRI)), Working Paper No. 3, October 1994.

— 'Academic Apartheid Revisited' (a publication of the Japanese Policy Research Institute (JPRI)), Working Paper No. 9, May 1995.

Hillman, R. S. (ed.), *Understanding Contemporary Latin America*, London: Lynne Rienner Publishers, 2001.

Hitchens, C., 'The Ghoul of Calcutta', *The Nation*, 13 April 1992.

— *The Missionary Position: Mother Teresa in Theory and Practice*, London and New York: Verso, 1995.

— Interview, Interviewer S. Capen, *Worldguide*, 24 December 1995.

— Interview, 'Christopher Hitchens on Mother Teresa', Interviewer M. Cherry, *Free Inquiry*, Vol. 16, No. 4, Fall 1996.

— Interview, 'The Missionary Position: Mother Teresa's Crimes Against Humanity', Interviewer D. Postel, *LiP Magazine*, 15 September 1998.

Hoare, S., 'All white at the top', *The Guardian*, 25 May 2004.

Howden, D., 'Shanty town in Albania built on toxic time bomb', *The Independent*, 7 June 2002.

— 'Back home: the child of six sold to traffickers', *The Independent*, 19 June 2003.

Huart, A., 'Mother Teresa: Joy in the Night', *Review for Religious*, September-October 2001, pp. 494-502.

Huntington, S. P., *The Clash of Civilizations and the Remaking of World Order*, London: The Free Press, 1996.

Ilirjani, A., A. Elbasani, and R. Peshkopia (eds), *Albanian Journal of Politics: 2005*, Vol. 1, Chapel Hill, NC: Globic Press, 2006.

— *Albanian Journal of Politics: 2006*, Vol. 2, Chapel Hill, NC: Globic Press, 2007.

Johnson, E., *Mother Teresa, From Teacher to 'Living Saint'*, London & Sydney: Franklin Watts, 2003.

King, R., 'Albania as a laboratory for the study of migration and development', *Journal of Southern Europe and the Balkans*, Vol. 7, No. 2, August 2005, pp. 133-55.

Kolodiejchuk, B., *The Soul of Mother Teresa: Hidden Aspects of Her Interior Life*, ZENIT News Agency, Rome, Italy, November-December 2002, <http://print.firstthings.com/ftissues/ft0305/articles/zaleski.html> (accessed 11 November 2006).

Kuper, S., 'Albania eager for action', *The Financial Times*, 24 March 2001.

— 'Good grass and gun law', *The Observer*, 25 March 2001.

Laszlo, T., 'Learning a lesson: the uncertain future of foreign academics in Japan', *American Chamber of Commerce in Japan Journal* (ACCJ), August 1996, <http://www.issho.org> (accessed 16 April 2004).

Lévi-Strauss, C., *Tristes Tropiques*, Trans. J. Weightman and D Weightman, New York: Penguin, 1992.

McBrien, R. P., and H. W. Attridge (eds), *The HarperCollins Encyclopedia of Catholicism*, San Francisco: Harper, 1995.

Mahroum, S., 'Europe and the Challenge of the Brain Drain', The Institute for Prospective Technological Studies (IPTS) Report, No. 29, November 1998, <http://www.jrc.es> (accessed 17 February 2004).

Malcolm, N., *Kosovo: A Short History*, London: Papermac, 1998.

Manji, I., *The Trouble with Islam Today: A Wake-Up Call for Honesty and Change*, Edinburgh and London: Mainstream Publishing, 2005.

Matto, K., "Mother' Teresa', <http://www.scionofzion.com/teresa/htm> (accessed 29 July 2003).

Metcalf, B. D., and T. R. Metcalf, *A Concise History of India*, Cambridge: Cambridge University Press, 2003.

'Mother Teresa takes pro-life message to Supreme Court', *Arlington Catholic Herald*, 4 February 1994, <http://www.ewtn.com/library/ISSUES/MTERSPCT.HTM> (accessed 11 November 2006).

Mueller, A., 'Tirana's true colours', *The Independent on Sunday*, 13 July 2003, pp. 17-20.

Muggeridge, M., *Something Beautiful for God: Mother Teresa of Calcutta*, London: Collins, 1971.

Mukherjee, B., 'The Saint Mother Teresa', *Time*, 14 June 1999.

Neill, S., *A History of Christian Missions*, London: Penguin, 1990.

Nelson, N., 'Brain drain', *The People*, 25 January 2004.

Northwest Family Services, 'Natural Family Planning', <http://www.nwfs.org/home.htm> and <http://www.nwfs.org/nfp.htm> (both sites accessed 11 November 2006).

Orwell, G., 'Boys' Weeklies', in J. Giles and T. Middleton (eds), *Writing Englishness: 1900-1950 – An Introductory Sourcebook on National Identity*, London: Routledge, 1995, pp. 177-85.

Pacitti, D., 'In search of justice: Italy is embroiled in a bitter diplomatic row over its *lettori*', *The Guardian*, 7 March 2000.

— 'Governments side with Italy's foreign teachers', *The Guardian*, 20 April 2000.

— 'Fourth court case for Italy's *lettori*', *The Guardian*, 18 December 2000.

Pacitti, D., and J. Meikle, 'Unfair exchange', *The Guardian*, 25 March 1997.

Pandya, N., 'Refugees are wasting their skills', *The Guardian*, 23 April 2005, p. 25.

Pettifer, J., 'The wild frontier', *The Times*, 28 March 2001, p. 2.

Pettifer, J., and M. Vickers, *The Albanian Question: Reshaping the Balkans*, London and New York: I. B. Tauris, 2007.

Ponsford, D., 'Gill cleared by PCC over "ferret faced" Albanians piece', 10 October 2006, <http://www.pressgazette.co.uk/article/101006/pcc_aa_gill_sunday_times_newspaper_journalism> (accessed 24 October 2006).

Porter, D., *Mother Teresa: The Early Years*, Oxford & New York: ISIS Large Print, 1986.

'Press Complaints Commission Report: 73 Adjudication', 22 September 2006, <http://www.pcc.org.uk/news/index.html?article=NDE1MQ==> (accessed 23 October 2006).

Racine, J. (ed.), *Calcutta 1981*, New Delhi: Concept Publishing Company, 1990 (originally published in French, 1986).

Rae, C., 'Mr Moaner and pals rap *Sun*'s spoof', 22 January 2003, p. 7.

Roberge, G., *Chitra Bani: A Book on Film Appreciation*, Foreword by Satyajit Ray, Calcutta: Chitrabani, 1974. (Also available in Bengali, *Cinemar Katha*, Calcutta: Bani Shilpo, 1984. *Chitrabani* or 'image-word', is the Bengali equivalent of 'sight and sound'. Chitrabani is the name of a media center in Kolkata.)

— *Mass Communication and Man*, Allahabad: St Paul Society, 1977. (This is an abridged version of *Chitra Bani*, specially made for high school students; a provisional edition was published by G. Roberge in 1971. The book is also available in Hindi, *Manab aur Samuha Sanchar.*)

— *Manab aur Samuha Sanchar*, Indore: Satprakashan Sanchar Kendra, 1978. (Hindi version of *Mass Communication and Man.*)

— 'Images of Calcutta: From Black Hole to Black Box', in J. Racine (ed.), *Calcutta 1981*, New Delhi: Concept Publishing Company, 1990, pp. 15-27 (originally published in French, 1986).

— *Mediation, the Action of the Media in Our Society*, Delhi: Manohar Book Service, 1979.

— *Films for an Ecology of Mind: Essays on Realism in the Cinema*, Kolkata: Firma KLM (P) Ltd., 1980.

— *Eisenstein's 'Ivan the Terrible': An Analysis*, Kolkata: Chitrabani, 1981.

— *Another Cinema for Another Society* (also in Bengali, *Natun cinemar Sandhane*, Calcutta: Bani Shilpo, 1984), Kolkata: Seagull Books, 1984 (reprinted 2005).

— *The Subject of Cinema*, Kolkata: Seagull, 1985 (reprinted 2005).

— *The Ways of Film Studies*, Delhi: Ajanta Book International, 1992.

— 'Images of Calcutta: Mirages of Development', in *India International Center Quarterly*, New Delhi, Spring-Summer 1993, pp. 225-42.

— (ed.), *The Chitrabani Jubilee Book*, Kolkata: Chitrabani, 1995.

— *De la morosité à l'espoir: Cinéma, Communication et Développement* (French translation of *Communication Cinema Development*), Editions OCIC: Bruxelles, 1996.

— *Communication Cinema Development. From Morosity to Hope*, Delhi: Manohar Book Service, 1997. (National Award (special mention) at the 46th National Film Festival of India, 1999; also available in Bengali, *Sanjog Sinema Unnayan*, Kolkata: Bani Shilpo, 2004; Hindi version in preparation.)

— *The Compassionate Face of Meaning: Fragments for a Mosaic*, Gujarat: Anand, Gujarat Sahitya Prakash, 2004.

— *Cyberbani: Being Human in the New Media Environment*, Gujarat: Anand, Gujarat Sahitya Prakash, 2005.

— *Satyajit Ray*, New Delhi: Manohar Publishers, 2007.

Robyns, G., *Geraldine of the Albanians: The Authorised Biography*, London: Frederick Muller, 1987.

Rojek, C., *Celebrity*, London: Reaktion Books, 2001.

Roth, I., 'Strict degrees of accreditation', *The Varsity* (University of Toronto's Student Newspaper), October 1997, <http://varsity.utoronto.ca> (accessed 26 May 2004).

Rowling, J. K., *Harry Potter and the Chamber of Secrets*, London: Bloomsbury, 1998.

— *Harry Potter and the Goblet of Fire*, London: Bloomsbury, 2000.

— *Harry Potter and the Deathly Hallows*, London: Bloomsbury, 2007.

Ruhs, M., and B. Anderson, 'Semi-compliance in the migrant labour market', 1 May 2006, <http://www.compas.ox.ac.uk> (accessed 2 May 2006).

Said, E. W., *Orientalism*, London: Penguin, 2003.

Sanness, J., 'Speech delivered on the occasion of the award of the Nobel Prize to Mother Teresa', Oslo, Norway, 10 December 1979, <http://www.dassk.org/contents.php?id=72> (accessed 23 February 2006).

Sebba, A., *Mother Teresa: Beyond the Image*, London: Orion, 1997.

Segal, L., 'The brain drain', *The Guardian*, 17 May 2002.

Sen, A., 'Tagore and His India', 28 August 2001, <http://nobelprize.

org/nobel_prizes/literature/articles/sen/index.html> (accessed 19 December 2006).

— *The Argumentative Indian: Writings on Indian History, Culture and Identity*, London: Penguin, 2005.

Shah, D., 'Mother Teresa's Hidden Mission in India: Conversion to Christianity', 2003, <http://www.indiastar.com/DhiruShah.htm> (accessed 16 August 2004).

Shakespeare, W., *The Tempest*, London: Penguin, 1994.

Shrimsley, R., 'Tirana saw us', *The Financial Times*, 3 March, 2005.

Smith, A., 'All in a good cause?', *The Observer*, 27 January 2002, pp. 45-7.

Spink, K., *For the Brotherhood of Man under the Fatherhood of God: Mother Teresa of Calcutta, her Missionaries of Charity and her Co-Workers*, Surrey, UK: Colour Library Information, 1981.

— *Mother Teresa: An Authorized Biography*, London: Fount, 1998.

Stafford, N., 'Brain drain? What brain drain? – Not all German scientists agree there's a problem with researchers abandoning Europe', *The Scientists*, 23 December 2003.

Tafaj, M., 'Considerations about massive brain drain from Albania and strategies attracting high-qualified scientists', <http:// www.see-educoop.net> (accessed 16 April 2004).

Tagore, R., 'Crisis in Civilization' (lecture delivered on 14 April 1941), Calcutta: Visva-Bharati Publishing Department, 1950, pp. 11-23.

— *The Religion of Man*, Calcutta: Visva-Bharati Publishing Department, 2000.

— *Selected Short Stories*, Trans. W. Radice, New Delhi: Penguin Books India, 2000.

— 'The Noble Prize Acceptance Speech', in R. Tagore, *Gitanjali: Song Offerings*, Trans. R. Tagore, New Delhi: UBSPD, 2005, pp. 291-300.

— *Gitanjali: Song Offerings*, Trans. R. Tagore, New Delhi: UBSPD, 2005.

Tarn, W. W., *Alexander the Great: Narrative*, Vol. I, Cambridge: Cambridge University Press, 1979.

Teresa, M., 'Nobel Lecture', 11 December 1979, <http://nobelprize.org/peace/laureates/1979/teresa-lecture.html> (accessed 11 November 2006).

— 'An address at the National Prayer Breakfast' (Sponsored by the US Senate and House of Representatives), Eternal Word Television Network (Global Catholic Network), 3 February 1994, <http://www.ewtn.com/New_library/breakfast.htm> (accessed 11 November 2006).

Tettey, W. J., 'Africa's brain drain: exploring possibilities for its positive utilization through networked communities', *Mots Pluriels*, No. 20, February 2002.

The New Jerusalem Bible, Standard Edition, Bombay, India: Darton, Longman & Todd Ltd and Bombay Saint Paul Society, 1985.

The Holy Bible, Containing the Old and New Testaments with Apocryphal/Deuterocanonical Books, New Revised Standard Version, New York and Oxford: Oxford University Press, 1989.

The Other Balkan Wars. A 1913 Carnegie Endowment Inquiry in Retrospect with a New Introduction and Reflections on the Present Conflict by George F. Kennan, Washington, D.C.: Carnegie Endowment for International Peace, 1993.

The Qur'an, Trans. M. A. S. Abdel Haleem, Oxford: Oxford University Press, 2004 *The Statesman*, 'Abortion criticized by Mother Teresa',

Kolkata, India, 11 December 1979.

Todorova, M., *Imagining the Balkans*, New York and Oxford: Oxford University Press, 1997.

Vidyalankar, P. S. (ed.), *The Holy Vedas: A Golden Treasury*, Delhi: Clarion Book, 1983.

Walker, M., 'Albania ready to talk tall', *The Guardian*, 5 September 2001.

Weber, M., *Economy and Society: An Outline of Interpretive Sociology*, Vol. I, G. Roth and C. Wittich (eds), Berkeley, CA: University of California Press, 1978.

— *The Protestant Ethic and the Spirit of Capitalism*, Trans. T. Parsons, London and New York: Routledge Classics, 2004.

Webster's Ninth New Collegiate Dictionary, Springfield, MA: Merriam-Webster Inc., Publishers, 1987.

Williamson, R., 'Interview with Gëzim Alpion – Fallen hero: how the clown prince of Albania got right up the nose of his greatest fans', *Sunday Mercury*, 9 September 2001, pp. 45, 46.

'Why the Berlin Wall was built', <http://www.guillotine.net> (accessed 30 May 2004).

Wolff, L., *Inventing Eastern Europe: The Map of Civilization on the Mind of the Enlightenment*, Stanford, California: Stanford University Press, 1994.

Zaleski, C., 'The Dark Night of Mother Teresa', *First Things*, No. 133, May 2003, pp. 24-7.

Index